Advance P  ld

"There is no greater threat to family life than the digital deluge we are facing. There is no better book than this one to guide you through the clever clutter of misinformation the device myth makers would have us believe. We are in the midst of a fifteen year social experiment that no one is controlling… and it's not going so well. Dr. Freed has crafted something here that is sensible, impeccably researched, fairly presented and most of all a message of hope."

—KIM JOHN PAYNE, M.Ed., author of *Simplicity Parenting* and *The Soul of Discipline*

"Before you buy a piece of technology for your child—or think of offering tech rewards to him or her—*read this book*. This is not a screed against all things tech, but rather a psychological profile of what technology can and cannot accomplish with children, puncturing many popular myths along the way. It also answers the question of why Steve Jobs limited his children's access to and use of technology."

—JIM TRELEASE, author of *The Read-Aloud Handbook*

"Every parent needs to read this book. Not only is it a treasure trove of significant research that can spur positive action, it also uncovers the underbelly of our industry-culture that intentionally perpetuates harmful digital myths at the cost of our children's optimal development. Get it. You might get mad, and that may be a good thing."

—GLORIA DEGAETANO, author of *Parenting Well in a Media Age,* coauthor of *Stop Teaching Our Kids to Kill*

"As marketers tout screen technology as a solution to myriad child-hood ills, parents need honest information about what's best for children in a digital world. In *Wired Child*, psychologist Richard Freed combines facts, real-life stories, and tips into a highly readable, timely, and much-needed resource for parents and anyone who cares about children's health and well-being."

—SUSAN LINN, Ed.D., instructor in psychiatry, Harvard Medical School; author of *Consuming Kids* and *The Case for Make Believe*

"An important book! *Wired Child* is a timely reminder that billion dollar tech myths don't hold up to scrutiny. Freed's insights spark a critical conversation on InfoTech myths and how kids can benefit from wise use of technology. His psychotherapist perspective is convincing!"

—RAFFI CAVOUKIAN, singer, founder of Centre for Child Honouring, author of *Lightweb Darkweb*

"*Wired Child* is a handy, readable, and all-too-timely volume on the myths that have gripped American families about the value of digital tools.... Practices alleged to improve kids' learning and family relationships actually harm them. Freed exposes the hype and fraud surrounding video games, social media, and other entertainment-based technologies, then concludes with the right corrective—not the elimination of technology, but their productive use."

—MARK BAUERLEIN, Ph.D., professor, Emory University; author of *The Dumbest Generation*

"This is an amazing book! A superb piece of scholarship and writing. This book *must* receive the maximum possible exposure, it is vital to the success and survival of our families and our way of life."

—Lt. Col. DAVE GROSSMAN, author of *On Combat* and *On Killing*, coauthor of *Stop Teaching Our Kids to Kill*

WIRED CHILD

Reclaiming Childhood in a Digital Age

by Richard Freed, Ph.D.

ISBN: 150321169X
ISBN 13: 9781503211698
Library of Congress Control Number: 2014920499
CreateSpace Independent Publishing Platform
North Charleston, South Carolina

To my wife Rae
and our daughters, Madeline and Elena

Contents

Introduction

Six months ago, Erin bought her seven-year-old son Jacob a tablet computer. What she heard in the media made her hope the device would give her son a leg up on learning. At his mom's urging, Jacob started playing games advertised to improve math skills, but he quickly discovered entertainment video games. His passionate desire to play these was like nothing his mother had ever seen in the child.

At first Erin found she could use the tablet as an incentive to get Jacob to do things like finish his homework or clean his room; however, as she told me in counseling for her son, Jacob's use of the tablet quickly became obsessive. He asked to game constantly, and he started to bargain about homework, saying he would do it, except only in exchange for more game time than they'd agreed. Erin felt her son was changing in other ways, too. Activities he had enjoyed, like playing outside and reading, became less and less frequent. Most recently, when Erin told Jacob to turn his game off, he threw a tantrum and fumed for more than an hour.

Are you feeling a disconnect between what is promised about children's technology and what you've experienced yourself? Do claims that technology will bring the family closer seem out of sync with kids who retreat to corners or back rooms with their mobile devices for hours at a time? Are assurances of technology's amazing learning opportunities contradicted by the reality that kids often prefer playing video games, social networking, and texting over doing their schoolwork?

What explains this disconnect? In *Wired Child,* I'll talk about how our children's technology use is defined by profound myths. These myths—many cultivated by those who sell kids their gadgets—encourage the wiring up of a nation of children at the expense of what science is now telling us about their developmental needs.

Marketing tugs on our heartstrings and tells us that all these distracting gadgets—somehow—will bring families closer. A stirring TV commercial for Apple's iPhone shows a young teen whose phone seems to keep him away from his family's holiday celebration. At the end of the ad, we learn he's been videotaping family moments. As the family watches his creation, it brings everyone together. The message to parents is clear: Don't believe your own eyes, your concerns are all wrong, buy your kids iPhones and they will be closer to you—even if it looks like they're ignoring you in favor of their phones. Many of those making YouTube comments on the ad said it brought tears,[1] however, such consummate salesmanship (the ad was nominated for a 2014 Emmy for Outstanding Television Commercial)[2] belies research that shows our increasing focus on gadgets is pulling the family apart.

A number of pundits claim traditional schooling has lost its value and that the latest tech gadgets offer kids the learning experiences they need most.[3] In reality, research indicates that technologies our kids typically spend so much time with, including video games and social networks, hinder their success in school. Moreover, we'll see that academic success has never been more important.

A FLOOD OF TECHNOLOGY

Our children's recreational use of screens and phones is exploding, up considerably from years past,[4] so that it is now the dominant activity in their lives. According to the latest Kaiser Family Foundation research, today's children 8 to 18 years old spend an astounding 5½ hours every day indulging in various *entertainment screen technologies*—including video games, social networks, online videos, and TV—about

7½ hours each day if screens that are used at the same time (e.g., the computer and TV) are counted separately.[5] High-school-age kids somehow manage to spend an *additional* 2½ hours each day texting and talking on the phone. The result is that our kids spend far more time playing with their gadgets than they do attending school.

There's no doubt that our young people need to learn to use technology productively, but the Foundation finds that kids spend a paltry 16 minutes a day at home using the computer for schoolwork.[6] The bottom line is that a remarkable portion of our children's and teens' lives is taken up with digital self-amusement. It's this incredible overuse of screen and phone entertainment technologies that, as we see in this book, threatens their connection to family, academic effort, and many other important activities.

DO YOU HAVE THE RIGHT TO GUIDE YOUR CHILD'S TECH USE?

Many popular media voices suggest that kids know more than their parents or teachers when it comes to technology. This parenting notion stems from the *digital native-digital immigrant* belief first articulated by video game developer Marc Prensky. He calls children "digital natives" because they have grown up with digital technologies and are therefore comfortable with them, while their relatively tech-inexperienced parents and teachers are "digital immigrants."[7]

Prensky holds that parents' proper role is to buy their kids lots of e-gadgets, sit back, and watch the magic happen.[8] Turning the traditional family hierarchy on its head, the digital native-digital immigrant belief marginalizes parents and teachers as technologically incompetent, and maintains that kids are better judges of how they should use their devices and time.

I will show that the digital native-digital immigrant belief is a myth. It confuses the ease with which our kids use their gadgets with something that is far more important: understanding how lives spent playing with devices affect kids' emotional health, academic performance, and chances of success. Parents understand these concerns because they have greater life experience, adult brain development, and better judgment. Nonetheless, the myth has convinced many parents to do what former generations would have considered unthinkable—to step away from guiding kids in the waking activity that takes up more of their time than any other.

WHY DIGITAL MYTHS PREVAIL

Why do digital myths triumph over science? Much of the reason is America's abiding trust in technology. Our country's emergence coincided with the Industrial Revolution. Our progress has been tied to advances in transportation, medicine, and other industries. We welcome new technologies, we adore our gadgets, and we revere those who make them. As Scott Keeter of the Pew Research Center notes, "If the US has a national religion, the closest thing to it is faith in technology."[9] Bill Gates, Steve Jobs, Mark Zuckerberg, and other industry leaders are today's gods.

The makers of the tech gadgets that our kids use almost exclusively for entertainment, including video games, phones, and even computers, have hitched a ride on our goodwill for technology. Even if it looks like kids game, text, and gossip endlessly on their devices to the exclusion of family and school, marketing and other popular culture elements tell us we've got it all wrong. Our concerns are misguided, and our kids need more and more gadgets most of all.

Media outlets that parents rely on to make effective decisions have financial ties to the producers of kids' technologies, so it's not surprising they help build and maintain technology myths. Think about how much TV and Internet technology news looks and sounds like advertising as it highlights the bells and whistles of the latest gadgets. To suggest that kids actually power down their devices and spend time with their families or schoolwork is bad for business, so it's not said.

Makers of kids' tech products use other channels to influence parents. Much as the tobacco industry once did, high-tech companies fund pseudo-scientific organizations that appear objective but promote a pro-industry agenda with little acknowledgement of objective current research. When information leaked that Facebook was considering opening its social network to children younger than age 13, many child development experts cautioned against this move. They warned that young minds don't have good defenses against cyber-bullying, and kids' use of social networks is linked to poor grades. Nonetheless, immediately following news of Facebook's expansion plans, the directors of ConnectSafely heaped praise on the possible move in high-profile national press.[10] Despite its parent-friendly name, ConnectSafely is funded by Facebook and other companies financially interested in getting kids to spend even more time using commercial technologies.[11]

Digital-age myths also triumph because high-tech devices have a remarkable ability to occupy children without caregiver attention. Industry claims that these devices babysit and educate kids exploit parents who have less time and resources available for their children than prior generations. The extended family—which played an important role in sharing the parenting burden since the beginning of history—is increasingly unavailable. Today's parents work and commute much longer hours than past generations, often leaving kids to fend for themselves. Assurances that more attention-grabbing gadgets can solve this challenge sound enticing but mislead parents.

Industry denials of the risks of technology addiction also keep parents from questioning the speed and intensity of our children's shift towards the virtual world. However, brain imaging shows that certain behaviors, such as gambling and video game use, work just like drugs, triggering an avalanche of dopamine, a powerful, reward-based neurotransmitter, into the brain.[12] Millions of children, teens, and adults in the US and worldwide now suffer from video game and Internet addiction. Countries such as China, South Korea, and Japan are acting to protect their children from tech addictions, yet the US has been slow to recognize the problem and its consequences.

In my work as a child and adolescent psychologist, it's abundantly clear that the symptoms children and teens experience fit the classic definition of addiction: continued use in spite of serious negative consequences. Over time, addicted kids require more and more technology to achieve the same amount of pleasure. Parents are tearful in my office as they describe how their efforts to limit their child's technology use are met by kids slamming their fists through walls, physical attacks, or kids becoming withdrawn and suffering from depression and thoughts of suicide.

Finally, as parents, our own love affair with technology makes it hard for us to recognize the costs of wiring up this generation of children. As a Microsoft marketer aptly describes, "As a society, we're in a moment of major gadget lust and overwhelming choice."[13] We are awed by the way our devices keep us continually in the know, entertained, and in touch with others; we develop powerful bonds to these machines. Despite every intention of engaging with our kids, we find ourselves taking another peek at our computer or phone, sending just one more email or text. "I'll be right with you sweetie…."

FROM MYTH TO SCIENCE

The understanding that myths define our children's technology use emerged from my daily efforts to help families. I have worked with hundreds of parents who were misled by our culture's "all-tech-is-good-all-the-time" hype, only to find things go very wrong as their children's gadget use distances them from family, detracts from school success, and sometimes leads to addiction. I became determined to expose these myths, and the result is this book.

In *Wired Child*, I make the case that we need to stop accepting on faith the gadget-dominated life thrust upon our kids, and I show that research makes a better guide for our decisions. We'll see that the push to give our kids so many playtime devices is based on widely held but inaccurate notions, and that our kids thrive most when they are connected to the two most crucial elements of their well-being: family and school.

Decades ago, we built families out of necessity. Now we must work consciously to create strong families. And while parents could once assume their children understood the responsibility to make a strong academic effort, in an era when tempting apps are released daily we need to be thoughtful about building our children's interest in education. Interestingly enough, we'll see that many leading tech execs provide strict limits on their own kids' use of digital devices.

This book's primary emphasis is on children's and teens' technology and screen use away from school, which constitutes the great majority of their time with devices. We'll cover technologies including video games, computer, Internet, talking and texting on phones, TV, online videos, and social networking. I will suggest screen and technology guidelines for kids, however, this book is not primarily a technology guide. I won't recommend how to monitor your child on various social networks or choose the right video game. I *will* help you provide a balanced life and suggest practical ideas and activities that science has proved support healthy development for children.

I want to make it abundantly clear: Kids' use of technology is not the problem. The problem is our kids' extreme *overuse of entertainment technologies* that is displacing the experiences that are fundamental to a strong mind and a happy, successful life. Together, we'll look at how to help our kids use technology productively, as a positive force for their future.

I write this book as a psychologist and also a parent. I know the challenges of limiting technologies and screens that can seem to make parenting easier and our kids happy. As we'll see, though, while technologies may appear to be a godsend at the outset, misused technology denies kids the connection with parents and other caretakers that's at the very heart of effective parenting and healthy child development. Furthermore, because it deprives them of the bond with parents and hampers their success in school, our kids' obsessive tech use leads them to be anything but happy.

One of my main goals is to help parents feel less alone if their child or teen experiences problems as the result of technology overuse. Immersed in 24/7 positive tech spin, parents often believe that their kid is the only one who developed compulsive tech habits, failed classes, or spurned family. Parents need to know that many, many families across America and the world are experiencing the same problems. Rather than feeling embarrassed or blaming yourself, it's time to peek behind the curtain of tech myths to understand why such problems are quite predictable.

It's especially important to tackle head-on the harmful digital native-digital immigrant belief that persuades parents to diminish their role in kids' lives. This falsehood is at the core of all the digital-age myths outlined in this book. What you almost certainly know in your heart is what science is now revealing: More than ever, our kids need us to be their guide, to help them on their journey to a happy and successful life.

In each of the following chapters, I highlight a specific digital-age myth that is undermining children's development. After refuting each myth, we'll then turn to scientific evidence as a better guide for raising healthy children. Finally, in each chapter I'll provide you with practical strategies to give your children a loving, rewarding childhood amid the challenges of this digital age.

1

Build the Strong Family
Your Child Needs

Thirteen-year-old Nina's parents were incredulous to discover their beloved daughter cutting her arms and legs with a razor—an unhealthy coping mechanism a growing number of kids rely upon in an attempt to distract themselves and seek relief from their loneliness, sadness, and anger. Nina's parents' first step was counseling. As Nina and I talked, it became clear that she was depressed, and her increasing sadness was driven by a widening emotional gulf between her and her parents. She was also experiencing a barrage of cyberbullying.

A major reason for Nina's problems became clear when I asked her to describe a typical day: "I come home from school, grab a snack, and then I'm upstairs in my room on my phone for most of the night," she told me. On the evenings she ate dinner with her family, she rushed to get back to her phone. Riding to and from school or on weekend outings, she was usually too busy texting or scanning social networks to engage with her parents. Nina's phone compulsion was driven in part by her efforts to defend herself from unremitting online harassment. A classmate believed Nina was the reason her boyfriend dumped her, so she and her cadre of friends were increasingly merciless in their targeting of Nina.

Because I was concerned that Nina's phone use isolated her from her parents, I asked the family how they felt technology impacted their lives. Nina and her parents raved about how their devices brought their family closer, telling me their phones and other technologies allowed them to be in contact with one another at a moment's notice. However, it was clear they rarely used technology for this purpose. Instead, they most often used their digital devices to engage with friends and work, or to distract themselves with entertainment.

I could watch technology's impact on Nina's family as they came and went from my office. In the waiting room, Mom, Dad, and daughter usually sat in silence, working their own smartphones. During our meetings, even when family members weren't actually using their phones, their preoccupation with the buzzing devices—and if that signaled a crisis at work or unfolding teen drama—kept them from being fully present with one another and limited their ability to join as a family. As they left my office, even after talking about weighty subjects such as Nina's cutting, they didn't acknowledge each other. Instead, everyone immediately reached for their phones to check what they had missed in the last hour. It was this connective void that had driven Nina to cut her arms, despite her parents' certainty that their daughter was perfectly fine.

PERCEPTION VS. REALITY

Like Nina's family, apparently most in the US are sure technology brings their families closer. In a survey of Americans' *perceptions* about the effects of technology, the Pew Research Center found our culture holds rosy beliefs, noting "A majority of adults say technology allows their family life today to be as close, or closer, than their families were when they grew up."[1]

A similar survey commissioned by the Microsoft Corporation also looked at American parents' *perceptions* of technology's family impact. Microsoft's poll found that 64% of US parents aged 22 to 40 believe technology helps bring their family closer. Younger parents are even more upbeat. Seventy-four percent of parents between 22 and 30 believe that technology brings their family closer.[2]

Popular media report such studies as *evidence* that technology supports family ties, but what's measured is *perception*, not the reality of how technology affects the family. In the next section, we'll look at research that measures the actual *effects of technology on family relationships*. It's increasingly clear that our perception doesn't match what's actually happening in our lives.

HOW CHILDREN'S TECH USE *REALLY* IMPACTS THE FAMILY

I see shining examples of technology bringing family members closer together. Kids with parents serving overseas can connect with them via video chat. Children with distant siblings or grandparents can catch up digitally. Unfortunately, many parents and kids often go separate ways, focused on their own devices as they walk in their front door. Most of us have seen families eating in restaurants individually engrossed in their gadgets at the expense of engaging with one another.

So what's the real effect of our increasing digital immersion on families? To find out, we need to look beyond perception to research that measures technology's impact on the family. When we do, increasing evidence shows that our kids' digital immersion *divides* them from family. In *Wired Youth,* technology researchers Gustavo Mesch and Ilan Talmud sum up their findings this way: "Most of the empirical evidence on the association between Internet use and family time shows a reduction in the time parents and youth spend together."[3]

The effects of tech use extend beyond time to other measures of family closeness. In a study published in the *Archives of Pediatrics & Adolescent Medicine,* teens who spend more time playing on the computer (not for homework) or watching TV were *less attached* to their parents than kids who spend comparatively little time with the screens. In this study, the level of a teen's bond with parents was determined by an objective measure of teen attachment.[4]

Interestingly, studies show that how kids use technology—whether as entertainment or school/education focused—impacts how it affects relationships with parents. While entertainment applications such as online gaming appear to hurt kids' relationships with parents, using the Internet to study for school does not.

As noted in a study of 4th to 6th grade Korean children which parallels the findings of studies from other parts of the world: "The impact of Internet use depends specifically on what children do online. Playing online games decreases both total time with family and time communicating with family members. However, for children who frequently use the Internet for homework and searching for educational information, the Internet is not a medium that threatens family relationships."[5] Unfortunately, as we will see in Chapter 3, kids use the Internet and computers primarily for entertainment rather than education.

Why does a child's use of computers and the Internet for entertainment negatively affect families? There's a simple explanation: Interactive amusement-based technologies negate the need for interaction with family. Instead, they offer the remarkably seductive alternative of gaming or connecting to life outside the home.

The exploding use of mobile technologies only amplifies kids' separation from family. The Kaiser Family Foundation reports that providing kids phones and other mobile devices dramatically increases their use of digital entertainment.[6] Kids using mobile devices are not only more distracted by screens, the devices also encourage children to retreat to their own spaces so that shared time with parents is lost. Even when kids use their mobile devices in the presence of family, the devices' engaging content often leads children to ignore family members. As noted by child advocate Raffi Cavoukian in his book *Lightweb Darkweb,* "Family space has been hijacked by the very devices that are supposed to enhance our lives. They've taken over the family dynamic."[7]

A Window into Gadget-filled Lives

A remarkable UCLA study brings what happens in today's gadget-filled homes to life. *Life at Home in the Twenty-First Century* describes how researchers videotaped everything a sample of middle-class families did throughout their homes from the time children and teens woke up until they went to bed.[8] They found that kids' use of electronic gadgets profoundly impacted these families.

Lead researcher Elinor Ochs says, "I'm not certain how the children can monitor all those things at the same time, but I think it is pretty consequential for the structure of the family relationship." Reviewing the footage of kids welcoming their dads home from work, Dr. Ochs tells us, "About half the time the kids ignored him or didn't stop what they were doing, multitasking and monitoring their various electronic gadgets." Commenting on how frequently parents play second fiddle to kids' devices, she says, "We also saw how difficult it was for parents to penetrate the child's universe. We have so many videotapes of parents actually backing away, retreating from kids who are absorbed by whatever they're doing."[9]

HOW PARENTS' TECH USE AFFECTS THE FAMILY

Does *parents'* tech use contribute to family disconnection? Debates about this frequently play out in my office. Gabe, a father of two, animatedly described how he used digital machines: "Technology's what allows me to be at home instead of spending evenings at the office. Email and texts are how I catch up with the kids." Gabe's wife, Rebecca, acknowledged these benefits, nevertheless, she had a different take on the attention her husband and kids devoted to their devices, telling me, "We may be at home, but often we barely notice one another. It doesn't feel like a family."

Like their kids', American parents' lives are increasingly screen-focused. Ball State researchers find that the average adult spends an incredible 6½ hours a day between television, computer, mobile phone, and other screens—with the majority of this use entertainment-based and outside of work. If screens used together (e.g., watching TV while using the computer) were counted separately, this would rise to 8½ hours.[10] How does all this parent screen time affect the family?

According to Stanford University researchers, each hour an adult spends on the Internet at home reduces family face time by 24 minutes. The researchers therefore concluded that the best way to represent adult Internet time is a "displacement" or "hydraulic" model.[11] This is what children in my practice describe to me, that the time their parent spends at home on the Internet and their phone tends to squeeze out time they would otherwise spend with them.

Researchers from the Center for the Digital Future at the USC Annenberg School for Communication report that our culture's move towards personal interactive technologies leads to increased relational distance between parents and kids. Measuring the time family members 12 and older spent together, these researchers found a significant decrease from 2005 to 2008, crediting that to individuals' increased online engagement.

Michael Gilbert, Senior Fellow at the Center, cautions: "Many technology issues are pulling on the family which, in the modern world, has enough pressures…. Certainly a lack of collective experience and face-to-face time will lead to a breakdown in communication, decreased opportunities to experience the world together, increased alienation of children." And he warns of a troubling outcome: "Family breakdown leads to destructive behavior."[12]

The Painful Reality of Wired Families

MIT professor and psychologist Sherry Turkle describes the consequences of our wired lives in her book *Alone Together*. Studying modern families, she finds a generation of children who often "contend with parents who are physically close, tantalizingly so, but mentally elsewhere."[13] Parents take the time to pick their children up from school, still they're so caught up in their phones that they don't acknowledge their kids.

Catherine Steiner-Adair, a psychologist at Harvard Medical School, is also looking at technology's distancing effects. She interviewed more than 1,000 children, 500 parents, and 500 teachers for her book *The Big Disconnect*. Like Sherry Turkle, she finds many children suffering from our embrace of 24/7 "connectedness." As seven-year-old Annabel describes, "My parents are always on their computers and on their cell phones…. It's very, very frustrating and I get lonely inside."[14]

Talk with parents, and they will often tell you they are "staying connected" using their phones and other gadgets. However, this focus on matters outside the immediate family can be at the expense of those who need our love and attention more than anyone else: our kids.

WHEN FAMILIES FADE AWAY
AND NO ONE NOTICES

Research showing that technology is distancing kids from their parents and parents from their kids matches what I see nearly every day in my clinical practice. Parents report their children attend dinner less and less because they are happier to game or text in their rooms. Children who a decade or so told me that their relationship with their parents was stifled by their parents' overuse of TV now say it's their parents' intense focus on phones—which extends screen use to out-of-home settings—that's denying them the ability to connect.

So why are we missing what we're missing? Parents' instincts to care for their children are quite powerful. One would think we'd see what's going on around us and act to strengthen our families—unless of course, we're misled by an industry that provides most of the media content the average American parent uses to make decisions, and which loses revenue every minute people shut off their screens.

Let's look at the messages the media/tech industry provides, especially to mothers who are viewed by the industry as the primary decision makers on family matters.

Ignore Your Concerns—Buy More Gadgets Now!

At the 2011 Marketing to Moms (M2Moms®) conference, two leading marketing firms described their sales approach in *Tech Fast Forward: Plug in to see the brighter side of life*.[15] This report identifies many concerns about technology's impact on children and the family, but it makes clear that the key to selling moms tech products is to ignore these concerns and instead promote the supposed benefits of technology, concluding, "It may be that having a positive attitude enables faster and more seamless adoption of technology."[16]

Tech Fast Forward is filled with selling points that show contempt for the science I describe in this book, including: "Digital distraction has its benefits," "Gaming our way to genius," and "Families that tech together stay together."[17] These typical industry catch phrases distract and confuse parents with faulty positives and get them to ignore the negatives research shows. This strategy is encapsulated by a key selling tactic suggested in *Tech Fast Forward*: "Mobilize tech optimism."[18] Media/tech companies use this strategy across many platforms, from the nightly news to online magazines, and the friendly "tech expert" the industry calls on to give parents advice. The intention is clear. Get parents to disregard concerns about technology and embrace the use of more digital machines.

The *Parents.com* article "Best Baby Apps" is an example of the push to "mobilize tech optimism." In spite of public health groups' concerns about using screens to babysit, the piece suggests the iPad is a cheap, effective childcare tool. "Best Baby Apps" calls on Katie Linendoll, identified as a "tech expert," to give the following guidance: "I call the iPad the ultimate babysitter.... Because it's very easy to use, there's no manual, and when the price point [for apps] is typically free or 99 cents, you can't go wrong in downloading a bunch and seeing what you like."[19]

A regular contributor to CNN, *The Early Show*, and *The Today Show*, Katie Linendoll is typical of authorities mainstream media and the technology industry use to dismiss parent concerns—promoters focused on selling tech products instead of children's needs. Her chief qualification? She hosts Spike TV's *All Access Weekly*, essentially a televised trade show promoting video games and other tech products.

The push to "mobilize tech optimism" is working in spades. A poll by the marketing agency Kids Industries found that 77% of American and British parents believe tablet computers benefit children.[20] Such goodwill gets parents to open their pocketbooks and doors to more and more devices. The Associated Press article "Squirmy Toddler? There's an App for That" shows parents are increasingly comfortable using tablets and smartphones as babysitters. One mother said the iPad keeps her three-year-old son busy for hours, and taking it away "is the greatest punishment ... he loves it that much." A mom of 3- and 6-year-old sons was equally forthright about her iPhone: "I'm buying my kids' silence with an expensive toy."[21]

Exploiting a Mother's Instincts

A particularly shrewd strategy is outlined in the 2012 Yahoo! and Starcom MediaVest (a market research agency) strategy report *Brave New Moms: Navigating Technology's Impact on Family Time*.[22] This study was a huge undertaking, as the marketers researched moms in nine countries through interviews, videotaping families, and reviewing moms' social network conversations.

At first glance, the Yahoo!/Starcom MediaVest(SMV) marketing report seems empathetic to today's moms fragmented by the demands of childcare, work, and technology: "We witnessed moms struggle with the power technology has to pull families apart."[23] They concede that more than half of moms "say their family is often distracted by technology during time together."[24]

During a poignant videotaped moment from the study, a mom somberly comments about the distancing effects of technology on her family: "Most people are going off into their own worlds, into their own space, doing their own thing, my husband and his iPad, my son with his DSI, and I'm on my laptop."[25] Another mom notes, "At my kids' birthday party the grandparents wanted to see the children, but could not because they were attached to the computer. They did not look at us or hear us talk to them."[26]

Yahoo! fittingly concludes that what today's mothers truly crave is time in which they can bond with their kids and families. However, Yahoo! is in the business of selling technology, and if moms focus on the hurtful effects of technology, it's bad for business. To solve this conundrum, the *Brave New Moms* marketers advocate for the use of some marketing judo. Companies should *exploit* a mother's desire to be closer to her children to sell her stuff via technology. As Yahoo! explains, this "desire by moms to create special moments with their families *creates an unprecedented opportunity for brands* [emphasis mine]"[27]—brands Yahoo! can insert via technology into the emotional space you and your child share.

The Yahoo! report cites a prime example of this marketing strategy—a Kraft Foods iPad app called "Big Fork Little Fork," purportedly developed to help parents teach their kids about healthy eating. The app features Kraft foods such as Cool Whip and Oreos, and provides parents lots of iPad videos on how to make Kraft-branded recipes. The app also keeps kids occupied with Kraft video games and videos featuring a Kraft Foods "mom" teaching kids cooking skills like how to crack an egg.[28]

The moments you share with your child in the kitchen can provide wonderful, attachment-building experiences. Even showing your child how to crack an egg is rife with bonding ingredients: you as guide, child as learner, the physical elements of eye contact and the holding of your child's hand as you crack the egg together, and sharing a laugh at the inevitable mess you make.

Experiences like this are important because they trigger the release of chemicals that promote pleasure and bonding into young brains; chemicals such as dopamine and oxytocin, released during close family times, facilitate your child's attachment to you. On a personal level, such loving moments are vital to building the relationship your child needs with you to grow up happy and successful.

What happens when we bring attention-demanding technologies like the iPad into moments like the one above? Are you and your child closer? Not likely, since iPads and their competitors are often used as babysitters precisely because of their uncanny ability to preoccupy children for long periods *without* parent attention. Today's interactive technologies and the sophisticated marketing they deliver are purposely designed to distract users of any age from attention elsewhere. In other words, why should your child crack an egg with you when there are cool videos to watch and video games to play?

DO TODAY'S KIDS REALLY NEED TO BOND WITH THEIR PARENTS?

My concern about technology's effect on parent-child relationships isn't due to a Norman-Rockwell-era sensibility. It's based on the body of scientific research on attachment and years of counseling families and children. Pioneering investigations by brain researchers Daniel Siegel and Allan Schore at UCLA, amongst others, show us children's brains are highly plastic, and that their interactions with parents have a powerful effect on brain architecture. As Siegel and child development specialist Mary Hartzell say in *Parenting from the Inside Out*, "Experience shapes brain structure. Experience *is* biology. How we treat our children changes who they are and how they will develop. Their brains need our parental involvement. Nature needs nurture."[29]

This applies to all caregivers who take on a parenting role, including foster parents, grandparents, childcare providers, teachers, and other caring adults who are invested in children's well-being.

The National Scientific Council on the Developing Child at Harvard University recently said that young children frequently left for hours at a time in front of the TV are prey to a type of under-stimulation that can damage brain development.[30] Today's parents may recognize why using television this way may be bad for children, however, they may be swayed by promises of a high-tech babysitter in the form of a tablet or smartphone. Yet often young children engage in exactly the same activity, watching TV (or its equivalent), on mobile devices. Moreover, the potentially addictive qualities of the newer technologies may prove even more powerful competition for caregiver interaction.

Children's relationships with their parents profoundly impact nearly every facet of their behavior. Kids with a healthy parent attachment regulate their emotions better, score higher intellectually and academically, and have higher self-esteem than kids without a healthy parent bond. Attachment remains vital into the teen years. Adolescents with healthy bonds to parents are less likely to be depressed; they also receive better grades in school and have fewer behavior problems. They're also less likely to abuse drugs or alcohol compared to kids with poorer family bonds.[31] There is also irony, in that a close relationship with a parent from birth to late adolescence fosters a child's autonomy. Kids raised in strong families are emboldened to explore the world and, as they grow older, have the courage to venture out on their own.

Healthy attachment also allows us to parent effectively. The emotional dependence associated with attachment is why kids consent to our guidance. What helps an 11-year-old girl realize the importance of putting effort into her homework? What would encourage a 13-year-old boy to resist drugs, cigarettes, and alcohol, unlike many of his peers? Children and adolescents bonded to their parents are more likely to make good decisions and respect parents' advice because they identify with their families and feel beholden to them.

THE CONSEQUENCES OF LIFE
WITH DIGITAL MACHINES

Popular culture portrays the most tech-involved kids as competent, happy and successful, but because the wired life costs our kids connection to their families, it's not surprising to see our "digital native" kids struggling emotionally and with other elements of their well-being. A Kaiser Family Foundation study notes that: "Heavy media users are also more likely to say they get into trouble a lot, are often sad or unhappy, and are often bored."[32] A study in the journal *Pediatrics* found that 10- to 11-year-old children who played on a computer (not for homework) for more than two hours a day were more likely to suffer from psychological distress than kids who used less.[33]

The plugged-in life also puts kids at greater risk for cyberbullying. As noted in a *Children & Society* journal article: "Cyberbullies and cyber-victims are generally heavy Internet users."[34] Likewise, kids who say they have high levels of Internet expertise are more likely to be a victim or perpetrator of cyberbullying than kids who don't claim such expertise,[35] and kids who attach high levels of importance to the Internet are more likely to cyberbully than kids who consider it less important in their lives.[36] Concerns about cyberbullying are serious because online harassment increases the risk that kids will skip school or consider suicide.[37]

Cyberbullying is more common among tech-heavy kids because children's tech time is spent almost entirely in entertainment domains, including social networks and online games, where mean things are easier said than in real life because kids don't have to face the target of their comments. Moreover, as we have seen, kids more engaged with technology are less engaged with parents—parents whose involvement could help kids treat others better. Research shows that a strong emotional bond with parents diminishes the risk that kids will be cyberbullied.[38]

A similar pattern emerges when we look at teens' involvement with sexting, the transmission of sexually explicit information using technology—most often on cell phones. Pew Research Center's *Teens and Sexting* shows us that teens who use their phone more often, tend to leave their phones on, or have an unlimited texting plan are at higher risk of receiving sexually suggestive messages. The Pew researchers identified which kids are more likely to sext, noting that they "are likely to be those whose phones are more central to their lives than less intense cell phone users."[39]

It's time to change our priorities, to make family (and school) central to our children's and teens' lives, not phones and other tech gadgets kids rely upon primarily for self-amusement.

HOW TO GIVE KIDS THE FAMILIES THEY NEED

While your child needs a close bond with you, there are obvious, real challenges to building this relationship in our myth-filled culture. We'll look at strategies to help you overcome these in the following pages.

The Sacrifice

Until fairly recently, no deliberate effort was needed to build a family, as a strong connection grew out of necessity. Families throughout most of human history have been faced with hostile landscapes and threatening circumstances that required all family members—parents, children, and teens—to work together to achieve success or simply survive. In our present age of abundance, characterized by our ability to spend so much of our lives being entertained by screens, there are fewer outside forces pushing family members together, and instead finely segmented commercial technologies targeting smaller and smaller demographic groups that are pulling us apart.

Every day, radio, TV, and online marketing promote the latest devices' and data plans' ability to provide moms, dads, younger kids, and teens 24/7 real-time access to whatever their own hearts could desire—online gaming, streaming TV, sports and fantasy football coverage, any of a number of social networks, and on and on. At the same time, because news sources have a tremendous financial interest in having us all stare at screens (Yahoo! is the most-read news site in the US with more than 100 million monthly viewers),[40] there is nary a mention of how devices are pulling us away from one another.

The result is that family members focus increasingly on their own screens rather than one another, splintering family, undermining it. Helping children requires that we see through the hype to understand that the self-amusement-focused life promoted as the height of progress and enjoyment is depriving kids of the families they need for health, happiness, and success. Parents can make a powerful contribution to improving their kids' well-being by making a sacrifice that our culture tells them they shouldn't: to not overindulge in their own screen and phone entertainment and instead devote all the attention and energy they can to their family.

I know that many of us work harder and spend less time in our homes than we used to, making it more challenging to be with our families. Yet somehow American parents and their kids have the ability to spend tremendous amounts of time recreating between screens and phones every day. If we make connecting with our kids rather than connecting with digital devices a priority, there's a lot of room for improvement.

Build Your Own Routines, Rituals, and Traditions

Earlier we saw how the media/tech industry is intent on inserting distracting technologies and marketing into loving moments you might share with your child. Thankfully, industry marketing materials also share how their strategists plan to accomplish this, which helps us thwart their efforts. Describing practices that are used across the industry, Yahoo!'s *Brave New Moms* recommends that companies sell their brands by targeting the "building blocks of family time," namely a family's *routines, rituals,* and *traditions.*[41] Yahoo!'s suggestion of inserting an iPad with a Kraft Foods app into the *ritual* of a mother teaching her child in the kitchen is a good example. The recent effort to copyright the tooth fairy and build a Web presence and product line around this tradition is another.[42]

Family routines, rituals, and traditions exist because they build strong ties and help raise healthy children. They give our children something tangible that says, "This is my family, this is what we do together, and this is how we connect." A family's togetherness suffers if we allow distracting technologies to compete for love and attention. We need to root family traditions in sources that don't have corporate profits as their first goal, and instead have our children's best interests at heart. These include extended family, friends, religious institutions, cultural heritage, and other trusted sources.

Consider the tradition of teaching your children cooking skills. Rather than looking to Kraft's iPad app, consider having a grandparent cook with your child. Experiment with your own food combinations in the kitchen, or host a barbeque and have your kids help make the meal. During everyday routines and rituals like doing errands or watching a sibling play soccer, keep gadgets out of sight, talk about plays, cheer for your team, or reminisce about something in your shared lives.

Carve Out a Family Space

Spending time together as a family is made easier by putting time on the books. Daniel, the father of pre-teen twins, says his family never skips a weekly bowling night together. Other families save a specific time in their week for family night, movie night, playing board games like Pictionary, or other traditions that get parents and kids together. Special moments don't necessarily mean spending money.

As eight-year-old Jeff told me with a smile on his face, "On Saturdays, I help my dad in the yard."

Read To Your Child

Kimberly, the mother of two young boys, told me about reading to her kids at least a couple of times a week: "I love this time and I think they do too. We snuggle up and it's a moment when time stands still." Science says Kimberly's on the right track. Younger children whose parents read to them frequently are more attached to their parents than children who are read to infrequently.[43] Reading builds kids' bonds to parents because they look to parents for the pleasure-filled activity. Moreover, books often provide a jumping-off point for remembering shared experiences ("I remember we saw animals like that at the zoo....").

The parent-child moments fostered by reading books together contrast sharply with the experiences of children sitting alone, getting stimulation from a digital device. In my work with families, a steady diet of tech-heavy, caregiver-light experiences—especially when kids are young—can form the basis of tech addiction. We'll look at this issue more closely in Chapter 4.

Rituals of Affection

Many kids get half-hugs or half-glances from parents as they come and go from school, head to bed, or otherwise transition, while parents keep one hand and one eye on their gadgets. Sherry Turkle found in her research that children often named the same three examples of being emotionally hurt and not wanting to show it when their parent was using a device rather than paying attention to them: at meals, during pickup either after school or an extracurricular activity, or during sporting events.[44]

We're all harried, but it's vital to make time to honor our kids' transitions by putting our phones away and offering our undivided attention. If we don't, our kids are likely to seek comfort in their own devices and shut us out in turn.

A Health-Giving Tradition: The Family Meal

Caught up in a whirlwind of recently-emerging technology myths, we too easily let go of family traditions that reach back into our distant past. For instance, the frequency of family meals is down greatly from prior generations, in spite of strong evidence for its benefit.[45] An article in the *Archives of Pediatrics & Adolescent Medicine* found that the more often families ate together, the less often adolescents (ages 11–18) smoked cigarettes or marijuana, drank alcohol, had poor grades, were depressed, or had thoughts of suicide.[46]

When families eat together, much more is shared than food. As educational consultant Kim John Payne and Lisa Ross note in their book, *Simplicity Parenting*, "The family dinner is more than a meal. Coming together, committing to a shared time and experience, exchanging conversation, food, and attention... all of these add up to more than full bellies. The nourishment is exponential. Family stories, cultural markers, and information about how we live are passed around with the peas."[47]

The good news is the desire for being with one another is there. The National Center on Addiction and Substance Abuse at Columbia University reports that 66% of teens and 75% of parents said they would give up a weeknight activity in order to have dinner with their family.[48]

Here are some tips to increase the frequency and pleasure of family meals:

- **Go distraction-free:** While it's common for kids and parents to text during meals (70% of parents allow this[49]), it's vital to set digital devices aside to allow the benefits of eating together. As noted by The National Center on Addiction and Substance Abuse at Columbia University: "Compared to teens who have five to seven family dinners per week without distractions at the table, those who have fewer than three family dinners per week and say there are distractions at the table are three times likelier to have used marijuana (12% vs. 40%) and tobacco (9% vs. 31%), and two and a half times likelier to have used alcohol (25% vs. 63%)."[50]

- **Accept imperfection:** If one member of the family can't share a family meal due to work or extracurricular obligations, don't give up the effort. The key is to have at least one parent or caregiver sit down to eat with kids. The meal doesn't have to be a traditional dinner. Kids tell me that the simple act of a parent sitting down to share a bowl of cereal with them in the morning helps them know the parent is invested in them, and helps them take on the challenges they face at school.

- **Keep it simple:** In my clinical experience, meals can separate rather than bring families together. Even after working a long day, parents may feel compelled to cook involved meals for kids and spouses. The result? Parents are kept busy in the kitchen while kids are occupied by screens. Offering leftovers or healthy frozen foods are better alternatives, as the parent-child bond is infinitely more important than gourmet meals. As kids get older, have them help make the meal and set the table as much as they are able.

Make Family Stories Triumph

My family is lucky. Our daughters revel in the captivating stories told by their grandfathers—both are true raconteurs. They also can't wait to tell me how much fun they had making cookies, banana bread, and other treats with their grandmothers. When children turn inward and recall their most treasured and vibrant memories, we—and they—need those stories to be about *us*—their parents, grandparents, teachers, and other real people who take care of them. We need our children's time with family to outshine their experiences with electronic toys.

Technology domination in the lives of children and teens I work with can be powerfully negative. As a matter of course, I ask the kids who are old enough to know what their parents do for a living. The shocking reality is that many have *no idea* what their parents do for eight-plus hours a day to support the family. Honestly, many of these kids don't care. The overriding narrative for these children is their superior gaming abilities or the latest social network gossip. A gap like this leads kids to lose touch with familial expectations about making an effort in school or helping out around the house.

Research shows us that kids are helped when families share moments together at home. A study in the journal *Attachment & Human Development* reveals that when parents help their preschool children talk about the emotional experience of shared parent-child moments, it builds kids' attachment.[51] Similarly, preliminary research suggests that helping preadolescent children reminisce about what happened that day or in the distant past helps limit emotional problems and acting-out behaviors.[52]

Take these steps to build family stories that will foster your child's connection to you:

- **Make time for family:** Kids' perceptions of how we choose to spend our time—playing with them even after a long day at work vs. indulging in our own screens—can win or lose a healthy attachment. Bonding occurs through sharing what could be considered ordinary moments: giggling over the ball that rolls down the gutter, chatting on a late-night walk to the ice cream shop, or laughing at the antics of a pet.
- **Make screen time shared time:** Watching a movie or a favorite TV show can provide moments when parents and kids can laugh or cry together. Such common experiences can be remembered together later ("My favorite part of the movie is…").
- **Don't miss opportunities:** "Yet when is there even *time* to talk?" bewildered parents ask me. In the fairly recent past, busy parents

and kids could talk while waiting for food to arrive at a restaurant or sitting at a doctor's office: "Is Billy still giving you a hard time at school?" "Hey, who do think will make it to the Super Bowl?" If you lose such moments to checking email or gaming on a phone, one day you may wish you could have them back to do over.

BUILDING A FAMILY DESPITE THE HYPE

The routines, rituals, and traditions you choose are deeply personal and unique to your family, however, key to all efforts—whether these are a day trip together, shared time at home, or even the ride to and from school—is to recognize how bonding moments are undone by a parent or child who is gaming, texting, checking scores, or responding to social network posts. Kids I work with tell me they don't want to have dinners or take trips with the family because their parents ignore them in favor of a phone, painfully dashing children's positive expectations.

Psychologist Catherine Steiner-Adair vividly describes how parent overuse of technology affects kids in *The Big Disconnect:* "The message we communicate with our preoccupation and responsiveness to calls and e-mail is: Everybody else matters more than you. Everything else matters more than you. Whatever the caller may say is more important than what you are telling me now."[53] When this happens day after day, kids are likely to "check out" of their families. They may live at home, but they begin to look elsewhere for comfort—often in technology.

I know it's difficult to contain our own technology use. Even though I'm acutely aware of how important it is to spend quality time with my kids, I struggle to break free of my computer. What helps? Consciously thinking each day about my priorities. I've learned from years of working with families that we only have one shot to raise our kids. There are no second chances.

2

Boost Children's Self-Control

Turn on the TV or read online parenting articles, and you may be prodded to expose your child to video games to help build a better brain. Consider these headlines: "High-action Video Games Benefit Brain" or "7 Games That Expand Your Brain."[1] A *Parents.com* article "8 Reasons Video Games Can Improve Your Child" claims: "Video games can help children's brain development."[2] Another online article declares: "Parents, the next time you fret that your child is wasting too much time playing video games, consider new research suggesting that video gaming may have real-world benefits for your child's developing brain."[3] These messages are enough to make you run out and buy your child a gaming system.

IT'S A FACT: VIDEO GAMES IMPROVE *CERTAIN* BRAIN FUNCTIONS

There's little doubt that the long hours kids spend video gaming is changing their brains. That's because of a neuroscience principle: "Cells that fire together, wire together." Activities stimulate development of particular areas of the brain, which in turn fosters children's ability to succeed at those activities. The reverse is also true: Brain areas that *aren't* stimulated tend to atrophy and become less able to support other skills.

Do video games improve children's brains? The answer is a qualified yes, as exposure to video games develops specific skills. For example, playing action video games slightly reduces *reaction time*, e.g., the amount of time it takes to push a button in response to a flash of light.[4] Playing action/violent video games also improves *visual attention.*[5] Visual attention includes the ability to rapidly process visual information—for instance the ability to detect objects in one's peripheral vision. As we'll see, this skill is much different than the ability to *focus and maintain attention* during challenging classroom activities.

Daphne Bavelier, professor of brain and cognitive sciences at the University of Rochester, whose research has shown how video games foster *visual* attention, describes how video games build better combat soldiers: "It is certainly good training for people in situations where they need to detect things in their visual environment at any time in any location, like ground troops going through uncharted territory."[6] Militaries around the world have turned to video games to train recruits. The US Army has invested tens of millions of dollars in its latest video game simulator, the *Dismounted Soldier Training System,* or *DSTS.* This simulator helps combat soldiers survive in war environments and uses the same technology as the popular off-the-shelf first-person-shooter game *Crysis 2.*[7]

BRAIN TRADE-OFF REVEALS A MYTH

While action video games prepare the brain for "kill-or-be-killed" environments, these same attributes appear to create a liability in settings where kids need the skill of *self-control* most. Technology writer Nicholas Carr brought attention to this trade-off in his book *The Shallows,*[8] a 2011 Pulitzer Prize finalist. Iowa State psychologist Douglas Gentile similarly suggests that while video games give, they also take away: "The same attentional skills that are learned by playing action games (such as a wider field of view and attention to the periphery) are part of the problem. Although these are good skills in a computer-mediated environment, they are a liability in school when the child is supposed to ignore the kid fidgeting in the chair next to him and focus on only one thing."[9]

Numerous studies show that the more children play video games or watch entertainment TV shows, *the more likely they will struggle with self-control skills needed for the classroom or homework.*[10] This may surprise parents who believe video games improve their child's focus abilities, because it's the one activity that can hold their attention. Still, think about the vast differences between the focus demands for slow-paced, complex ideas vs. video games, which use constant movement and reward to keep users' attention. Christopher Lucas, associate professor of child psychiatry at New York University School of Medicine, notes that focusing on school and most other real-world activities requires "sustained attention in the absence of rewards," while video games and TV rely on "frequent intermittent rewards" to keep kids staring at the screen.[11]

Self-control, which encompasses the ability to not only focus attention, but limit impulses, belongs to a set of brain skills referred to as *executive functions.* Executive functions get that name because they manage other brain areas and help people apply their intelligence to a wide range of challenges at work, home, and school. The power of executive functions to influence our lives and success is so profound that the brain area that controls them, the prefrontal cortex (or PFC), is referred to as *the brain's CEO.* Of the executive functions governed by the PFC, none is more important to our kids than self-control.

So while digital immersion changes our children's brains, it's a myth to say that they're changing for the better. There's no evidence that the combat-like skills enhanced by video games help children in the real world. Instead, as we'll see next, there are strong signs that the self-control skills which appear to be harmed by gaming are vital to our kids' health and success.

HOW IMPORTANT IS SELF-CONTROL? CONSIDER A MARSHMALLOW

Walter Mischel, a psychology professor at Columbia University (and formerly Stanford), has long studied how children's self-control skills affect their lives. In the late 1960s, he tested four-year-olds' self-control using a simple but ingenious procedure he calls the "Marshmallow Test." At a nursery school on the Stanford University campus, a researcher would put a marshmallow in front of a child, who was then left alone in a room. The child was told that if he or she could resist eating the treat until the researcher came back (about fifteen minutes later), the child would get a second marshmallow and be able to eat both. About 30% of four-year-olds could resist that first marshmallow.

After the original experiment wrapped up in the early 1970s, Mischel continued to have casual conversations with his three daughters (who attended the same nursery school as the kids in the study) about how the original participants' lives were going. These talks led him to suspect that self-control played a powerful role in later life success.

As the original study subjects approached adulthood, Mischel tracked them down and was able to prove his hunch correct. Subjects who had been able to delay gratification as young children (resist the marshmallows) generally had fewer behavior problems during adolescence than those who showed less self-control as young kids. Moreover, those who avoided eating the marshmallow at age four went on to perform much better academically than subjects who were unable to resist eating the marshmallow, scoring an average of 210 points better on their Scholastic Aptitude Test (SAT).[12]

Is Self-Control More Important than I.Q.?

Since the Marshmallow Test, Mischel and many other researchers have continued to demonstrate the profound importance of children's self-control. A New Zealand study followed subjects from birth to 32, and discovered that those who possessed greater self-control at ages 3 to 5 performed better in numerous domains throughout their lives. They were less likely to abuse drugs and alcohol, to be convicted of a crime, or to have financial problems. In good news for parents, the scientists also found that children's self-control can be improved, and this is associated with better life outcomes.[13]

In another compelling study, researchers at the University of Pennsylvania compared the effects of self-control vs. intelligence in 8th graders. Teens who had greater self-control spent more time on homework and less time watching TV, were more likely to be accepted to a competitive high school, and had higher grades. In what should give us all pause, the researchers found that a child's level of self-control was *more than twice as important as intelligence* in predicting his or her academic success.[14]

Why Self-Control is Vital in a Digital World

How important is self-control in an age of flashy gadgets that can capture even the most distractible child's attention? It's more than important; it's crucial. As Walter Mischel remarked, no matter how smart a child is, he or she still needs to do homework.[15] Nonetheless, getting kids to open schoolbooks after they arrive home is harder than ever. The afterschool entertainment I was offered years ago consisted of *Leave it to Beaver* and *Gilligan's Island* reruns on an old TV. Today's kids have 24/7 access to profoundly enticing digital distractions. They desperately need self-control to resist the temptations of games and social chatter for the long-term payoff of algebra, chemistry, and other academic subjects.

THE DISTRACTED GENERATION

Many parents and teachers are noticing that something is not right with our wired-up kids. In 2012, the *New York Times* reported that surveys showed, "There is a widespread belief among teachers that students' constant use of digital technology is hampering their attention spans and ability to persevere in the face of challenging tasks."[16] Many parents see the same thing. When I talk to parent groups at schools, I sometimes ask the audience what one word gamers use to describe school. Every time, parents call out in unison "Booorrrring!"

The increase in children's screen-focus is implicated as a reason for the exploding rate of attention deficit hyperactivity disorder (ADHD), a behavioral condition in which self-control is compromised. In March 2013, the *New York Times* reported the rate of children 4 to 17 diagnosed with ADHD is up an alarming 41% in the last decade. The same article, reporting Centers for Disease Control and Prevention data, said that almost 1 in 5 high-school-age boys now receive a diagnosis of ADHD.[17]

I've tested a number of children for ADHD, only to find that their symptoms, falling grades and lack of homework completion, were caused by overuse of video games and TV. Once parents got control of these children's tech habits and provided structure around homework, the symptoms went away. Would these kids have been diagnosed with ADHD if no one asked questions about their screen habits? Probably.

I believe the problem often goes deeper than behavioral symptoms. It's even more serious: Our children's early and heavy exposure to screens may be altering their brains and denying them the ability to develop self-control skills. Attention deficit hyperactivity disorder or its characteristic symptoms can result. Seven-year-old Caleb is typical of many kids I see. From the time he was a toddler, he was raised on cartoons and, later, high-action video games. His mother says he never seemed interested in reading or playing creatively at home. Now in 2nd grade, Caleb is struggling—understandably—with slower-paced classroom and homework tasks. His mother and teacher have asked for professional assessment of a possible attention disorder.

In meetings with Caleb, he tells me that he finds real-world tasks intolerably slow and dull. While we talk, he fiddles with the game player buried in his pocket and then impulsively pulls it out to show me the games that are the love of his life. His mother and teacher tell me they've tried many things to help Caleb sit still and complete schoolwork, but no matter what they try, he can't seem to focus.

Caleb's mom and teacher are right. His low levels of self-control suggest that he *does* have ADHD. Would he have the same difficulties, or to the same level, if he had grown up in an environment that fostered patience and perseverance rather than the quick-twitch skills gaming hones? My belief is he would not. Has Caleb's brain actually been changed by extensive screen exposure? I believe it has.

PROMOTING CHILDREN'S SELF-CONTROL

How can you promote your child's self-control? By following the "cells that fire together, wire together" principle that says a child's prefrontal cortex is much like a muscle. If we want our kids to be able to focus on slower-paced, less immediately-rewarding activities such as schoolwork, we need to engage them in activities that exercise similar skills, and minimize their exposure to activities likely to diminish their self-control capacity. The remainder of this chapter suggests strategies to achieve this goal.

LIMIT SCREEN COMPETITION

It's vital to recognize that your efforts to promote your child's self-control can be undermined, or even negated, by kids' unfettered access to digital technologies and TV. Parents often tell me they can't interest their children in activities like reading or playing creatively, which demand focused attention. When I ask them what their child does instead, the answer is often, "Play video games and watch TV."

Unless *you limit* your kids' access to screen technologies, it will be difficult, if not impossible, to interest them in much else. As we'll see in Chapter 4, the makers of entertainment technologies purposely design their products to keep users fixated on their screens at the cost of other pursuits. The activities kids need for healthy brain development just can't compete.

I suggest you follow the American Academy of Pediatrics' (AAPs') recommendations. Don't expose kids to *any* screen media before they're 2, and limit kids 2 and older to 1–2 hours a day of total screen time.[18] When young children begin to watch TV, slower-paced educational programming is a better choice than fast-paced cartoons and other entertainment technologies. A study in *Pediatrics* found that viewing educational programming—shows with a clear intent to educate—from birth to age three was not associated with children developing attention problems, however, viewing entertainment television during this period in a child's life was linked to attention difficulties.[19] We'll look more closely at recommended screen limits in Chapter 3.

HOW READING DEVELOPS SELF-CONTROL

Clearly reading benefits children of all ages, as kids who frequently read have more advanced language development and get better academic grades than kids who read less.[20] Still, even more is happening when children are read to or read themselves: It helps develop their brain's ability to maintain self-control. The practice of reading, or listening to a book being read, requires that kids focus attention on a challenging activity without the attention-grabbing sights and sounds of TV cartoons or video games. As Daniel Willingham, Professor of Psychology at the University of Virginia, said in a recent *New York Times'* article, reading teaches kids that there's value in "doing something taxing, in delayed gratification."[21]

The following steps will help you promote your child's reading, and in turn build self-control skills.

Limit Screens that Discourage Reading

There's little question that children's use of screens gets in the way of their learning to read or learning to read better. A study by University of Michigan and University of Texas researchers shows children ages 10–19 who play video games spend 30% less time reading compared to non-gamers.[22] Similarly, the more TV kids watch the less they read and the less proficient readers they become.[23] Consistent with the theme of this book, challenge digital-age myths by strictly limiting your child's TV and amusement-based tech use to promote reading.

Create a Home Conducive to Reading

To promote our children's reading, what we *do* is more important than what we say. No matter how much we tell our kids to read, if we spend a lot of time watching TV or playing on the Internet, our kids will likely do the same. A classic study in the *Journal of Education Research*, which pre-dates the digital revolution, shows that parents' home activities and the environment we surround kids with has a profound influence on their interest in reading. Kids of kindergarten age were much more likely to take an interest in reading if their parents read to them daily, took them to the library, or kept books in their room. Also, these same-age kids were more likely to find reading appealing if their parents' leisure activities were focused around reading rather than watching TV.[24]

Choose Traditional Books Over Bells and Whistles

E-book apps designed for tablet computers and other electronic devices are heavily promoted as the ideal method for getting kids to read. Their *interactive features*—sound effects, videos, games, etc.—are supposed to captivate kids and entice them to read. While there's no doubt that e-books grab children's attention, there's concerning evidence about their effect on kids' reading skills.

A recent study by the Joan Ganz Cooney Center *Print Books vs. E-books* compares parent-child interactions while reading print books, basic e-books (without interactive features), and enhanced e-books (with interactive features). The study finds that children's use of both types of e-books, but especially the enhanced e-books, led parent-child pairs to have more *non-content related actions* as compared with print books.[25] In other words, when using e-books, parents and kids spent time focusing on non-reading matters such as the device itself, or parents had to push their kids' hands away from the device. This isn't surprising as the engaging features of e-gadgets can make it difficult for parents to help their kids stay focused on a story.

Print Books vs. E-books also compares how different types of books affect children's ability to recall a story. Perhaps not surprisingly, kids who use an enhanced e-book recall fewer story details than kids who read print or basic e-books. As the authors of the study conclude, "Some of the extra features of enhanced e-books may distract adults and children alike from the story, affecting the nature of conversation and the amount of detail children recall."[26]

Another common complaint about e-books by parents I work with is that kids left alone with the devices often don't read, but use them to video game or play around on the Internet at the expense of schoolwork. Such problems with e-books lead me to suggest that parents rely on traditional books, kids' magazines, and other printed materials, not e-books, to develop their children's reading skills.

Dialogic Reading

If fancy machines aren't well suited to teach children to read or read better, what is? *Dialogic reading*. This term may sound intimidating, however, it's a custom that parents have long used with their children. In dialogic reading, parents engage their children in discussion (*dialog*) about a book that they read together. Instead of parents doing all the talking while their children sit silently, parents encourage their kids to talk about the book's content through questions ("Oh, what's going to happen to the children?"). This helps elicit kids' responses, which parents can then expand on or follow-up with more questions, perhaps tying the book's content to their child's own life ("Do you remember when we saw the lion at the zoo?... What did he do?").

Dialogic reading helps kids use more words, speak in longer sentences, score higher on vocabulary tests, and have better expressive language skills.[27] That's because it helps kids practice *using language*. Dialogic reading also fosters children's language development because it helps kids associate books with loving moments with adults, and in turn encourages their desire to read as they grow older.

SELF-CONTROL IS CHILD'S PLAY

What's another way to build children's self-control? Let them play—a lot. While it may seem counterintuitive, kids' dramatic play is incredibly important for strengthening the brain's self-control abilities.

Dramatic play is the pretend or imaginative play of children. It often includes more than one child and involves symbolic representation of experiences kids see every day in life or books, i.e., playing school, parent, firefighter, space crew, or vet. Dramatic play supports problem solving, language, and social skills. Yet Russian psychologist Lev Vygotsky was the first to understand how dramatic play also builds children's executive functioning, cleverly observing, "A child's greatest self-control occurs in play."[28]

At first glance, children's dramatic play may appear carefree, but if you look more closely, you'll see that it's all about control. There are roles and rules to be followed, and if children step out of line or don't fulfill their responsibilities (for example, if a kid playing the firefighter role doesn't do the right thing), other children will help bring him into line.

What's magical in dramatic play is that children are motivated by *the play* to push themselves to self-regulate. In one study, four-year-olds who were asked to stand still could not do so for more than a minute, yet when the same kids were engaged in dramatic play guarding a factory, they could stand still, focused on their role, for more than four minutes.[29] Over the course of months and years, such experiences build brain connections that regulate self-control.

Contemporary researchers are now testing Vygotsky's principles. The innovative preschool program Tools of the Mind engages 4- and 5-year-olds in a curriculum designed around dramatic play. After a year in the program, participating kids exhibited substantially more self-control (such as the ability to contain impulsive behaviors) than children the same age in a more traditional preschool program.[30]

Promoting Dramatic Play

In previous generations, no one had to encourage children in this kind of play, which comes naturally to kids and is remarkably rewarding. Sadly, in an age of digital machines that provide addictive-level distractions, we need to actively support dramatic play to help our kids prosper.

Turn off screens to give play a chance. Ever try to get your child's (or spouse's) attention while he or she is staring at a screen? Impossible, really. Evolution has provided us with lower brain structures, such as the brain stem, that draw our focus to sudden movements in the environment. Referred to as the *orienting response*, this trait once helped us find food and kept us from becoming food for other creatures. The frenetic pace of today's fast-action video games and TV triggers the orienting response, and an unfortunate result is the loss of undistracted space needed for dramatic play. A report in *Pediatrics* found that the more children from birth to 12 years watched TV, the less they were involved in creative play.[31] So Step One in fostering play? You've guessed it by now—limit kids' screen time and regulate all family members' use of screen entertainment in the home.

Give your child play scenarios. You also may need to help your children develop a mental storehouse of play scenarios to draw from. How? It's pretty simple, actually. Expose your kids to a wide range of experiences in real life and through literature. Have your children cook with you; tour a local firehouse, airport, or farmers' market; expose them to travel and museums. Take advantage of a local children's theatre or band performance. Go to a sports event. Share enriching experiences outside the daily routines to foster your child's imagination.

Help your child appreciate all that's behind seemingly simple life experiences. While you and your child are waiting for an appointment with the pediatrician, keep your phone in your pocket and talk with your child about the roles of various medical staff and how a hospital or medical office works. At the grocery store, talk about how the products get there. When your child plays, he or she will have the material needed to generate ideas and be an active and knowledgeable participant.

Be a play coach, especially for tech-obsessed children. Children who have grown up in environments conducive to dramatic play usually do it instinctively, but the screen-heavy lives of the current generation of kids deprive many of the knowledge and ability to play. Parents therefore may need to guide their children's early forays into play. For example, you can help kids plan play activities by asking them, "If you're going to play doctor, who's going to be the nurse? What does a nurse do if someone is sick?" Parents or grandparents can play one of the roles and offer kids guidance until the play gets going. Once your children become comfortable with dramatic play, the play itself will be its own reward, and you can step away.

Provide opportunities for play. Solitary pretend play may help build children's self-control, however, it's also important to provide lots of opportunities to interact with other kids in unstructured ways. Siblings are good play partners; if you have an only child, ask cousins or your child's friends over for play dates. Quality childcare centers can provide an ideal setting for dramatic play, so look for programs that understand the value of play and also limit screens.

Props matter. "In all my games, I kill someone," seven-year-old Ben told me matter-of-factly, as he made it clear the only things he had to play with at home were violent video games. Many kids I work with don't have playthings that encourage positive play experiences. Instead, they either are solely engaged with screens or have toys that are movie or video game spin-offs. By their nature, spin-offs come with prepackaged character identities and purposes that can limit rather than foster dramatic play.

Look for toys and props that promote child-centered, open-ended play. "The best toy is 10% toy and 90% child," says Susan Linn, author of *The Case for Make Believe*. "We've got all these toys embedded with computer chips that talk and sing and play and dance at the press of a button. But what they do is deprive children of the ability to exercise their creativity. The toys that really foster creativity just lie there until they're transformed by children."[32] A box of discarded, colorful clothes and hats is great—the same item can connote a firefighter one day and a pilot the next. Dolls and stuffed animals that aren't media-character tie-ins, doctor's kits and cash registers, kids' tool kits and strollers also promote dramatic play.

WHAT FUELS SELF-CONTROL: MOTIVATION FROM WITHIN

"If you do your homework, you can play video games" or "If you get good grades this semester, I'll buy you a phone." Parents often rely upon their children's profound desire for tech gadgets as a carrot to motivate them to put effort into academics. Many well-meaning parenting experts recommend this strategy, and the immediate results may look positive, as the promise of technology for completed schoolwork can persuade even the most uninterested kid to put pencil to paper. What gets lost is the long-term consequences of using *extrinsic rewards* like video gaming time or the promise of a phone to influence our kids' behavior. As we'll see next, the common practice of trading technology rewards for school effort compromises our kids' self-control and chances of long-term success.

Intrinsic vs. Extrinsic Motivation

A technology incentive for completing homework is an example of *extrinsic motivation*, something external (e.g., video games) for the behavior we are asking of our kids (e.g., school effort). Other extrinsic rewards include money, ice cream, or other enticements we give kids in return for their performance. This contrasts with *intrinsic motivation*, internal factors that influence children to put strong effort into meeting a goal. Examples of intrinsic motivation include curiosity about how living things work which spurs interest in biology, or students' focused study to reach the goal of becoming a pilot, musician, or doctor—because that's what they've always wanted to be.

What's most effective to motivate your child to work hard, extrinsic or intrinsic motivation? It's intrinsic motivation by far. *Intrinsic motivation works because it promotes children's self-control and self-interest.* Kids motivated from within are focused, don't give up easily, and are driven to perform at their best level. Think about yourself. Are there activities at which you excel? Chances are it's because they intrinsically motivate you. If you enjoy them, you *want* to do well. Sure, a reward like a paycheck is nice, but what really gets us to try our best day in and day out is wanting to do well and taking pride in what we do.

Why Choose Intrinsic Motivation?

My recommendation to move away from extrinsic rewards and to embrace intrinsic motivation may sound foreign, especially since many trusted sources recommend using video games or other technologies as incentives for completed tasks. I fully agree that extrinsic rewards seem to make common sense, however, science sometimes reveals the unexpected, and in this case it shows why our kids will do better if we cultivate intrinsic motivation, especially in school.

Extrinsic rewards hurt intrinsic motivation. Perhaps the most disturbing effect of extrinsic rewards is that they *decrease* children's intrinsic motivation,[33] essentially robbing kids of the enjoyment in, and the effort they would otherwise put into, learning. Offering children extrinsic rewards inadvertently sends the message that schoolwork, for instance, isn't worth doing in its own right—what is really important is the video game or other reward. The long-term result is that kids put less effort into schoolwork. While it may seem that your child would never be motivated from within to study, this may be because using extrinsic rewards is diminishing the pleasure he or she otherwise could experience from learning and mastery provided by the activity itself.

Extrinsic rewards lead kids to choose easier tasks. Extrinsic rewards also limit success because they encourage kids to choose easier tasks.[34] If children know they'll receive a reward for schoolwork, they tend to do *just enough* to get the reward. The reward takes precedence over the learning. When kids choose easier work or classes, they avoid challenging tasks that really could bolster their learning and satisfaction.

Intrinsically motivated kids perform better academically. The best proof of the superiority of intrinsic over extrinsic motivation may be in the results. Researchers at Stanford and Columbia universities, and Reed College, found that the more 3rd- through 8th-grade children were intrinsically motivated, the better their grade point average and standardized test scores. The same researchers also found that extrinsically motivated kids had lower grade point averages and standardized test scores.[35]

How to Foster Kids' Intrinsic Motivation

The following actions will encourage your child's intrinsic motivation for school and other learning activities.

Shift away from extrinsic rewards. If you have been trading the use of video games, smartphones, or other technologies for your child's school effort, start to shift away from this practice. While this may be challenging, remember that—over time—extrinsic rewards actually lessen the chances that kids will put genuine effort into learning. For children who have grown used to having screen time as a reward for effort, I suggest having an age-appropriate talk with them about how rewards can make school seem less interesting and reduce their chances of success. For this reason they should be phased out. Over a period of weeks or months, begin to ask your kids to put in more school effort for less extrinsic reward, working towards eventually stopping the use of extrinsic rewards.

Moving away from extrinsic screen rewards demands that kids use much less entertainment technology and TV than is now typical. A number of parents I work with have found eliminating video games and TV Monday through Thursday inspires their kids to do well in school. A system of this sort gives kids a chance to put effort into their studies, appreciate what they are learning, do their homework without rushing, and achieve. I know this is a radical departure from how most American children live, but as we'll see in the next chapter, our kids—caught up in long hours of digital playtime—are academically underperforming compared to their peers in the developed world. We need strong action to change this.

If these weekday screen limits seem like too much to ask of your family, an alternative is to provide a "screen-free space" (e.g., no entertainment technologies or TV) after school, perhaps until after dinner or a set time like 8 p.m. This minimizes children's incentives to rush through homework or falsely claim that it's done just to get to digital playtime sooner.

Children with learning difficulties, ADHD, or some other challenge that makes school tasks more difficult can struggle to gain intrinsic motivation for academic learning. Limited use of extrinsic rewards may be necessary to get these kids started on tasks. If this is the case, as soon as possible make efforts to fade or minimize extrinsic rewards.

Create a home environment that inspires intrinsic motivation. The research of Adele and Allen Gottfried[36] shows how we can create a home environment that encourages children's intrinsic desire to learn:

- **Promote curiosity**: Pay close attention to your children's interests, whether these are how the human body works or how things are put together. Help an interested child learn more about these subjects by taking trips together to the bookstore or library or by assisting in an Internet search for age-appropriate information. Many research institutions and museums now offer real-world sites for exploration and experimentation; some even allow children to participate in real research. If museums or natural environments that promote these interests (a quarry, a nature center, an observatory) are available, consider a visit.

- **Help your child experience success**: Get to know your children's strengths—whether these are in putting things together or writing stories—so that you can help them achieve success. When kids master a learning activity, it helps them say to themselves, "I've done this before, and so I can do it again." When your kids struggle in certain tasks, as we all do, be there to support them and demonstrate that your love isn't contingent on a particular outcome. Help them to figure out what might work better and improve the end result. This can give our kids the strength to try again and again, even when they fall short of their original expectations.

- **Expose kids to learning-focused environments**: When your family takes a daytrip or vacation, include visits to historic points of interest, science centers, or other sites that broaden your kids' experience. Support these visits by reading up on them with your child before and after the experience.

Help kids find the value of academics. The relevance of acquiring skills learned in school is frequently lost on digitally-transfixed kids. "I won't need math (or science or English) when I'm older," kids tell me. College and career are often a distant abstraction, something assumed, or to be considered later, much later. What's very real *now* are the social networks or entertainment devices that kids log onto the second the afternoon school bell rings. Unable to make the connection between academic effort and later life success, kids lose the intrinsic motivation they need to succeed.

We need to help our children recognize that school-based learning is useful to *them*.[37] For younger ones, this may involve showing them how reading can help for baking a cake or navigating a zoo. As our children progress through elementary school, we can play board games like Monopoly that use and develop math skills or Scrabble for language skills. For preteens and teens who plan to attend college, it's important to help them appreciate why they need to put in all that effort in middle and high school. Kids I work with have commented that visiting college campuses with their parents or an academic club has helped make tangible what they were shooting for and increased their sense of purpose.

Used correctly, some rewards help. While material extrinsic rewards (e.g., time online, phones, or TV) diminish kids' intrinsic motivation, verbal praise encourages that motivation if it is:

- **focused on strong effort and persistence rather than performance**, e.g., a compliment for working hard, not only for an "A"[38]
- **used sparingly**, not every time a child completes a task[39]
- **specific to the task rather than general**, saying, for instance, "You studied really hard for that math test and that helped you a lot,"[40] instead of a generic, "Good job"
- **genuine**, focused on something the child realistically sees him or herself as doing well, as kids see through insincere compliments[41]

3

Promote Kids' Academic Success

The image of kids sitting at school with pencil and paper can seem old-fashioned compared to the high-tech, gadget-filled world they embrace the moment the school day ends. It's not surprising that some pundits suggest video games, social networks, and other entertainment technologies are invaluable to children's learning and success in the 21st century. Some go so far as to say video games promote kids' learning *better* than school. One of the first proponents of this philosophy is author James Paul Gee, who declared: "The fact is, when kids play videogames they can experience a much more powerful form of learning than when they're in the classroom."[1]

The video-gaming's-better-than-school mantle has more recently been assumed by video game developer Jane McGonigal, author of *Reality is Broken*. She proclaims: "There's this big misconception about games that they are a waste of time, but 10 years of scientific research show that playing games is actually the most productive thing we can do, more productive than most of what we spend doing in work or at school."[2]

Others make claims about the learning value of social networks. In an effort to justify why kids younger than 13 should be allowed to use Facebook, the company's co-founder Mark Zuckerberg declared it vital to young kids' learning: "My philosophy is that for education you need to start at a really, really young age."[3]

Such cheerleading for video games and social networks is frequently picked up by the popular press and reported as being based in fact. The message to parents is quite clear: Encourage your children to use fun-based digital applications and the devices that access them—phones, tablets, computers, gaming consoles, etc.—and be less concerned about focusing kids on school-based learning tasks. That sure would make parenting a lot easier, yet are such claims true?

HOW IMPORTANT IS SCHOOL TODAY?

To determine how entertainment technologies affect children's learning and chances of success, let's begin by judging the value of traditional schooling, then look at how screen technologies impact school performance. It's relatively straightforward to determine the value of college, so let's start there, then consider the value of earlier schooling that prepares kids for college.

There are valid concerns about the fast-rising costs of college education, but no doubt about its benefits. In 2010, the US Census Bureau estimated that college graduates made $19,550 more per year than high school grads, and this gulf has increased in the interim.[4] Moreover, according to a study by the Pew Charitable Trusts, while it's challenging for college grads to find a job today, this pales in comparison to the struggles of those without a college degree.[5]

Clearly, going to college remains a critical element of our children's success. What can we do to ensure that they have the best chances of getting there? We can help them master the academic fundamentals high schools teach, as colleges select students based on their proficiency in 9th to 12th grade subjects, including math, English, and science. Colleges also evaluate students based on their performance on standardized college admissions tests like the SAT and ACT (the Scholastic Aptitude Test and the American College Testing Program), both of which test reading and math abilities.

The path to high school and college achievement actually starts early in kids' lives. A report from ACT states: "College and career readiness is not something that suddenly 'happens' when a student graduates from high school but instead is the result of a process extending through all the years of a student's education. College and career readiness is not a high school issue—it's a K–12 issue."[6] Because young brains are so sensitive, I would add that learning experiences from birth to kindergarten also play a crucial role in preparing kids for college and later life success.

The bottom line: The learning skills children gain in school are remarkably important to their success. Nevertheless, to gauge the value of traditional schooling, we also need to consider the effects of kids' school involvement on their health and well-being. According to Johns Hopkins Professor of Medicine Robert Blum: "Research has shown that students who feel connected to school do better academically and also are less likely to be involved in risky health behaviors: drug use, cigarette smoking, early sex, violence and suicidal thoughts and attempts."[7] So add emotional well-being to the benefits kids' school involvement offers.

TECHNOLOGY'S IMPACT ON ACADEMIC PERFORMANCE

How does our children's use of technology affect their academic performance? To answer that question, *it's important to recognize that various types of technology affect kids' learning quite differently.* There's no doubt that we need to provide our kids the skills to use technology productively. However, our kids only spend 16 minutes a day using a computer at home for school-related learning.[8] So the far more pressing question is how do the gaming, social networking, TV, and other entertainment technologies that occupy the equivalent of a full-time job in our kids' lives affect their ability to be successful in school and life?

Video Games, Social Networks, and TV—The Same Story

Numerous studies show that the more high school or college kids use *video games* or *social networks*, the less well they perform academically, as evidenced by lower GPA and other performance markers.[9] Family physician and psychologist Leonard Sax notes the effects of gaming on academics in *Boys Adrift*: "A series of studies over the past seven years has demonstrated clearly and unambiguously that the *more time your child spends playing video games, the less likely he is to do well in school*—whether he is in elementary school, middle school, high school, or college [emphasis in original]."[10] Similarly, as noted in a study of kids' (ages 9 to 17) use of social networks, heavier users receive lower grades (a mix of Bs and Cs or lower) than students who use them less frequently.[11]

The effects of video gaming and social networking on academic success echo the effects of earlier TV technology—negative. Why? Because kids use these newer technologies much like television. American kids watch very few educational TV programs. Instead they indulge in entertainment programming that displaces reading and homework and therefore hurts school performance.[12] Likewise, a study in the *Archives of Pediatrics & Adolescent Medicine* finds that children aged 10–19 who play video games spend 34% less time on homework and 30% less time reading than nongamers.[13] And kids' top three social networking activities are posting messages, downloading music, and downloading videos[14]—activities that often supersede schoolwork.

The displacement of school-based learning by video games can start early. A study by researchers from Denison University that explored the impact of giving 1st- to 3rd-grade boys a video game player reads like an obituary for kids' school effort. Four months after receiving the player, the boys were gaming more, had lower reading and writing scores, and had more teacher-reported academic problems. What were the reasons for the decline? The researchers described something quite similar to what I see in my practice almost every day: increased gaming displaced time spent in afterschool learning activities like homework, reading, listening to stories, and writing.[15]

The amount of entertainment screen time that puts kids' academic performance in jeopardy is actually quite small. A *Pediatrics* study of 5th to 8th graders found that kids who used more than 1 hour of video games or 3 hours of TV per weekday were more likely to have below average academic performance than those who used less.[16] Another study found that boys ages 6 to 9 who played video games an average of about 40 minutes per weekday scored lower academically than boys who played for about 10 minutes per weekday.[17]

Texting

The more college students text, the less well they perform academically as measured by GPA.[18] Research has yet to look into the effects of texting on academics for middle- and high-school students. There are reasons for concern, however: In a recent study looking at how texting affected the study habits of middle-school, high-school, and college students, these students reported that texting was the number one reason they were *drawn off task from studying*.[19]

Computers and the Internet

Determining the effects of computers and the Internet on children's academic performance is challenging because these technologies can be used for entertainment *or* education. Evidence suggests that effects hinge on how these technologies are used. A study of Taiwanese middle-school students shows that the use of the Internet to *search for information* was associated with higher scores on a high-school entrance exam, but using the Internet *to game or socialize* was associated with lower scores on the exam.[20]

Unfortunately, as we have seen, our kids' use of technology, including computers and the Internet, is dominated by entertainment applications. According to the Kaiser Family Foundation, the top three computer activities for children ages 8 to 18 are social networking, gaming, and watching online videos.[21] In spite of all the promise computers offer our kids, it's disappointing that two out of the three greatest components of their computer use (social networking and gaming) are associated with lower academic performance. While there hasn't been study of how kids' watching online videos affects school performance, it's a very similar activity to watching TV, an activity we know hurts kids' school success.

It's therefore not surprising that Duke University researchers found the introduction of computers or high-speed, broadband Internet access into homes led to lower academic scores for 5th- through 8th-grade kids.[22] As researcher Jacob Vigdor observed, when adults aren't supervising computer use, kids "are left to their own devices, and the impetus isn't to do homework but play around."[23]

THE HIGH COSTS OF A MYTH

We've seen that traditional schooling is immensely important to children's success and that overusing entertainment technologies undermines academic performance. If claims that video gaming or social networking boost children's learning were true, these technologies would need to provide tremendous benefits to kids in domains other than school. Unfortunately, while the time kids spend playing around on their gadgets may teach them certain skills, no convincing research shows that these skills translate into real-world success, especially when weighed against the costs amusement-based technologies pose to academic achievement.

In his book *What Video Games Have to Teach Us About Learning and Literacy*, gaming advocate James Paul Gee says that video games teach problem-solving skills.[24] There is no doubt that children and teens who play video games are learning something, and they may become adept at solving the problems created by video games. However, there is no evidence that such skills are preferable to the problem-solving skills kids gain from non-tech-based classroom exercises, science projects, or enrichment programs. Meanwhile, we have abundant research that our kids' overuse of gaming hinders their academic performance and, as we will see in Chapter 4, puts them at risk of addiction. In other words, video games and other entertainment technologies provide questionable benefits yet known risks to kids' learning success.

The risks posed by video gaming are generally ignored by their advocates, some of whom claim the superiority of the technology over real life. For example, in *Reality is Broken,* Jane McGonigal says, "Compared with games, reality is pointless and unrewarding. Games help us feel more rewarded for making our best effort," and "Compared with games, reality is disorganized and divided. Games help us make a more concerted effort—and over time, they give us collaboration superpowers."[25] Yet in reviewing McGonigal's book, *New York Times* William Saletan says her assertions about the benefits of gaming lack "reliable evidence." Similarly, Andrew Klavan's *Wall Street Journal* review of the same book says McGonigal "seems to confuse states of feeling with facts."[26]

Some of the most recent claims about the learning benefits of entertainment technologies are described by Clive Thompson in his book *Smarter Than You Think.* He says, "[Video] Games evoke modes of thinking that can be enormously valuable in education." Nonetheless, Thompson relies upon hypotheticals and anecdotes for corroborative support, while neglecting the mounds of evidence in peer-reviewed journals that show the negative impact of video games on kids' academic performance.

Thompson's failing is that his captivating narratives disregard a basic reality of American kids' technology consumption: profound overuse of entertainment technologies which displace school-based activities such as homework and therefore lead to kids' academic struggles. Nonetheless, contentions about the benefits of gaming and other entertainment technologies are often reported as fact in the popular media.

The myth that entertainment technologies advance our kids' learning has unfortunately encouraged a nation of parents to feel good about loading their kids with tech gadgets, while paying less attention to indicators of school success. I see the consequences in my work. I meet with many families whose children or teens are struggling academically because they overuse digital self-amusements. The parents often don't bat an eye as their kids describe typical afterschool schedules: "First I come home and watch funny YouTube videos, then check Facebook, and then hop on *Call of Duty*, but I'm always texting.... Oh ... when do I do homework? Sometimes late at night if I have time...." When I ask these kids' parents if they'll consider making school a bigger priority, many see no such need. "He'll be fine," they tell me.

FALLING DOWN ON THE WORLD'S STAGE

Loyalty to the belief that entertainment technologies advance kids' success is costing our children greatly, as our tech-obsessed kids have less time and inclination to learn educational fundamentals. The Program for International Student Assessment (PISA) tests and compares the academic performance of 15-year-old students from countries around the world. The latest results (2012) were disappointing to say the least. America now ranks 30th in math, 23rd in science, and 20th in reading compared to the 64 other countries that took the exam.[27]

American kids' 2012 scores remained stagnant from the previous test while numerous countries surpassed us. In 2009, 23 countries outperformed the US in math, 29 did so in 2012. While 18 countries outdid the US in science in 2009, 22 did so in 2012. And 9 countries surpassed the US in reading in 2009 compared to 19 in 2012.[28] In the 2012 testing, 18 countries scored higher than the United States in *all three subjects*, including perennial standouts such as Korea and Japan, yet also Poland, Estonia, Ireland, and New Zealand. This should spur concern, as the PISA measures the skills colleges use to evaluate high-school students for admission.

While America seems enchanted by kids' ability to multitask between video games, TV, social networks, and texting, our biggest global competitors recognize that educational fundamentals are essential. China and India are embarking on bold programs to increase their investment in public education (China is spending $250 billion each year.[29]) A recent report, *The Competition that Really Matters*, warns that our competitors' greater emphasis on schooling will pose increasing risks to our nation's ability to compete globally.[30]

How can we help American kids compete on at least equal footing with children from other nations? A first step is moving beyond the belief that educational funding is a political issue to recognize it as a matter of national economic interest. Yet as three-time Pulitzer prize winner Thomas Friedman and Johns Hopkins professor Michael Mandelbaum note in their book, *That Used To Be Us*, adding resources to education won't help unless American students dramatically cut back their amusement-based technology habits and instead focus on school.[31]

WHAT CAN WE ASK OF OUR KIDS?

Can we really ask our kids to put more effort into schoolwork? High rates of psychiatric disorders and self-injurious behaviors such as cutting show American children are significantly stressed.[32] A series of annual University of California, Los Angeles (UCLA) surveys shows that a growing number of college freshmen report they felt "overwhelmed by all I had to do" during their senior year of high school.[33] Do high homework demands drive this stress? Let's take a look.

The same UCLA study asked how much time these kids spent doing homework during their senior year of high school. Since the study only includes students attending college, we would expect them to report more homework than the average high-school student. Counter-intuitively, about 6 in 10 kids said they spent less than an hour per night on homework as seniors. Only about 10% of kids spent more than two hours on homework each night.

There is no doubt that a minority of kids are overburdened academically, and this problem should be addressed. However, UCLA's study corroborates research that shows the majority of American teenagers actually spend little time studying compared to the tremendous amount of time they spend video gaming, social networking, texting, and watching TV.

So why are our kids so stressed? I believe it's time to look critically at what's changing dramatically in our kids' lives. That's the exploding use of entertainment technologies that chokes off their connection with family and school—both vital to kids' emotional health.

Does Homework Help Kids?

Homework is a hot-button issue, as the popular media questions whether it benefits kids and, if it's helpful, what's the right amount. Harris Cooper, Professor of Education and Chair and Professor of Psychology and Neuroscience at Duke University, and the author of *The Battle Over Homework,* is an authority on these matters. He's an advocate for not overloading kids with homework, yet he's found that homework benefits children significantly if the amount is appropriate for their developmental level.

Cooper's research finds that educators' traditional "10-Minute Rule," which multiplies a child's grade by 10 minutes (e.g., 6th grade x 10 minutes = 60 minutes), provides a good basis for how much homework is appropriate. For high school, especially if a teen is enrolled in honors classes, there may be advantages to increasing this guideline. Cooper says that the maximum amount of time high-school kids should spend on homework is 1½ to 2½ hours per night, after which there are diminishing returns.[34] Contrast this with the research that indicates most American teens—who average 5½ hours of entertainment screen use plus 2½ hours of texting and talking on phones each day—put in less than an hour per night on homework.

Some children may benefit from less homework, including kids with ADHD or learning disabilities. Consult with your children's teacher or counselor, especially if you feel they are spending too much time on homework. Still, I believe the evidence is clear that most American children would gain from powering down their devices and spending more time with their school books open.

In the remainder of this chapter, we focus on strategies to help our kids shift their attention from digital amusements to school-based learning.

TECHNOLOGY USE GUIDELINES

To foster your children's school success, I suggest setting screen time and cell phone limits very different from what the average American child or teen experiences. I believe a good place to look for guidance is the American Academy of Pediatrics' recommendation that children and teens (ages 2 and older) should be limited to 1 to 2 hours or less of total entertainment screen time per day—including TV, computer-based entertainment, and video games.[35] (I will address children's use of cell phones in the next section.)

If your family puts high importance on children's academics, there is support for even greater limits on screen use, especially on weekdays.[36] Parents I talk with have found that eliminating screen use from Monday to Thursday, and limiting *total* screen time to two hours per day on weekends (Friday to Sunday) puts their child or teen in the best position to succeed in school.

Some parents I talk with understandably question the need to set screen limits, even if their kids spend a great deal of time with entertainment technologies, because they are doing well enough in school, perhaps getting As and Bs. And it's true, sometimes intelligent kids can get by in school without exerting a great deal of effort—especially in the earlier grades.

In my experience, however, such kids often pay a price in high school, when greater homework demands become a poor match for a lack of study skills. I also think about lost potential—what could these kids have achieved if they hadn't spent so much time playing with gadgets? Finally, as I mention in Chapter 9, I recommend that parents and teens become aware of today's increasingly rigorous college admission demands. For example, the high school GPA of admitted college freshman to many schools is often quite remarkable.

THE MYTH OF MOBILE

Industry promises that mobile devices, such as smartphones and tablets, are essential for children's learning have helped drive a meteoric rise in our kids' use of these gadgets. The devices are remarkably powerful, but their effect on children's learning success doesn't match the hype.

The Mobile Industry Sales Pitch

Emotion-eliciting commercials show kids using mobile devices to achieve dazzling learning feats. A commercial for Google's tablet computer, the Nexus 7, shows a boy about 12 retreating to his own spaces with the device to study public speaking in order to overcome his speech anxiety.[37] He studies so hard that his mother has to tip-toe into his room at night to pull the tablet away from the sleeping boy. The message is clear: Buy your kids this gadget and learning will take care of itself.

While heartwarming, such marketing is disingenuous. As we see throughout this book, our kids focus their technology use largely around gaming and other entertainment applications. Parents I work with tell me that, just like in the commercial, they find their kids using tablets late into the night. The difference is they find their kids using the devices to sneak in more game time. As Mike Vorhaus, a media research consultant responding to a recent survey of kids and adults, says, "The great majority of tablet owners love tablet gaming, and the tablet is becoming their go-to device for gaming."[38]

Tech corporations commission their own studies to sway the public. The cell phone company Verizon funded a study that found about a third of the middle-school students surveyed reported using their smartphones and tablets for homework.[39] Verizon then issued a press release touting: "Kids FINALLY have a case for why they are using mobile devices for homework."[40]

Verizon claimed that the study's findings might change the minds of parents and teachers who see for themselves how mobile devices can hamper learning. As the press release noted, "Many parents and teachers see these devices as distracting to kids, but this national study proves that even this young age group deserves more credit for how they're using them as 1 in 3 are using mobile device for homework and they're helping them learn better."[41]

Yet do mobile technologies really help children learn? The Verizon study doesn't tell us that. It doesn't report the surveyed kids' grades. It can't determine if kids would have been better off spending their time doing something else, or how much these devices distracted kids from their studies. However, we're fortunate that emerging research is revealing the true impact of mobile technologies on kids' school success. So back to the science.

Mobile's Impact on Kids' Connection to Family and Learning Success

One clear effect of mobile devices is that they *dramatically increase the amount of time kids spend using entertainment technologies.* As noted by the Kaiser Family Foundation: "The transformation of the cell phone into a media content delivery platform, and the widespread adoption of the iPod and other MP3 devices, have facilitated an explosion in [recreationally-based] media consumption among American youth.... Today, the development of mobile media has allowed—indeed, encouraged—young people to find even more opportunities throughout the day for using media, actually expanding the number of hours when they can consume media, often while on the go."[42]

Kids' top uses for their smartphones include gaming, texting, social networking, and TV watching (all entertainment-focused).[43] Look over kids' shoulders to see how they're using their phones and tablets and you'll find them watching TV, a lot of TV, in settings where kids once read a book or did their homework. The Kaiser Family Foundation reports: "Television content [kids ages 8–18] once consumed only by sitting in front of a TV set at an appointed hour is now available whenever and wherever they want, not only on TV sets in their bedrooms, but also on their laptops, cell phones and iPods."[44]

In essence, mobile technologies act as portals for children and teens to gain increased access to entertainment technologies, that, as we've seen in this book, pull kids away from involvement with family and a focus on schoolwork. This contrasts with the tech industry's claim of benefits, however, it's a reality we need to face if we are to help our children thrive emotionally and succeed academically.

COUNTERING THE MYTH OF MOBILE

The following strategies will help you push back against an industry determined to wire up kids with ever more mobile devices.

Don't Lose Control of Your Kids

Even champions of children's use of technology acknowledge that mobile devices *reduce* parents' ability to manage their kids. The Online Mom organization tends to be an industry-friendly advocate of kids' tech use, but co-founder Monica Vila acknowledges what happened when she provided her kids access to mobile: "I used to regard myself as one of those tech-savvy moms.... I even had my kids' tech habits under control. There was a strict 'no-tech-before-homework' rule, parental controls on all the computers and a total of three hours a week set aside for video games. It worked well for about a year. Then everything went mobile and I lost control."[45]

Vila is right. Mobile technologies weaken your ability to oversee your children's use of technology and provide the structure to do well in school. "She's in her room and I walk in and she's on her phone instead of doing her homework," a mom told me about her 14-year-old daughter. "But she tells me she was just texting a friend about a homework assignment.... I'd like to believe her yet she's on her phone all the time." Privately, many teens tell me that their inability to manage their phone use is hurting their school grades, which is quite understandable considering their struggle with impulse control as we will discuss in Chapter 9.

What's the best way to maintain control of your kids? Don't buy smartphones, tablets, and other mobile devices for your child. It's much harder to limit misuse once your kids have the 24/7 ability to use time-wasting applications out of your sight. Just as the best way to limit kids' use of sugary soda is to not bring it home, the same is true of mobile devices.

Why Kids Deserve a Basic Phone Rather Than a Smartphone

As a parent, I understand the instinct to be in contact with our children. I also appreciate that we all want the best for our kids, for them to have nice clothes, the latest sports equipment, etc. Understandably, this has led many parents to decide that when their child gets a phone, it may as well be a smartphone, perhaps one with all the bells and whistles. However, it's increasingly clear that smartphones pose more risks than rewards to kids. I therefore suggest that when kids are of the age that they need a phone, they are better served by basic phones that don't provide Internet access and unlimited texting with peers. This can be achieved by purchasing a basic phone and then accessing parental controls on the phone or through your cell phone provider.

"So at what age... ?"

"So what's the right age for a child to get a smartphone (tablet, or other mobile device)?" This question is often asked by parents who believe mobile technologies help children learn, yet as we've seen in several contexts, the opposite appears to be true. There doesn't seem to be an age when the risks mobile devices pose to academics fade, as the possession of such gadgets encourages both younger kids and adolescents to overuse entertainment technologies. I therefore believe it's time to stop viewing children's ownership of mobile devices as a beneficial rite of passage and to recognize it as a threat to family connection and school success for kids of all ages.

Specifically regarding cell phones, I think that kids are better served by basic phones than smartphones through their high-school years. Although this runs counter to the direction our culture is moving in, the very nature of kids' smartphone use (providing addictive entertainment technologies away from parental oversight) makes it likely that children with smartphones will be indulging in digital amusements harmful to their well-being. If you feel it's important for your kid to reach you during the school day, give him or her a phone that provides *only* that capability without Internet access or the ability to text peers.

I realize that parents may feel that their child will feel left out without a smartphone or tablet. If you feel at some point that your child should have a device due to social pressure, it's understandable. That said, we best serve our children by working together as parents, schools, and a nation to use research rather than corporate-sponsored myths in making decisions about our kids' use of mobile devices.

Redefining Luxury

One of the reasons kids demand smartphones is that they want them as status symbols. Marketing research shows that if we can be convinced a product connotes "luxury," we are more likely to demand it for ourselves,[46] so cell phone makers try to convince us that their products are indicators of wealth and status.

Yet the mobile industry appears to be a victim of its own success. Cell phone companies have sold so many smartphones to families of all economic levels that it's undermined their ability to claim their products are a luxury item. As noted in the 2013 *Teens and Technology* report by the Pew Research Center and Harvard's Berkman Center: "Teens living in the lowest-earning households (under $30,000 per year) are just as likely as those living in the highest-earning households ($75,000 or more) to own smartphones."[47]

I suggest that it's time to redefine luxury in order to shift consumer demand. What is in fact increasingly rare for today's children and teens is to have undistracted, device-free moments with their parents or school studies. If we begin to view the parent-child bond and academic success as luxury goods, we may make more effort to attain them.

An Exception for Devices that only Play Music

The mobile devices that pose the most risk to children's learning are those that facilitate video games, social networks, video, and texting. There isn't evidence that listening to music detracts from children's school performance, so I don't think that you should be concerned about providing kids devices that are designed to allow music listening without other features. That said, I believe parents should insist that personal music-listening devices not be used to shut parents or siblings out of kids' lives, e.g., these devices shouldn't be used during moments when family members could converse, such as during drives to and from school.

If Kids Have Mobile Devices, Limit Their Use Because Kids Can't

If you decide to provide your child a mobile device, you need to limit how it is used, as we'll see the addictive potential of the content mobile devices make available in Chapter 4. The combination of addictive content and a child's or teen's less-developed prefrontal cortex (the brain's judgment center) is a poor match.

Even fully mature adults struggle to control their technology use. In a *Huffington Post* article, Jennifer Meer, mother of two, says, "Last week, I almost killed my daughter."[48] She says that she put her 3-year-old daughter in the tub and started the water, and then went to another bathroom to start the shower for her 5-year-old son. Before she got back to her daughter, she heard the ping of her iPad, saw an email from a friend and felt compelled to respond to it. Doing so, Jennifer left her daughter alone in the tub for about two minutes. When Jennifer returned to her daughter, she found her asleep, slumped against the side of the tub. By tremendous fortune, her daughter had not slipped under the water.

Describing why she reached for the iPad, Jennifer said, "Because it's an option, I feel compelled to exercise that option.… The choice is there so I feel compelled to act on it."[49] Most of us can empathize. That said, if a loving, responsible mom unconsciously chooses her mobile devices at the risk of her daughter's life, what can we realistically expect from our children and teens? Our kids need our help.

Changing the Way Our Kids Do Homework

Tech industry spin has convinced many parents to place no limits on their kids' smartphone use, with a resulting dramatic transformation in how our kids do homework. While most parents wouldn't consider allowing their children to study with the TV on, today's parents generally think nothing of allowing their kids to study with a constantly buzzing, pinging, flashing smartphone that distracts and detracts from homework much like the TV.

I suggest that you set the same limits on smartphones as you do the TV during study time. That means prescribing the hours when kids can use smartphones, if you permit them at all, especially during weekdays after school. If you don't limit TV during homework, start to do that, too. For example, you could allow your teen to use the phone from 9 to 10 p.m. on weekdays. This seems to work better than saying kids can't use their phone until homework is done, to circumvent the incentive for kids to rush through their studies.

Of course kids will complain that they need their phones to communicate with peers about homework. This argument belies the truth of how our kids really use their phones. There's also no doubt that many kids will protest denying them continual access to texting, gaming, social networking, and the like, yet such tech habits have emerged from a culture taken with industry-sponsored myths. What is very real is that American students need to catch up with the rest of the world academically. To do so, we need to make tough choices.

How Parents Can Set Limits on Mobile

Let me be clear. The best way to set limits on kids' use of mobile devices is to not provide them with a smartphone or other mobile device in the first place. If a child *has* a mobile device, make every effort to limit its use. Setting such limits starts with you being a good role model. Are you using your own device to play indiscriminately or do you use it primarily for work or necessary tasks?

I also suggest following the advice of Rosalind Wiseman in *Queen Bees and Wannabes:* "There needs to be a family rule that, when people walk into your house, their cell phones go in a basket in the hallway or the kitchen. You get a pass if you are a doctor or therapist and you're on call—but only when you're on call. This also should go for any other child who is over at your house."[50] You also can place limits on kids' phones by using parental control features (accessed through your cell phone provider) that limit how much and when they can be used.

How can kids stay in touch with their peers? I suggest you maintain a home landline for this purpose, and once kids reach middle-school-age, it's also appropriate for them to converse with friends via email on a computer. Phone calls or emails that come in during dinner and other family moments, as well as during homework time, can be returned later. The alternative, of kids having continuous access to mobile, means that their attention to family and schoolwork are continually threatened by a compulsion to return a text, check social networks, or game.

Kids should never be allowed to sleep with phones or other mobile devices in their bedrooms, as many do. Preteen and teen drama and the desire to game can go late into the night, denying kids the sleep they need to perform well at school.

How Schools Should Address Kids' Smartphones

Because kids' smartphone use is centered around entertainment technologies shown to hurt academic success, I believe it detracts from teachers' ability to do their job. I therefore suggest that schools place strong limits on kids' use of smartphones, and that parents ask for them. For example, rules that kids should keep their phones at home or in their lockers better support learning than allowing them at passing periods, lunch, etc.

BUILD UNITASKING, NOT MULTITASKING, SKILLS

Mobile devices have fueled an increase in kids' efforts to multitask between entertainment technologies and schoolwork. Fifteen-year-old Sherry's study habits are typical of the kids with whom I work. "I do my homework better if I'm texting and have the TV on," she insists. The latest Kaiser Family Foundation study found more than half of kids aged 8 to 18 multitask during homework either most or some of the time.[51] Because multitasking is typically applauded by popular sources, you may believe you have little reason to be concerned about your child's ability to split focus.

The Multitasking Mirage

The belief that kids (or adults) can competently multitask is another invention of our present-day culture. As developmental molecular biologist John Medina says in his book *Brain Rules*, "The brain cannot multitask. Multitasking, when it comes to paying attention, is a myth. The brain naturally focuses on concepts sequentially, one at a time."[52] To put this in practical terms: Although the brain can complete two *simple tasks* simultaneously (e.g., walking and chewing gum), it simply cannot attend to two *attention-demanding tasks* (e.g., texting a friend and completing chemistry homework) at the same time. Attempting to multitask results in toggling attention back and forth between various tasks, increasing the time to complete them and the chance of errors.

Many kids (and adults) claim they can effectively multitask. Can they be right? Not likely. Stanford University researchers found frequent multitaskers are actually more distractible and more likely to be sidetracked by irrelevant information than those who multitask less or not at all.[53] To explain this, the Stanford scientists suggest that the brains of heavy multitaskers may become primed to attend to distractions, and end up being more disrupted by them. As study co-author Clifford Nass said of those who claim to multitask well, "They're suckers for irrelevancy.... Everything distracts them."[54]

Evidence of the costs of multitasking is emerging. A recent study observed the learning habits of middle-school, high-school, and college kids, and found that those who checked Facebook at least once every 15 minutes had lower grade point averages than kids who were less frequent Facebook users.[55]

Teaching Kids to Unitask

The good news is that unitasking is a skill that we can help our children (or ourselves) develop. Because the brain works much like a muscle, by setting up the environment to encourage unitasking, this skill can build over time. Consider the following strategies to help your child develop focus skills.

Clear your child's study environment of phone and screen distractions. Earlier in the chapter, I suggested ways to limit the distractions of mobile devices. It's also important to keep TVs off during homework time; even having a TV on in the next room can rob kids of the focus they need to do their best in school. If siblings have completed homework, encourage them to read or go outside rather than turn on a TV that will distract their brother or sister.

Keep computers off unless kids need to use them for an assignment. For kids who are especially prone to digital distraction, consider using the computer's parental control features or purchasing parental control software so they can only access the functions they need. If you don't feel you have the technical know-how, turn to a relative or family friend who can help.

Designate a family study time. One family I worked with had two teen boys who were failing their classes because of incessant multitasking. Nothing the parents tried made things better until they implemented a family study time. Working alongside your child in a common area can make for pleasing, relaxed family time—and it also limits kids' tendency to shift away from studying. Balance your checkbook, read, or catch up on some work while your kids get their homework done.

Build in study breaks. Study breaks help keep the mind focused and limit potential technology distractions. Because unitasking is a learned skill, children may need more frequent study breaks as they develop this ability. Go for non-technology breaks, since kids who turn to gaming, texting, or TV find it difficult to return to homework. Running around the yard, jumping rope, playing with the dog, listening to music, or engaging in conversation are break options to reinvigorate kids' minds and help them do their best work when they get back to their studies.

FINDING DOWNTIME IN A 24/7 CULTURE

Limiting kids' engagement with screens and phones provides them the *downtime* vital for memory formation and other thinking tasks.

When kids give their minds a break, by resting on the couch or running around outside, the hippocampus (a brain structure vital to creating memories) can communicate with the cortex (the brain's outer layer where memories are stored) to create long-term memories. "Your brain is working for you when you're resting, so rest is important for memory and cognitive function," New York University cognitive neuroscientist Lila Davachi explains. "This is something we don't appreciate much, especially when today's information technologies keep us working round-the-clock."[56]

A study in *Pediatrics* reveals how kids' use of one entertainment technology may threaten the downtime our kids need to remember what they've studied. Mirroring typical academic demands, researchers gave 12- to 14-year-old boys vocabulary words to study in the late afternoon. They divided the boys into three groups that engaged in different activities later that evening. In one group, the kids didn't use any screens at all, a second group watched an exciting movie, and the third group played an action-oriented video game. Remarkably, when the kids were tested on the vocabulary words the following day, those who video gamed showed significantly lower performance than the other two groups.[57]

Why would video gaming interfere with the creation of memory? The answer may be related to the very high level of dopamine gaming triggers. Throughout human history, dopamine has served an evolutionary function. Emotion-filled events vital for people to remember, such as a chance encounter with a predator, prompt the brain's release of dopamine, which gives the memory priority over the thousands of other mundane events that happen in a day. For today's kids, the amount of dopamine produced by emotionally-engaging video games may lead kids' brains to prioritize gaming memories over school experiences.

You can encourage downtime for your child by following the American Academy of Pediatrics' recommendation to make kids' bedrooms an electronic-media-free environment—including Internet-connected devices such as computers, smartphones, and tablets.[58] You can make an exception for listening to music without video, since it isn't associated with lower academic performance.

HOW CAN SCHOOLS AND COLLEGES CHALLENGE DIGITAL MYTHS?

We know the tech industry is quick to blame failing education systems when disappointing PISA scores or similar reports highlight American children's learning struggles, and that they suggest the solution is even more access to ever newer e-gadgets. You've also seen how the same industry ignores the fact that our kids use these gadgets primarily to gain access to entertainment technologies that drag down academic performance.

For the most part, schools and teachers have not countered such claims, in spite of surveys showing that teachers believe kids' overuse of digital technologies reduces their ability to learn,[59] and despite the fact that many hold schools and teachers almost solely responsible for students' learning deficits.

I suggest that schools, from elementary to high school, take leadership on the issue of children and technology. Parents and other members of the public need to understand that no matter how good teachers are, students can't succeed in the face of continuous exposure to digital amusement.

When I speak at forums that bring groups of parents and teachers together, such as parent-teacher meetings and back-to-school nights, I recommend that schools encourage parents to limit kids' entertainment technology in the interest of learning success. I also suggest that schools share pertinent research and talk directly with students to help them recognize that overusing entertainment technologies threatens the goals kids have for themselves, including getting good grades and attending college.

Colleges Should Also Challenge Digital Myths

With evidence that gaming, social networking, and texting diminish the academic achievement of young adults, I believe universities and colleges will benefit their students by helping them understand the risks posed by obsessive use of entertainment technologies. While this will help both genders, such discussions are especially important for young men because, as we will see in Chapter 5, boys and young men spend much more time with entertainment technologies, especially video gaming, than do girls and young women. Sadly, I have talked with many parents whose bright young men have been asked to leave university for failing grades caused by the overuse of video games.

Colleges should emphasize prevention. Build awareness by talking openly with incoming freshman at orientation and welcome week. Make systematic efforts to catch problems early. Encourage resident assistants and school counselors to watch for signs of tech obsession or addiction, and to be aware of resources that can treat the problem before it leads to student failure.

I also suggest colleges encourage their students not to multitask in the classroom to establish a better learning environment for all students. A study published in *Computers in Human Behavior* showed that college students who multitasked with Facebook or texting during class had lower grades than students who did not.[60] Another study simulated a typical college classroom to find that multitasking not only hurt the performance of the multitasker, but also nearby students who became focused on what the multitasker was doing.[61]

4
Protect Children from Video Game/ Internet Addiction

An episode of Katie Couric's talk show, *Katie,* focused on video game addiction. Guests included Mark Petric, whose 16-year-old son Daniel murdered his mother and shot his father because they took away his *Halo 3* video game.[1] Daniel had become obsessed with *Halo,* playing the game for up to 18 hours a day, stopping only to eat, sleep, and use the bathroom. He became enraged when his father took the video game away because of its violent content.

The day of the murder, Daniel's parents were relaxing on the couch. The teen walked up to them and said, "Would you guys close your eyes? I have a surprise for you." Mark said he expected something pleasant. Instead, the teen shot his father in the head—he was severely injured yet survived because the bullet missed his brain—and then turned the gun on his mother, Susan. He shot her in her arms, chest, and back of the head.

A few minutes after the shootings, Daniel's adult sister arrived with her husband to watch a baseball game. They found Daniel trying to clean up the horrific scene with a bucket and cloth. While the others attended to Susan and Mark, Daniel ran out of the house and drove away in the family van. Apprehended a short time later, the only item Daniel had taken from home was his *Halo 3* video game.[2]

Trial judge James Burge sentenced Daniel to 23 years in prison for the murder of his mother and attempted murder of his father.

Judge Burge said the evidence led him to conclude that video gaming played a significant role in the violence. In his closing statement, the judge expressed hope that the tragedy would inspire a greater understanding of video games and addiction, and that this would help "achieve a greater sense of justice."[3]

UNDERSTANDING IT'S AN ADDICTION CHANGES THE GAME

In more than 20 years of working with families, I have encountered many, many kids addicted to technology, primarily video games. Typical of these cases is 15-year-old Cameron, whose mother, Gloria, brought him to treatment because she couldn't understand what was happening to her son. She said he regularly gamed online past 2 a.m. on school nights barking orders to fellow gamers, and that his gaming obsession had led him to neglect his homework and fail classes.

In the week prior to bringing Cameron to therapy, Gloria had approached her son about her concerns, but he ignored her. When she insisted that he limit his gaming, this six-foot teen slammed his fist through a wall, then stood over her and got her to back down. That's when she decided to seek help. In our first meeting, in contrast to his mother's distress, Cameron was calm, even distant. He told me that he saw nothing wrong with his gaming and insisted his life was going well. He said school was overrated, and he planned to work in video gaming. When I asked how he felt about his aggression towards his mother, Cameron was unapologetic. He blamed her, saying she had no right to limit his gaming.

YOU'RE NOT ALONE

Because addiction to video games or the Internet is rarely discussed in the popular media, many parents, like Gloria, don't recognize what their children are experiencing when they show profound anger or other symptoms as the result of the addiction. If they do understand their child is struggling with a tech obsession, they tend to feel alone with their problems and that their child or teen is experiencing something unique. However, pediatricians and mental health providers across the country and around the world see increasing cases like Cameron's. As a result, video game and Internet addiction has been extensively researched, and there are now hundreds of high-quality published studies that collectively support the addictive potential of certain technologies.

Video games (especially those played online) appear to have the greatest potential for addiction, followed by social networks.[4] In turn, an increasing number of kids show unhealthy attachment to the devices that deliver this content, such as video game players, computers, phones, tablets, and handheld gaming devices.

Who's at risk? *Any child, teen, or adult.* Some suggest that tech addiction is really just a sign of an underlying psychiatric problem, e.g., the reason a kid is stuck gaming in his room is because he's depressed or anxious. And it's true that tech-addicted kids often suffer from other psychiatric problems. However, a study of 3rd, 4th, 7th, and 8th graders published in the journal *Pediatrics* found that symptoms of obsessive gaming often came *before* signs of anxiety or depression.[5] This evidence, along with other research, suggests that tech addiction is its own disorder and that other psychiatric problems are often the result of the addiction. This is what I see frequently in my practice: previously high-functioning kids who first become addicted to technology and *then* develop anger, defiance, and/or depression.

The research does show there are subgroups who are at greater risk for a tech addiction, including adolescent and young adult males, as well as kids with ADHD or an autism spectrum disorder.[6] In my experience, it's boys starting about the 5th grade who are more likely than other populations to show signs of addiction. Yet because boys' obsessive use of video games is so common, as discussed in Chapter 5, this may be normalized by parents.

"Why did my kid develop a problem when his (or her) friends didn't?," parents demand to know. Unfortunately, I don't have a good answer for them, as science may never be able to predict with certainty which children will develop a tech addiction, only that certain groups of kids are at greater risk. It's much like drug addiction, as some adults can use cocaine, methamphetamine, or other drugs many times and put these substances down for good while others develop a destructive habit soon after the first use.

What we can say is that tech addiction is becoming more commonplace. Whether measured in the United States, Europe, or Asia, the rates of technology addiction—what is often called "pathological video game or Internet use"—range from about 7% to 11% of teen and young adult gamers.[7] That means tens of millions of kids now suffer from this syndrome. Because tech addiction is less understood and recognized in the US, addicted kids are often labeled as having problems with depression, anger, anxiety, learning, or focus—when their core problem is really a harmful obsession with various technologies.

THE ADDICTED BRAIN

The latest brain imaging techniques, including MRI and PET scans taken during real-time experiments, reveal that gambling and video gaming impact the mind in a similar way to drugs and alcohol. This is one reason why the medical and psychiatric communities now believe addiction is best understood not as the compulsive use of a substance but as something that *occurs in the brain* as the result of substance use or the performance of certain behaviors.

Imaging studies show that *video gaming triggers the release of dopamine at levels comparable to an intravenous injection of amphetamine,*[8] a powerful and addictive psychostimulant. Other imaging studies show that video gaming mirrors the effects of drugs and alcohol as it stimulates the brain's pleasure pathway.[9] Areas of the brain impacted by video gaming include the cingulate gyrus (an area involved in motivation) and the prefrontal cortex (the key area affecting insight, self-control, and decision making). This helps explain why kids can become fixated on digital devices, cease to care about the things that once mattered to them most, and yet have no insight regarding their problem.

Such research has helped pave the way for widespread acceptance of both gambling and video gaming/Internet use as two behaviors capable of causing addiction. In 2013, after decades of investigation, gambling was the first behavioral addiction to be recognized in psychiatry's chief guidebook, the *Diagnostic and Statistical Manual of Mental Disorders (DSM-5)*. While video game/Internet addiction was seriously considered as a diagnosis, the *DSM-5* committee decided that more research should be done before official acceptance—it took decades to formally recognize gambling addiction—so the *DSM-5* now identifies Internet Gaming Disorder as a condition that warrants further study.[10]

As research adds to the substantial literature on video game/Internet addiction, the US medical and psychiatric communities will likely move in the direction of China and South Korea. Both countries are overwhelmed by youth video game/Internet addiction, recognize it as a diagnosis, consider it to be a leading public health problem and a threat to their economies, and have devoted hundreds of treatment centers to address it.[11] In the film documentary, *China's Web Junkies,* a mother says of her son who has been placed in a boot-camp-style treatment center, "Since my son started playing online games, he changed to another person.... He became very cruel."[12]

The Chinese and South Korean governments are so concerned about the effects of video game addiction that they have enacted national rules to limit children's access.[13] Other countries are waking up to the crisis. Japan's Ministry of Education estimates that more than 500,000 Japanese children between the ages of 12 and 18 are addicted to the Internet.[14] The Ministry is therefore investing heavily in research on the disorder and provides tech "fasting" camps for children.

SELLING A MYTH

In contrast, in America, flip on the TV or read the average online parenting article and you will see news reports hyping the advantages of children's use of video games, social networks, and the Internet without mentioning the risks of addiction. Why? Those bringing us our news are often part of conglomerates that have financial ties to companies that sell kids gadgets and apps. Moreover, news sources frequently depend upon ad revenue from an increasingly powerful industry, which can influence the slant of news stories.

Just considering video games, the worldwide market for video game titles, gaming consoles, online mobile and PC games reached $93 billion in 2013, up from $79 billion in 2012.[15] Adding further to the "everything's good" message about kids' tech use is the steady drumbeat of industry PR. Rich Taylor of the Entertainment Software Association (ESA), the video game industry's lobbying and public relations arm, claims: "There simply is no concrete evidence that computer and video games cause harm."[16]

WHAT TECH ADDICTION LOOKS LIKE

Because various addictions show similar patterns in the brain, it's not surprising their symptoms mirror one another. The hallmark of any addiction is that a person *continues the behavior in spite of significantly harmful consequences in real life,* often in multiple areas: e.g., the alcoholic who keeps drinking even though his habit cost him his job, or the teen tech addict who keeps gaming even though his obsession has led him to fail classes and ravaged his family relationships.

The effects of a tech addiction are often tragic. Highly capable teens give up their educational and career aspirations in order to spend more time playing with technology. Loving, honest kids turn cold to their parents' touch and habitually lie to cover up their habits.

Parents of addicted children who try to reduce their kids' tech use are met with threats of suicide or physical attacks.

The focus of this chapter is on tech-addicted children but the condition also afflicts adults. A number of parents I work with have divorced primarily because their ex-partner was addicted to gaming. Other parents describe their current partner as cut-off from them, their children, and real life by technology-related behaviors. As a result, children suffer from an overwhelming feeling of loss and anger, and are more likely to become addicted to technology themselves.

Researchers and practitioners often use the symptoms of substance or gambling addiction as a guide to deciding if a person is addicted to video games or the Internet. I have modified the *DSM-5* gambling addiction symptoms to identify technology addiction.[17] While these signs should not be used definitively, they are a good starting point for assessing how much someone is harmed by their use of technology.

Signs of Unhealthy Technology Use

- Needs to spend increasing amounts of time video gaming or using the Internet in order to achieve the desired excitement
- Is often restless or irritable when the use of video gaming or the Internet is stopped or decreased
- Repeated unsuccessful efforts have been made to control, cut back, or stop video gaming or using the Internet
- Is often preoccupied with using video games or the Internet
- Often uses video games or the Internet when feeling distressed (e.g., anxious or depressed) in an effort to feel better
- Often lies to conceal the extent of involvement with video gaming or the Internet
- Has significantly damaged relationships with family members, or academic or work performance because of video games or the Internet

The more of these signs a person shows, the more serious their problem with technology. If most or all of these signs are present, this suggests a possible addiction.

TRICKS OF THE TRADE

How did this phenomenon develop? The extremely competitive environment of the consumer tech industry provides possible answers. Corporations have found that the most profitable tech products— those that keep users coming back again and again—greatly stimulate the brain's reward center. As tech industry executive Bill Davidow says in his *Atlantic* article "Exploiting the Neuroscience of Internet Addiction": "The leaders of Internet companies face an interesting, if also morally questionable, imperative: either they hijack neuroscience to gain market share and make large profits, or they let competitors do that and run away with the market."[18]

How do tech corporations hijack our brains? They use the same behavioral psychology techniques the gambling industry uses to attract and manipulate gamblers. One strategy, *variable ratio reinforcement*, provides random rewards to users (think slot machine) and is well known to develop compulsive responses in people as well as animals. Video game makers create experiences in which players never know how and when points will be metered out, or when they will stumble on a special prize. Similarly, social network developers create ideal environments for variable ratio reinforcement—users never know when they will receive a "like" or a positive post.

Compulsion loops are another method tech developers use to get players to spend more time online, and, after they leave, to feel the itch to return. Compulsion loops reward a player's efforts with more game time or increasing levels, making it difficult for players to walk away. In the Facebook video game *Farmville*, for example, once players plant a crop, they have to wait before they can return and harvest the crops, at which time they're rewarded with "farm cash" to buy more crops, etc. Players feel compelled to return time and time again, keeping the loop going. Game designer Adrian Hon, originally trained in neuroscience at Cambridge and Oxford Universities, states: "Farmville is basically a compulsion loop dressed up in plants, with goals being doled out on a player-controlled schedule and new content (crops, buildings, decorations) always tantalizingly within range."[19]

The qualities of today's tech environment also allow for the use of behavioral manipulation techniques beyond what the gambling industry can employ. Game makers use the principles of *avoidance* (players must continue to play to avoid being punished by losing points, having crops die, or seeing animals get sick) and *arousal* (violent and sexualized images stimulate users to continue).

Like many alcoholics who face pressure to continue to imbibe from their circle of drinking friends, social factors play a role in getting and keeping kids hooked on tech products. Beginning in elementary school, many boys face extreme peer pressure to give up their lives to online gaming communities. For girls, more than boys, the *need to belong* on social networks is a powerful motivator to never let go of their phones. As Joel Bakan, professor of law at the University of British Columbia and author of *Childhood Under Siege*, notes: "What the rapid rise of social networks suggests, and what kid marketers are now coming to understand, is that the lives and dramas of kids themselves are likely the stickiest content of all."[20]

These are just a few tricks that the industry uses to manipulate kids' behavior. If these techniques are combined in just the right way, disguised in the compelling content of games or social networks, kids don't know they're being manipulated. They believe they spend so much of their lives gaming or on their favorite social networks because they want to, because it's fun.

RATS IN A MAZE

To understand the pivotal role that behavioral psychology plays in the development of entertainment tech products, it's helpful to start at the beginning, with the research of B.F. Skinner. This experimental psychologist designed a tool commonly known as the Skinner Box, a chamber in which behavioral manipulation could be scientifically tested on lab animals. Skinner found that the right mix of rewards and punishments could get rats, pigeons, and chimps to do just about anything. Skinner believed that for this purpose, humans are no different than animals. Our behavior is shaped primarily by outside forces, not our own free will. He concluded that for humans, freedom is an illusion. It's just a matter of who's controlling us.

In 2001, while receiving his Ph.D. in behavioral and brain sciences, John Hopson wrote a paper titled "Behavioral Game Design," now considered a seminal work in the video gaming industry. He described how techniques learned from Skinner's experiments on lab animals can be used to manipulate video game player behavior. Hopson answered questions such as "How to make players play forever" and "How do we make players maintain a high, consistent rate of activity?" He says, "This is not to say that players are the same as rats, but that there are general rules of learning which apply equally to both."[21]

Hopson is extremely intelligent, however his description of using behavior manipulation techniques tested on lab animals to influence video game players is frightening and sad. For corporations that make entertainment technologies, these techniques have been revolutionary, greatly influencing the design of video games and social networks. When his paper was published, Hopson was contacted by Microsoft, which offered him a position in video game development. He says his work at the company helped inspire the development of the Xbox Live, Microsoft's online gaming system. He also helped develop Xbox games popular with kids, including those in the *Halo* series.[22]

BIG BROTHER

Since the mid-1990s, experimental psychologists, neuroscientists, and other experts in the brain and behavior, traditionally involved with lab studies of animal and human subjects, have found a home in the consumer tech industry. Increasingly, they oversee game development.

As a result, the content of today's video games, whether it's about tough-guy soldiers or cute fuzzy creatures, matters less and less. What increasingly drives product development is *user research*. User researchers are experts in behavioral psychology and the manipulation of human behavior who rely upon detailed statistical analyses of our behavior to tweak products to be extraordinarily enticing and hence more profitable.

On its Redmond, Washington, campus, Microsoft has a sophisticated human research lab called Playtest.[23] At this sprawling facility, Microsoft psychologist and User Research Lead Tim Nichols and his staff study children as they video game, delve deep into their minds, and collect mounds of data to create products that perfectly exploit the proclivities of young brains. Because of such efforts, Microsoft is considered the gold standard in user research.[24]

Across the video gaming industry, scientists bring kids and young adults into state-of-the-art labs to observe them as they game. One-way mirrors and cameras record the facial expressions of subjects while they play. If children look away from the screen, they're questioned to find out why. Behavioral techniques are used to fine-tune the game to make an end product kids can't look away from, and can't put down.

The industry's increasing use of experts in human behavior combines with advancements in measurement techniques to push the bounds of user research. Popular video game maker Valve employs experimental psychologist Mike Ambinder. At his lab, players are hooked up to biofeedback devices that measure skin conductance (which shows player arousal level) and track their eye movements (to gauge where players are looking in real time). Results inform game development.[25]

The video game industry has come a long way since John Hopson wrote his paper describing how tests of lab animals should influence game design, but in many ways little has changed. Experimental psychologists and similar experts continue to study lab subjects to find the best methods to influence behavior. What is different? The subjects now include children.

A DANGEROUS TIPPING POINT

The tech industry publicly claims that its intimate analyses of our behavior are intended to improve user experiences, that the primary purpose is making video games or social networks more usable or fun. These words hide a darker truth: a cut-throat business environment that fosters the development of consumer technologies so perfectly designed to capture attention that they promote addiction.

Sucking Kids' Lives Away

Bill Fulton is a game designer trained in cognitive and quantitative psychology. He started Microsoft's Games User-Research group and led it for seven years before founding his own consulting agency. He's up front about the intent of today's gaming industry, saying: "If game designers are going to *pull a person away from every other voluntary social activity or hobby or pastime* [emphasis mine], they're going to have to engage that person at a very deep level in every possible way they can."[26]

That's a remarkable description of game designers' motives. For children, "voluntary" activities include running around outside, spending time with their family, or putting effort into homework. A multi-billion dollar industry devoting its resources to developing entertainment technologies that *intend* to suck kids away from the rest of their lives is scary, yet it helps illuminate why frustrated parents can't get their children to do much besides sit in front of the computer or play with their phone.

Choosing the Virtual World Over the Real One

While writing her trilogy of books on our relationship with technology, psychologist Sherry Turkle became increasingly concerned that children would begin to prefer the virtual to the real world.[27] Tech-addicted children have reached this tipping point. We see the result: Kids who extensively use the games and social networks our society labels appropriate for them, and end up preferring that world to the real one. This is the nature of addiction: People become involved with a substance or behavior at the expense of their real lives.

Why do many kids gravitate to the virtual world? It happens because real life is difficult. It's tough to pay attention to not-so-exciting school tasks, to struggle through homework, and then to get up the next day and do it all again. Months and months of hard work are required to obtain a single report card grade stamped on a transcript. In contrast, kids' increasing access to phones and other handheld devices means that they can get a big shot of dopamine just about any time they want. Unfortunately, evolution has led our brains to often choose easy rewards over tough ones: Why walk over a hill to get water when it's available at your feet?

Parents I work with tell me that despite their best efforts they can't interest their tech-obsessed kids in anything but more entertainment technologies. The latest neuroscience research suggests why. Imaging studies show that the brains of tech addicts appear to get used to the very high level of dopamine that gaming releases into the brain by raising the threshold for what feels pleasurable.[28] The result is that, just like drug addicts, video game and Internet addicts may have a diminished ability to enjoy real-life experiences. Doing well in school or going on a family outing doesn't feel good, so kids refuse to put effort into these activities.

Why don't kids recognize they're wasting their time in these virtual wonderlands, that they're reducing their chances of going to college or becoming successful? It's for the same reason that an alcoholic keeps drinking despite losing a job and family. He suffers from an addiction. The overpowering rewards provided by certain entertainment technologies can rewire the brain and overwhelm its judgment center.

PREYING ON WEAKNESS

An increasing number of industry insiders are questioning the use of behavioral psychology methods to manipulate the members of the public, especially children.

Adrian Hon, the neuroscientist who became a game designer, suggests that the industry should become more socially responsible and acknowledge its ability to influence and potentially harm users. Hon says that in the current environment there's simply too much economic incentive for exploitation, because it's in the interest of corporations to "keep people playing as much as possible, for as long as possible. With investors and shareholders' demands for constant growth, it's hard to resist the siren call of techniques like compulsion loops and avoidance. The question of 'fun' becomes incidental—what matters is making money."[29]

This "anything goes" ethic shows in the advice of video game designer Teut Weidemann, who outlines how to profit in an increasingly competitive environment: "We have to bring them in and keep them addicted and make them keep playing." He, too, is up front about the methods used, saying, "We are monetizing all the weakness of people."[30]

PROTECTING OUR KIDS FROM ADDICTION

Ramin Shokrizade is a game designer originally trained in neuroscience who is troubled by the gaming industry's manipulation of children, noting: "I think it is inevitable that some companies will iterate towards even more exploitation of children in games. The most aggressive companies will hire soft and hard scientists like myself, in addition to quantitative scientists, to optimize the exploitation of youth. The ultimate result will be national regulation, which is already happening in some parts of Asia. In the meantime, such agents will try to make as much money as possible in this Wild Wild West of gaming."[31]

What about regulating the industry's use of behavior manipulation methods on kids? Corporations would surely fight such efforts tooth and nail, claiming their products are protected under the First Amendment as art forms and speech. However, the industry's increasing reliance on the same techniques the gambling industry employs to hook users shows us something more is taking place. It's also illogical to believe that children can protect themselves from rooms filled with neuroscientists who use lab-tested techniques to keep kids staring at screens.

The makers of children's tech products will also try to frame their argument as a case of government telling parents how to parent, that government shouldn't be Big Brother and that parents should be the only ones to guide their children's tech use. Yet how can you help your kids when all you hear from industry is that their products are safe and fun—not potential sources of addiction? It's also clear that Big Brother is already here—not in the form of government, but in tech companies that study kids like lab rats and control their behavior the same way.

A NASTY COMBINATION

Quite intelligent, fifteen-year-old Jake could get by in school with minimal effort, and this allowed him to devote himself to his primary passion of video gaming. Jake's parents, however, felt strongly that school, not gaming, should be Jake's primary focus and they were increasingly disappointed by his slipping grades. Getting mostly Bs and Cs, and an occasional D, Jake said he was "passing his classes" and that this should be enough to keep his parents from "nagging" him about his gaming and a lack of school effort.

In the weeks before they came to see me, arguments between Jake and his parents had escalated after the latest progress report showed that he was failing two classes because of missing and late homework. One night, fed up, Jake's father walked into the teen's room and told him to pull off his headphones, shut off his computer, and said that he couldn't play video games until his grades got better. Jake became enraged, and during the ensuing fit threw his chair against a wall with all his might and threatened to kill himself. Understandably fearful of their son's behavior, Jake's parents called the police. By the time the officers arrived, Jake had calmed down. He convinced the police he wouldn't hurt himself or his parents, so the officers suggested the family follow up with counseling.

Jake's parents were hopeful that bringing him to me would be helpful, that I could help him understand why school should take precedence over gaming, and that I could help him "see the light." I also was hopeful and did my best to get to know Jake and help him and his parents. Nevertheless, it was clear from our meetings that Jake saw no reason to change. He insisted that he would find a career in gaming, although Jake could not realistically outline how this would become a reality. He also insisted that school "isn't that great" and saw little reason to put in any effort. During one session, when I tried to suggest that school is a kids' primary "job," Jake responded by saying he didn't feel therapy was helping and therefore wanted to stop coming.

What I confronted with Jake, as I do many other tech-addicted teens, is a profound struggle with *insight* and *judgment*. As we discuss in Chapter 9, dramatic changes that normally occur in the adolescent prefrontal cortex and other brain areas compromise these abilities in teens. But adding a tech addiction to the mix is a nasty combination, as addictions hijack the same brain structures that are already compromised in teens, further diminishing their ability to recognize they have a problem and make good decisions about their future.

As my work with Jake had stalled, I informed his parents that the method of treatment would need to shift so that I could work with them to set limits on their son's gaming at home. Jake's parents rightfully understood that such limit setting risked further explosions from Jake and the possibility of more violence in the home, the police being called, and Jake being psychiatrically hospitalized as the result of being a danger to himself or his parents. Jake's parents said they couldn't tolerate these risks and as a result gave up treating their son's video game addiction and stopped attending counseling.

WHY RELYING ON THE TREATMENT OF TECH ADDICTION FAILS KIDS

There are two basic options for protecting children from technology addiction: *prevention* or *treatment*. America, following the industry's lead to load up ever younger kids with more and more alluring devices, has unwittingly eschewed prevention, which leaves treatment as the default option. Yet as we saw in the case of Jake, the treatment of tech addiction holds many perils:

- **Consequences that can't be undone**: The effects of a technology addiction are serious enough that they may not be fully reversible. One or more failed semesters of high school can dramatically alter a teen's life trajectory. The breach of trust that results from a child's habitual lying (e.g., claiming that school is going well when homework isn't being done or sneaking devices in the middle of the night) may take years to heal.
- **Addicted kids don't want help**: Tech-addicted kids generally don't wake up one day and say, "Video games are ruining my life. I better quit." Like other addictions, obsessive tech use is associated with intense denial. Kids insist they don't have a problem and are certain that everything's their parents' fault. Moms and dads resort to dragging their children to treatment where kids often refuse to participate. Alternatively, teenagers in particular may refuse to attend counseling at all. Parents end up doing much or all the work themselves by attempting to limit their addicted children's use of entertainment technologies—a daunting prospect for any parent.

- **Video game/Internet addiction is exceptionally difficult to treat**: As psychiatrist Jerald Block notes in an article in the *American Journal of Psychiatry*, tech addiction is resistant to treatment.[32] Parents may therefore, after numerous unsuccessful efforts to help their child, decide that the struggle isn't worth it. They may end up compromising with their child, e.g., "All we ask is that you pass your classes and you can play all the games you want." As a result, even if kids' school performance gets marginally better, many never reach the potential that existed prior to the addiction.[33]

- **The dangerous consequences of a technology addiction**: Those who are unfamiliar with child tech addiction sometimes suggest to parents, "Just take it away." Parents of addicted kids know that their problems are much more serious than that. Trying to limit an addicted kid's access to video games or the Internet frequently results in threats of, or actual, violence. Doors are broken down, parents are bullied, moms and dads are pushed or hit, and the police may need to be called. Kids faced with the loss of their beloved devices also can experience depression or thoughts of suicide. There are no easy, sometimes not even good, solutions to these problems once they're well established.

WHAT TO DO IF YOUR CHILD IS ADDICTED

If you believe that your child or teen shows signs of technology addiction (as described earlier in the chapter), I suggest that you not attempt to treat this problem yourself. Seek professional help. Treating addicted children and teens poses the serious challenges and risks outlined in this chapter. Pediatricians and school counselors or principals are often good resources for finding a counselor.

In looking for a prospective counselor to treat a child's or teen's technology addiction, I suggest finding someone with experience in that area, or someone willing to research the problem. You also need a counselor who is comfortable working with both your child and you, as this is a problem that kids can't overcome without parents' help. And look for someone who understands the seriousness posed by tech addiction. Be concerned if a prospective counselor attempts to minimize the issue by telling you how easy treatment should be.

It's always a good idea to meet with a counselor for an initial session to decide if you feel comfortable continuing to work with him or her. Judgments about the counselor's effectiveness should be made by parents because tech-addicted kids generally don't like anyone who is trying to get them to change their habit. Also, don't expect immediate results as treating a tech addiction is remarkably challenging for the reasons I've described. If the addiction proves to be severe, out-of-home wilderness and residential treatment programs that have traditionally treated oppositional kids now increasingly offer specific therapies for technology addiction.

Many families I've worked with have hoped their struggles could be brought to light so that other parents would be able to learn from their experiences. What these families consistently say is that they'd give anything to turn back time, to have been able to act in a way that prevented the problem.

TWO TECH POLICIES THAT PUT KIDS AT RISK

Clearly, relying primarily on *treatment* to address kids' tech addiction is a flawed strategy, and instead we should be looking at how to *prevent* this increasing problem. However, before I mention steps to prevent tech addiction, I want to show how two policies commonly applied to children's use of technology—*increased access* and *moderation*—may do more harm than good.

The Failings of Increased Access

Digital-age myths have helped convince many parents that typical technologies bring kids closer to their family, build better brains, and help kids learn. All the while, the risks posed by technology addiction either are not mentioned in the media or downplayed. So it makes sense that many parents believe kids will benefit from gaining *increased access* to tablets, phones, and more of the latest gadgets. Is this really true, or does increased access put our kids at risk for addiction?

A known risk factor for substance addiction in kids is *greater physical access:* the more easily kids can get their hands on cigarettes, alcohol, or drugs, the more likely they will develop an addiction to them. Does providing kids greater *physical access* to technology similarly put them at greater risk for tech addiction?

Research suggests that's the case. As reported in "Internet Addiction in Adolescents: Prevalence and Risk Factors," "Widespread Internet accessibility appeared to contribute to the likelihood of being addicted to the Internet, as adolescents who used it in the kitchen, on their mobile phones, and via WiFi were more likely to be addicted to the Internet than the adolescents who did not have extensive access."[34] This makes sense, as the child and teen brain has not yet developed the self-control abilities to limit using devices in easy reach.

Another type of *access* relates to the *age* at which kids are provided digital devices. As we know from studying substance addiction, the *earlier kids start to use* alcohol and drugs, the more likely they will become addicted later on. Not surprisingly, we see that the younger children are when they start playing video games, the more likely they will show signs similar to tech addiction as they grow older.

The study "Dependence on Computer Games by Adolescents" reports the following: "The earlier children began playing computer games it appeared the more likely they were to be playing at 'dependent' levels."[35] Similarly, as noted in the study "Pathological Video-Game Use Among Youth Ages 8 to 18": "Pathological gamers had been playing for more years, played more frequently and for more time."[36] Again, this makes perfect sense. Young brains are more likely to be captivated by powerful, dopamine-triggering technologies than mature brains with a better-developed judgment center. The bottom line is that the policy of *increased access* appears to put kids at greater risk of technology addiction.

Why Moderation Doesn't Prevent Tech Addiction

Another commonly used policy to guide children's use of technology is *moderation*, a line of thinking that suggests providing a child of any age with any device is fine, as long as parents attempt to keep its use under control so as to ensure kids lead a balanced life. Unfortunately, parents who attempt to moderate their children's use of digital devices frequently find this fails. The plan to have kids use their tablet or phone for only a few minutes a day quickly spirals out of control, and kids' lives end up revolving around a device.

Why? Because the addictive draw of today's gadgets overrides parents' ability to have kids use technology in a limited fashion. Six-year-old Jonathan's example, shared by his mother, is common in my practice: "He got a tablet for his birthday and we didn't think much of it. But it became increasingly difficult to pry from his hands. Now even though we try to limit its use, he only wants to game.... I can't get him to do anything else. And when we won't let him play his games he clenches his fists and scowls at us. Recently, he's hit me when upset."

Unfortunately exposure to even small amounts of technology can lead to disturbing craving symptoms. A *US News* report highlights the issue. Seven-year-old Ollie's parents struggled to limit his use of Webkinz, a social networking site designed specifically for children. "The issue is not the amount of time," Ollie's father, Brian, said. "We can control that. It's the fact that he gets up before everyone else and sneaks onto the computer. It's like he sets his internal clock so he can play Webkinz."[37]

As parents describe to me nearly every day, the hunger that children show towards entertainment technologies is unmatched. The very high levels of dopamine triggered by video gaming make it extremely difficult to find alternative activities that kids find equally gratifying. Many parents say they do their best to provide children with a variety of activities (e.g., sports, reading, outdoor and creative play), while permitting minimal entertainment technology. Yet the same parents become immensely frustrated because the child's desire for phone or video game play time overwhelms his or her interest in other activities. Even on child-oriented vacations, all kids can say is, "When can I play my game?" Such cravings deprive children of the ability to appreciate real-life rewards.

These cravings may also form the underpinnings of future addiction. As tech-obsessed kids grow older, smarter, and increasingly able to circumvent limits, they no longer put up with their parents' rules. Instead, they become progressively more willing to do anything to get what satisfies them most, even if it causes significant problems in the rest of their life.

As parents, we instinctively know moderation isn't a good way to protect kids from drug and alcohol addictions. Responsible parents don't consider giving children—especially when they are young—moderate amounts of alcohol, tobacco, or recreational drugs, because we know young brains struggle mightily with self-control. Our increased understanding of the addictive potential of entertainment technologies suggests that we also rethink the use of the policy of moderation to prevent video game/Internet addiction.

MAKING THE PREVENTION OF TECH ADDICTION A PRIORITY

Given the failings of both moderation and treatment, we need to focus our attention on preventing kids from ever developing a tech addiction. How can this be achieved? We need to greatly limit kids' access to tech gadgets and the entertainment they offer. We especially must (1) reverse the move to provide younger and younger kids with amusement-based technologies, and (2) as kids grow older, curb their access to these technologies.

In the book they wrote soon after the Columbine shootings, *Stop Teaching our Kids to Kill*, military science scholar Lt. Col. Dave Grossman and media-literacy educator Gloria DeGaetano offered prescient advice: "The trend of giving video games to toddlers, preschoolers, and elementary school children must stop. Even if parents are introducing only nonviolent video games at this stage of development, it is going to be so much more difficult to keep the kids away from violent ones. Just the nature of video games in and of themselves make them potentially addictive. Video game systems are just not developmentally appropriate for children."[38]

Of course, almost all kids will try video gaming and social networking at some point. Yet what parents need to know is that the later we introduce these technologies (if at all), the less risk there appears to be of kids developing addiction: high school is better than middle school, and middle school is better than elementary school. Grossman and DeGaetano suggest that if parents are going to provide kids video games, that waiting until kids are at least 12 to 14 is best.

Sure it can be difficult to set strict gaming limits on young kids, but the challenges of doing so pale in comparison to the struggles of many families who introduce gaming and then watch it take over their kids' lives. And while social networking appears to pose a lower risk of addiction than video games, the risk of addiction to these products remains. I therefore suggest following Grossman and DeGaetano's recommendation for gaming, and waiting as long as possible before introducing social networks to children.

I fully recognize that these recommendations are more conservative than what many others recommend. However, because of emerging research and my own experience of seeing families turned upside-down by children's tech addiction, I can't in good conscience recommend any other course of action. So I am hopeful that you will consider the steps to limit exposure to entertainment technologies described in prior chapters. And in the remainder of this book I will introduce many more actions to limit kids' use of technologies that pose the risk of addiction.

5

Tackle the Unique Tech Problems
Faced by Boys and Girls

Sheryl Sandberg, Facebook's Chief Operating Officer, has strong words of advice for parents. To increase girls' chances of success in today's high-tech work force, she says, "Let your daughters play video games. Encourage your daughters to play video games!"[1] Boys tend to video game more than girls, and males tend to dominate the computer science field,[2] however does video gaming help kids become successful?

BOYS: FALLING HARD FOR TECHNOLOGY

In the US, boys have immersed themselves in digital entertainment technologies far more than girls. Boys spend *over an hour more each day* using entertainment screen technologies (excluding phones) than girls: 5 hours, 56 minutes for boys compared with 4 hours, 51 minutes for girls.[3] Looking at the details of this difference, boys typically spend more time than girls using the computer for entertainment, for example watching online videos, but video gaming time makes up the biggest difference. Among kids who use video gaming consoles such as Xbox and PlayStation, boys spend nearly an hour more each day gaming than girls.

How Are Our Nation's Tech-Heavy Boys Doing?

If Sheryl Sandberg's suggestion that video gaming promotes success is correct, we would expect our gaming-heavy boys to thrive compared to our gaming-light girls. So how are our boys doing? Not well. Just as Chapter 3's research showing that entertainment technologies hurt academic performance would predict, boys now earn significantly lower grades in elementary, middle, and high school than girls—including in math and science.[4] Girls also dominate the high school honors ranks.[5]

Boys' poorer performance in high school is an important reason they struggle more than girls do to gain college admission. Young men once dominated the college ranks, yet they now represent only 43% of college admissions,[6] despite the fact that some college counselors acknowledge giving admission preference to males in order to attain gender balance in the student body.[7] Factors other than gender tech-use differences likely play a role in college admission differences, including changing social norms. However, we shouldn't ignore the negative impact of gaming and other entertainment technologies on academic performance because it's so well documented.

Male *college students* also video game at significantly higher rates than their female peers.[8] Unfortunately, evidence shows that their greater gaming time hurts college academic performance,[9] and is likely a reason college-age women earn higher grade point averages and more college honors, and graduate at higher rates than men.[10]

Considering that a college education is an important prerequisite for getting many jobs and it also raises lifetime earnings, we shouldn't be surprised that the relatively tech-heavy, education-light lives of today's boys lead to less career success. Although males dominate the computer science field, they are increasingly losing out to women in many other professions. According to recent research from the Massachusetts Institute of Technology, males' lower level of college achievement erodes their prospects for workforce success.[11]

Boys' and young men's overuse of technology is not the sole reason for their current woes. We face a difficult economy and the US is losing manufacturing jobs that allowed generations of young men to earn a good living. Video game advocates will say the presence of such non-tech factors negates the possibility that boys' overuse of entertainment technologies is hurting their chances of school and career success. Yet there are surely multiple factors explaining the struggles of our boys and young men. And it's getting difficult to ignore this basic formula: overuse of entertainment technologies hurts pre-college and college academic performance, boys use significantly more of these technologies than girls, and therefore boys are paying a price in an economy that increasingly demands a college education.

Boys' Struggles Are Not Going Unnoticed

A number of authors are calling attention to the academic and life struggles of boys and young men, associating them in part to the overuse of entertainment technologies. Family physician and psychologist Leonard Sax, in *Boys Adrift*, notes: "The destructive effects of video games are not on boys' cognitive abilities or their reaction times, but on their motivation and their connectedness with the real world. These boys may be highly motivated, but their motivation has been derailed: I've seen boys who care much more about their success at *Halo* than about their grade in Spanish…. The video game world is more real to them than the world of homework and grades and college applications."[12]

Psychologist Philip Zimbardo and Nikita Duncan raise similar concerns in *The Demise of Guys*, in which they describe a generation of boys and young men who, from very young ages, are "seduced into excessive and mostly isolated viewing and involvement" with various technologies, especially video games.[13] Echoing Sax, they state, "The disadvantage of playing video games, especially a lot of exciting video games, is that it can make other people and real life seem boring and not worthwhile in comparison."[14]

I run into this phenomenon frequently in my work with boys and male teens. For them, the real world simply doesn't stack up to the virtual one, so they gravitate towards the enticing world of gaming—especially the games offered online. However, their parents are less apt to show concern because of the ubiquitous culture of boys' gaming. "He doesn't game any more than his friends," the mother of 14-year-old Matthew told me. But Matthew's four-hour daily habit of gaming was clearly hurting his school grades.

Why Boys Get Hooked on Games

Stanford University researchers' use of functional magnetic resonance imaging (fMRI, brain scanning that shows active areas of the brain) confirms many parents' observations that their boys are more drawn to gaming than their girls. The scans showed that video gaming activates the mesocorticolimbic center—an area of the brain associated with reward and addiction—much more in men than women. This study's authors conclude: "These gender differences may help explain why males are more attracted to, and more likely to become 'hooked' on video games than females."[15]

Helping Our Boys

Serious problems in tech-obsessed boys are commonplace in my practice. Seventeen-year-old James' family was new to me, however the family's problems were not. Over the past year, James and his parents were increasingly at each others' throats but couldn't understand why. The reasons emerged in our first meeting.

Like most parents, James' mother and father had an unconscious archetype of what an older teen son should be: hardworking, responsible, and ready to take on the world. Their archetype increasingly clashed with their son's real life: gaming alone in his room with no real plans for the future. James' parents were increasingly agitated and even downright angry, even if they didn't understand why.

I helped James' parents bring their unconscious expectations to the surface. This began when I asked them to describe the life they envisioned for James. They told me they wanted him to realize he would be 18 in a short time and to recognize what this meant. Their expectations were not ambitious, still they wanted their son to take visible steps towards his post-high-school life, looking into college or work options.

I asked James' parents to describe their son's current life. "He just stays in his room and does nothing," they told me. "Nothing?" I asked. They went on to describe James' fixation on video gaming, and how this habit prevented him from helping around the house or doing schoolwork. In the process, James' parents began to realize that the 40 or so hours a week their son spent gaming wasn't only an activity he did because he couldn't figure out what else to do, but that it also diverted him from becoming productive and taking steps towards growing up. In our work together, James' parents also were helped by learning that their teenage son's less developed prefrontal cortex meant they would have to provide more structure to help him control his gaming.

With his parents' help, James was able to distance himself from gaming. He started to gain the perspective to recognize that real life was right around the corner, and that he needed to plan for his future. The last I heard, James was doing well at junior college and considering transferring to a four-year-school.

WHY GIRLS DO BETTER YET HAVE THEIR OWN CHALLENGES

Today's entertainment tech-heavy boys can learn much from the entertainment tech-lighter girls around them. In Chapter 3, we looked at how video gaming displaces reading and homework. It's therefore not surprising that girls, who game less than boys, tend to read more than their male counterparts.[16] Likewise, University of Pennsylvania researchers found that 8th-grade girls started their homework earlier in the day and spend almost twice as much time on it as boys.[17] Since reading and homework completion are vital to learning, these gender differences help explain why girls outperform boys in high school and college admission.

What's the Bad News?

While girls use *less* amusement-based technologies than boys, they still spend nearly five hours a day using entertainment screen technologies.[18] The research described in Chapter 3 and my experience with families suggests that even this lesser time spent in digital self-amusement poses risks to academic performance and can separate girls from their families.

There are also two important exceptions to the general rule that girls use less entertainment technology than boys: compared to boys, girls spend significantly more time social networking and using cell phones to talk and text with friends.[19] While typical high-school-age boys spend 1 hour and 42 minutes talking and texting every day, high-school-age girls spend an incredible 2 hours and 36 minutes doing the same.[20] While boys average 50 text messages per day, for girls, it's double this amount.[21] Remember, all this time with phones *adds to* the time kids spend with other screens.

Just as gender differences in brain physiology help explain why boys are more attracted to gaming than girls, developmental differences between genders help us understand why girls are drawn to social networks and texting. Mirroring what many parents see for themselves, research shows that girls are more driven to seek out peer relationships and are more influenced by them than boys.[22] The connections and politics played out on social networks and cell phones can therefore be an almost irresistible draw for girls.

Shifting from a Life Online to Life in the Real World

Fifteen-year-old Sarah's life was typical of many high-school-age girls I work with. Much like our National Security Agency monitors electronic chatter, Sarah constantly checked posts on Facebook, Instagram, Twitter, and a host of other social networks. She scanned for conflict between peers, especially if she was involved. She worried that if she didn't have a strong online presence, or if she wasn't there to stick up for herself and her friends, her social world would crash and burn in an instant. So she checked her phone first thing in the morning, at breaks during school or sometimes during class, lived on her phone after school, and was online until late into the night. "Things were really going last night," she told me, looking exhausted, "It didn't quiet down until past one in the morning."

This hyperawareness of everything online undermined Sarah's focus on the two things that should matter most to her: family and school. She had a hard time engaging in conversations with her parents because she couldn't keep her mind off online peer drama. Even if she wasn't on her phone in the moment, she was preoccupied by the possibility of a returned text or a flare-up between enemies or even friends on social networks. Teen gossip, which for prior generations used to quiet down at the end of the school day, now continues around-the-clock for kids like Sarah because of their continual access to technology.

Additionally, Sarah's attempt to fit homework between texts and posting to social networks hurt her grades. "I'll probably go to college," she told me. I tried to bring up how much effort she'd need to make in high school to accomplish this goal, but she wasn't really listening. She was too distracted by peeking at the phone clutched in her lap.

What helped Sarah? I talked with her parents about how their daughter's overpowering connection to her phone affected the rest of her life. I asked Sarah and her parents if they spent time together as a family. They replied that traditions like family dinners or trips no longer happened because family members were all so busy. However, looking more closely, Sarah and her parents actually were often home at the same time; it was their respective screen engagement—Sarah on her phone in her room and her parents watching TV downstairs—that kept the family from coming together.

I talked with Sarah and her parents together about how important family is, even to teens. Sarah's parents decided to change the dinner hour. They created a new family ritual. Everyone would meet in the kitchen several nights during the week to prepare and eat meals together—with all devices turned off. Sarah complained that she *couldn't* be without her phone. Then we all took a look at what had happened to Sarah's grades after she'd received her smartphone about a year earlier—how As had turned to Bs and Cs, and how this could put her college chances at risk. This helped persuade Sarah to put her phone away for family and study time at home.

Helping Girls Take an Interest in Computer Science

So what about Sheryl Sandberg's claim that video gaming will help girls gain the skills needed for success in the high-tech workforce? First, we need to remember video gaming's negative impact on academics as noted in Chapter 3. And, as we will see in Chapter 10, high-tech companies typically hire computer scientists out of college or graduate engineering programs—schooling that kids are less likely to obtain if they game a lot. I therefore question the industry's advocacy of girls' video gaming. There's no proof that video gaming turns kids on to computer science, but lots of evidence that gaming hurts important stepping stones to the profession.

There *is* evidence of what can increase girls' interest in computer sciences from Stuyvesant High School, an academically competitive public school in New York City. In *The New Republic,* Lydia DePillis describes how Stuyvesant—with the encouragement of computer science teacher Michael Zamansky—tackled the underrepresentation of girls in computer science. It required that all students at its coed campus take an introductory computer science class in order to graduate.[23] The result: Female students now say they're more comfortable taking computer science classes because they aren't the only girl in class. Stuyvesant's policy has also encouraged girls to take advanced computer science and software development classes.

Stuyvesant's efforts work for many reasons. One is that adults who have teens' best interests in mind developed the program. Also in contrast to Sandberg's solution of more video gaming, Stuyvesant's computer science classes help provide the structure kids need to use technology effectively.

HOW TO HELP BOYS AND GIRLS IN A DIGITAL AGE

As seen throughout this book, biological and developmental vulnerabilities make both boys and girls susceptible to overusing their gadgets. Our kids need our help if we hope to protect them from an industry intent on exploiting these vulnerabilities. In the following chapters, we'll explore more actions to address the real challenges of reducing children's and teens' immersion in entertainment technologies and increase engagement with family, school, and productive technologies.

6

Be the Loving, Strong Guide
Your Child Needs

Until quite recently, parents have been considered the primary family authorities since children and teens need substantial guidance to become healthy adults. More recently, the belief that kids' use of technology is the key to their happiness and success has left us susceptible to a destructive myth about the defining qualities of effective parenting.

In 2001, video game developer Marc Prensky described his vision of what should be the appropriate relationship between children, parents, and technology in his article "Digital Natives, Digital Immigrants."[1] He called children "digital natives" because they've been raised amidst technology, while parents and teachers are "digital immigrants," suggesting they're much less sophisticated on tech matters. He argued that by virtue of growing up "surrounded by and using computers, videogames, digital music players, video cams, cell phones, and all the other toys and tools of the digital age"[2] kids gain wisdom that their parents and teachers don't possess.

In his 2006 book with the telling title *Don't Bother Me Mom—I'm Learning!: How Computer and Video Games Are Preparing Your Kids for 21st century Success—and How You Can Help!*, Prensky uses the digital native-digital immigrant narrative to inform moms and dads how to parent. He lavishes praise on video-game-focused kids while reserving criticism for parents who he says just don't understand the value of gaming and instead have unfounded "fears about games."[3] Prensky is also disparaging of teachers, noting that game-playing kids "are totally frustrated by their parents' and teachers' uninformed attitudes, and who, given half a chance, would happily explain why video and computer games are a positive part of their life, and why they spend so much time playing them."[4] With absolute faith in gaming, he asserts: "Kids learn more positive, useful things for their future from their video games than they learn in school!"[5]

Prensky therefore argues for a reversal in the traditional family hierarchy: Parents should obey their children when they demand more video games, cell phones, portables, and online subscriptions.[6] For parents who are concerned about allowing children to decide how much they should video game, Prensky has an answer: "The true secret of why kids spend so much time on their games is that they're learning things they need for their twenty-first century lives."[7]

A DESTRUCTIVE PARENTING MYTH

While the digital native-digital immigrant belief has gained widespread popular acceptance, it doesn't hold up to scientific scrutiny. As noted by Sue Bennett, Senior Lecturer at the University of Wollongong in Australia, "The idea of the digital native captured the imaginations of teachers, parents, journalists, commentators and academics. Closer examination of Prensky's arguments, particularly in his influential 2001 paper ["Digital Natives, Digital Immigrants"], reveals little in the way of evidence to substantiate his claims, however. He relies on anecdotes, conjecture and speculation. Nonetheless his ideas have often been uncritically repeated and cited as if fact."[8]

The research simply doesn't support the idea of a generation of young tech experts who are more adept than prior generations—after all, prior generations created the technologies kids now use. Neil Selwyn, formerly with the Institute of Education at the University of

London and now a professor in the Faculty of Education at Monash University in Australia states, "The findings show that young people's engagements with digital technologies are varied and often unspectacular—in stark contrast to popular portrayals of the digital native."[9] Similarly, we have seen in this book that our kids' technology use is marked by an overuse of entertainment technologies at the expense of a focus on family and school, and is putting them at risk of addiction.

The digital native-digital immigrant belief is in fact a remarkably harmful myth. Simply growing up in a world surrounded by digital gadgets does not give children the ability to understand how the use, or frequently the overuse, of such devices affects their lives. Kids can be astoundingly adept at swiping through phones or tablets, however parents—by virtue of their more developed brains and greater life experiences—are much better able to understand how technology can impact emotional well-being, academic growth, and life success. And that is far more important than knowing how to access all of a phone's features or rack up points playing a video game.

A PARENTING MYTH THAT IS ALIVE AND WELL TODAY

Prensky's original description of the digital native-digital immigrant belief came one year after the new millennium, so many of those he would have considered digital natives are becoming parents themselves. Nonetheless, the main thrust of the native-immigrant belief continues to be advanced: that by virtue of growing up with the latest technologies from ever younger ages and for greater amounts of time, each new generation of kids supposedly knows more about how digital gadgets should be used than their parents.

The website advertising the recent book *Toddlers on Technology: A Parents' Guide* notes: "Does your toddler seem to know more about the iPad than you do? Welcome to the world of the Digitods: the young children born into the era of mobile technology. These kids are learning faster and better than any generation that has come before them. And they are loving it!"[10] Reminiscent of Prensky's argument, it's by virtue of being born amidst the latest digital devices that gives kids a leg up on their parents.

Likewise, Hanna Rosin advocates for modern-day digital-native-digital-immigrant-parenting in her recent *Atlantic* article "The Touch-Screen Generation," as she says: "This term [digital native-digital immigrant] took on a whole new significance in April 2010, when the iPad was released."[11] She argues that today's "touch-screen generation" understands technology in a way that their parents simply can't, noting of her four-year-old son, "To us (his parents, I mean), American childhood has undergone a somewhat alarming transformation in a very short time. But to him, it has always been possible to do so many things with the swipe of a finger, to have hundreds of games packed into a gadget the same size as Goodnight Moon."

Like Prensky, Rosin demeans parents who are concerned about technology's effect on their kids, suggesting this is based on their own "neurotic relationship with technology." She also suggests there has been a shift of power on matters of technology from parent to child. Reflecting on her toddler son's use of the iPad, she writes, "I must admit, it was eerie to see a child still in diapers so competent and intent, as if he were forecasting his own adulthood. Technically I was the owner of the iPad, but in some ontological way it felt much more his than mine." Rosin therefore decided to provide her toddler son what she termed "Prensky rules" for the iPad: "Whenever he wanted to play with it, I would let him."

TELLING PARENTS NOT TO PARENT

It's often argued in modern culture that kids' adeptness at swiping screens and manipulating gadgets should trump the traditional family structure, that parents don't have the right to guide their kids' use of screen technologies. This suggested shift in family power is remarkable because kids spend more time with entertainment screen and phone technologies than any other waking activity—far more than school. Essentially, parents are being encouraged to back away from guiding kids in the activity that now dominates their lives.

However, kids don't have the ability to understand how an overfocus on gadgets denies them the connections with parents they need for emotional health. They don't get that time spent gaming or social networking is time spent away from activities that help them prepare for their future. Whether they are toddlers or teens, kids are simply not capable of this level of insight and instead will enthusiastically disappear into cyberspace amusements for hours or even days on end. Parents therefore have a responsibility to help kids make good choices about the use of screen and phone technologies.

When Parents Back Away, Corporations Profit

While kids need strong guidance about technology from their parents, tech corporations have a multi-billion dollar stake in parents not setting limits on their children's use of technology—as kids with few or no media rules use significantly more technology products.[12] So it's not surprising that the tech industry advises moms and dads to back off.

Like Marc Prensky, Danah Boyd, author of *It's Complicated*,[13] is a vocal advocate for getting parents out of the business of guiding their kids' technology use, including social networks and cell phones. In her *Time* magazine parenting article "Let Kids Run Wild Online," she repeats the theme of belittling parents who are concerned about their kids' tech use, labeling those who set limits as "fearful." She also rehashes a main point of the digital native-digital immigrant belief that parents should not guide their kids' use of technology. Instead, she claims, "The key to helping youth navigate contemporary digital life isn't more restrictions. It's freedom—plus communication."[14]

Danah Boyd's bio printed at the end of her article mentions she is employed by Microsoft as a researcher, but she says nothing in the article about this conflict of interest—Microsoft is a leading producer of the entertainment technologies Boyd suggests kids be turned loose with. Unfortunately, failing to disclose such conflicts of interest is common practice by industry-connected pundits so that parents really don't know what financial interests lurk behind the advice they are given.

Boyd's advice also sets up a double standard because her parenting recommendations as a Microsoft researcher conflict with the child rearing the company's co-founder Bill Gates and his wife Melinda provided their own children. In the Reuter's article "Bill Gates keeps close eye on kids' computer time," it's reported that the Gates parents set strict limits on their daughter's gaming, and their son had his own screen limits. Bill Gates quipped, "My son said, 'Am I going to have limits like this my whole life?', and I said, 'No, when you move away you can set your own screen limits.'"[15]

The International Society for Technology in Education (ISTE) also advocates that parents back off from guiding their children's technology use. The organization portrays itself as a research-based organization; it creates official "standards"[16] intended to guide schools and parents about how kids should use technology. In truth, leading purveyors of the tech products kids use for entertainment (including Microsoft, Apple, and cell phone company Verizon) help fund the ISTE, and it acts as a lobbying and marketing body for its funders, e.g., advertising its ability to help corporate members "gain visibility and build brand awareness."[17]

Is it surprising that the ISTE encourages parents not to limit their kids' tech use? The organization hosted Marc Prensky as a speaker at a recent conference and articles on its website suggest that kids know what they're doing with technology and adults should largely stay out of their way.[18] In "The Many Benefits, for Kids, of Playing Video Games," author Peter Gray asserts: "Children are suffering today not from too much computer play or too much screen time. They are suffering from too much adult control over their lives and not enough freedom."[19]

FALSE FREEDOM

I agree with an assertion Danah Boyd makes in her *Time* parenting article, that the freedom prior generations of kids had to explore the real world, e.g., ride their bikes and visit friends, was helpful to their development, and I am a believer in having modern-day kids be able to experience this. However, I strongly disagree with her contention that turning today's kids loose in cyberspace results in their greater freedom.

Kids can tweak their games, avatars, social network profiles, or phones in innumerable ways, but this only provides an illusion of control. Malleability is purposely built into these products to encourage kids to spend more time in for-profit domains looking at ads and racking up digital minutes. Children and teens are also tracked and data mined on these sites so that content and advertising can be better tuned to their whims—all for the sake of the corporate bottom line. This in no way resembles the relatively unconstrained lives of former generations of youth. A sad irony is that all the "freedom" present-day kids have on their gadgets displaces the educational experiences that would provide greater long-term independence by increasing their job choices and incomes.

WHEN PARENTS STOP PARENTING

Tech corporations should be quite pleased with the present state of affairs. When the Kaiser Family Foundation measured US parents' rules for the use of TV, video games, and computers, they found: "The majority of 8- to 18-year-olds say they don't have any rules about the type of media content they can use or the amount of time they can spend with the medium (there is one exception—a bare majority of 52% say they have rules about what they're allowed to do on the computer)."[20]

Specifically, today's kids have few if any rules about the technologies that, as we saw in Chapter 3, are shifting their focus away from school and hampering academic performance. For example, the Foundation reported that few seventh to twelfth graders have *any* rules about how much they can talk or text on the phone (27 and 14 percent respectively), while a meager 18 percent of American kids ages 15–18 have *any* rules whatsoever about how much time they can spend playing video games.[21]

FLAWED PARENTING IN THE DIGITAL AGE

Research by Diana Baumrind at UC Berkeley and Eleanor Maccoby and John Martin at Stanford University shows that parenting is defined by two factors: 1) *responsiveness* (a high or low measure of warmth and attachment in the parent-child connection), and 2) *demandingness* (a high or low measure of how much parents supervise and provide expectations for their children).[22] From these factors emerge four types of parenting: *authoritative, authoritarian, permissive, and uninvolved.*

Parenting Styles Informed by Baumrind, Maccoby, and Martin		
	High Demandingness	**Low Demandingness**
High Responsiveness	*Authoritative*	*Permissive*
Low Responsiveness	*Authoritarian*	*Uninvolved*

Authoritative parenting has a high level of responsiveness and a high level of demandingness. Authoritative parents do their best to maintain a strong, loving relationship with their child, while providing high expectations and definite limits that help kids to meet parental expectations. There is a clear hierarchy in which parents are the primary authorities in the home, although this is conveyed warmly to kids through a close relationship rather than coercion.

Authoritarian (different than *authoritative*) parents tend to score low on responsiveness but high on demandingness. They are less concerned with a loving connection yet set strong limits for kids. *Permissive* parents are high on responsiveness but low on demandingness. They tend to be loving, have relatively low expectations, and there is no clear hierarchy in the home. Finally, *uninvolved* parents score low on responsiveness *and* demandingness. They tend to be relatively disconnected from their children's lives and there is a lack of hierarchy in the home.

Of the four parenting styles, *authoritative parenting* produces the best emotional health and academic outcomes. Children raised using this parenting style have higher self-esteem and life satisfaction, and lower levels of anxiety, depression, and delinquent behavior than those raised using other parenting styles.[23] Kids raised with *authoritative parenting* also are more likely to be engaged in school, and tend to have a higher GPA in both high school and college than kids raised with other parenting methods.[24] *Uninvolved parenting* leads to the unhealthiest outcomes, while *authoritarian* and *permissive parenting* outcomes tend to fall somewhere in between.[25]

How is our children's immersion in entertainment technologies affecting how they are parented? As we have seen throughout this book, kids' high usage of entertainment technology diminishes the parent-child connection (responsiveness) and school performance (demandingness), creating an environment best characterized by the least effective parenting style: *uninvolved parenting*. Nevertheless, our culture's message to parents to step away from guiding children's use of technology is highly seductive, as *uninvolved parenting* demands less effort and involvement from parents than *authoritative parenting*.

Myth-Inspired Uninvolved Parenting

The *uninvolved parenting* style is evident in many of today's families. Parents heavily rely upon tablet computers and other e-devices as babysitters for infants and toddlers, displacing positive interactions with parents or other caregivers. Many preschool- and elementary-age kids carry mobile devices around the home, on car rides, to appointments, and elsewhere—minimizing parent-child exchanges and displacing the reading that supports school success. By high-school, many teens are in full retreat to their rooms where they play on their phones and other e-gadgets until late into the night.

Moms and dads using *uninvolved parenting* also have been convinced that they don't have a right to oversee their kids' use of gadgets. In my office, many parents look at me quizzically when I suggest they need to limit their kids' use of fun-time gadgets to promote school involvement and success. "But I don't know if I can limit how much she uses her phone... she gets so angry when I try to say no," parents tell me. The same parents would never let kids make their own rules about curfews, chores, etc., yet a digital-age parenting myth has helped convince numerous parents that children should run the show regarding tech matters at home.

KIDS NEED *AUTHORITATIVE* PARENTING

I suggest that you take your rightful place as your kids' leader by using authoritative parenting strategies at home. How can we provide our children *responsiveness* and *demandingness* in this frenzied digital age? It's less about what we say to our children and more about the environment we provide.

While it's great to tell our kids that we love them, taking actions that limit distracting technologies and provide kids a strong family connection are hallmarks of responsiveness (See Chapter 1 for reminders). To provide demandingness, take the steps provided in Chapter 3 including setting up a home environment that limits playtime devices. The good news is that it's never too late to start using authoritative parenting.

While sitting at the top of the home hierarchy, authoritative parents don't simply lay down rules. They make an effort to explain the reasoning behind their rules in a developmentally-appropriate fashion. Authoritative parents also listen to their children's viewpoints, especially as kids grow older, and consider adjusting the rules based on their kids' concerns, although parents maintain final say.

Authoritative Parenting in Action

What does authoritative parenting look like in real life? The following examples show how authoritative parenting is used to address typical technology issues.

Scenario 1: A nine-year-old boy complains to his parents that they don't allow video gaming during the school week.

Authoritative parent response: "I know many of your friends game during the week, and I understand that you feel the rule's not fair—if they can, why can't you? Well, lots of scientists have found that too much gaming hurts kids' schoolwork, so we need the rule. I am willing, however, to negotiate with you about having a friend over once or twice during the week."

Authoritative principle applied: Parents set high standards for children and explain that rules are set in the context of those standards.

Scenario 2: A preteen with increasingly obsessive technology use and falling grades protests the computer being removed from his room.

Authoritative parent response: "I know how much doing well in school is important to you, and since it's so easy to get distracted on the computer when you're all by yourself, moving it to the family room will help you stay focused. "

Authoritative principle applied: Discipline is applied respectfully, and the remedy applied logically flows from the problem.

Scenario 3: A 13-year-old is pushing her parents to buy her a smartphone with Internet capability—something that parents don't believe will serve her well.

Authoritative parent response: "I understand that you want an Internet-capable phone. However, I think the negatives outweigh the positives. We've talked about how digital devices tend to make families feel disconnected and hurt schoolwork, and I know those are two things you care about."

Authoritative principle applied: Explaining that rules are set out of concern for children's well-being encourages kids to be agreeable to parents' requests.

Scenario 4: A 16-year-old girl says she won't follow the rule that phones need to be turned off at 9 p.m.

Authoritative parent response: "I would like to hear why you feel you need the phone later in the evening, and I will consider your thoughts when I make a decision."

Authoritative principle applied: Parents value their children's point of view and take this into consideration, especially as kids get older, although maintain the role of primary decision maker in the home.

ADDRESSING CONCERNS ABOUT HELICOPTER PARENTING

While authoritative parenting is by far the most effective parenting style, applying its principles to kids' use of technology is often criticized in a culture that embraces the notion of a generation of young tech experts. For example, Microsoft's Danah Boyd equates parents' setting of tech limits with *helicopter parenting.*[26] Described by psychologist Madeline Levine in *Teach Your Children Well,* the term helicopter parenting (also called *hyperparenting*) refers to parents who hover over their children and teens, doing for them what they would better be off doing themselves.[27] An example would be parents completing schoolwork for kids who didn't take the time to do it.

Why is setting limits on kids' technology *not* helicopter parenting? Clearly our kids' profound overuse of entertainment technologies signals they need our help. Also, as we saw in Chapter 4, there's no way for kids to withstand the sophistication of psychologists and other experts in human behavior who deploy behavioral manipulation knowledge to shape products that kids can't put down. Moreover, kids' less developed judgment abilities make them highly susceptible to industry marketing selling "must-have" products. If we use the principles of authoritative parenting, we recognize kids' limitations and see the need for parental guidance. As Levine points out: "There is an important distinction between good and bad parental involvement."[28]

Ironically, in my work, I actually find that it's parents of tech-obsessed kids who rely most on helicopter parenting. Such kids are less likely to put in the necessary academic effort for success, so parents constantly have to stay on their case about missing homework assignments, lack of studying, and other consequences of that tech use.

HOW A DIGITAL-AGE PARENTING MYTH AFFECTS KIDS

When you consider setting serious limits on your children's use of entertainment technologies, you may rightfully question how he or she will respond. That's because the digital native-digital immigrant and similar parenting philosophies haven't only influenced how parents raise their kids. They also affect how children respond to parenting. In industry marketing, TV shows, and throughout our culture, children are bombarded with messages that kids rightfully should demand unlimited amounts of entertainment technologies and that their parents should simply acquiesce.

An Associated Press article highlighted the latest American Academy of Pediatrics (AAP) technology guidelines, clarifying that the recommended total screen entertainment limit of 1 to 2 hours per day included computers, TV, and video games. The article featured 16-year-old Mark, who said that he spends about four hours each day using the Internet for homework, Facebook, YouTube, and watching movies. He remarked that the AAP recommended limits "would be catastrophic" and that kids wouldn't follow the advice. "They'll just find a way to get around it," he said.[29]

This defiance may be minimized as typical of today's children and adolescents, but such attitudes are promoted by the industry-sponsored parenting myth that kids should be in control of their electronic and digital gadgets. Even though limits will foster their happiness and success, kids have been led to believe that unlimited access to screen-based and networking devices is essential to growing up. They rebel, refuse to follow their parents' direction, and suffer as a consequence.

HOW TO PARENT AUTHORITATIVELY IN AN UNINVOLVED CULTURE

So how can we parent authoritatively in a culture that encourages parents to provide kids open access to screens and similar gadgets, and conditions children to reject their parents' guidance? There are steps we can take to help us overcome these obstacles and encourage our children to work with us on the issue of technology. We'll explore these in the remainder of the chapter.

AUTHORITATIVE PARENTING THROUGH ROLE MODELING

To provide our children the *high expectations* and *strong limits* of authoritative parenting requires that we establish authority over our children. This power comes less from what we say ("Turn that thing off!"), and more from a strong parent-child connection and the characteristics of the home environment. One of the most important aspects of this environment is the way we ourselves model technology use.

When parents overuse technology, not only will kids copy our example, they can feel abandoned and will demand their own devices to keep them company. It's therefore vital that we limit our own use of phones, laptops, and TV, and instead engage with our kids—not all the time but a lot. Connecting with our kids opens a door for us to guide their tech use, as they are much more apt to listen to caregivers who show a strong investment in them.

If we listen, we may notice our kids asking us to be better media or technology role models. "I resent having to do my homework when you're watching TV or playing computer games," a teen boy divulged to his father. Since the beginning of time, kids have learned valuable habits by working alongside their parents, however today's kids are often denied this positive role modeling because they so often see their mother or father being entertained by a screen.

Most parents are tired after a long day's work. Many engage with entertainment screens as a break from other responsibilities, yet our kids generally don't see us at work. Instead they learn primarily from what they observe of us at home. If we want our kids to engage in activities like reading and homework when at home, we need to role model good work habits for them. So as your child sits at the kitchen table to complete his or her homework, read a book, do some chores, or use the computer for work rather than entertainment (kids notice the difference).

It's important that we limit our use of technology even for work when we're at home with the kids. If you have to take a call now and

121

then, no big deal, but kids are affected when their parents are constantly pulled away by work texts, calls, and emails. An eight-year-old boy told me that when he is with his dad kicking a soccer ball, his father constantly puts him "on hold" while he takes a call or returns a text. A 13-year-old girl explained to me that she is reticent to open up to her mom because her efforts to do so have been undermined by her mom stealing looks at her phone.

As mother and blogger Meredith Sinclair reported in a *New York Time's* article, kids are painfully aware when their parents attempt to multitask between gadgets and the parent-child relationship. "You can't really do both," Ms. Sinclair said, "If I'm at all connected, it's too tempting. I need to make a distinct choice."[30]

Parents' ability to attend to children is increasingly threatened by employer pressure to be available 24/7, because technology makes that feasible. Unfortunately, digital-age myths that push the benefits of technology while neglecting kids' attachment needs have misled parents about how costly such distractions are. Finding a healthy work-family balance is also made difficult because we are spending much more time working than generations past.[31]

There are no doubt tough choices for parents to make when considering the demands of work and family. I believe what's helpful is to be honest with ourselves about the needs of our kids and think clearly about our priorities, even if it means taking a job that pays less but offers the benefit of more devoted time with our kids. Kids need undistracted quality time with us far more than a bigger home or an expensive vacation.

I also suggest doing all you can to have technology help rather than hurt family connections. Do what you can to limit the use of real-time technologies, such as texting, that show little respect for the undistracted family moments our children need. Instead, I suggest using technologies such as email that you can check when you have taken a break from the kids. Employers also need to allow us undistracted time with our families at home. However, as Catherine

Steiner-Adair, author of the *Big Disconnect*, notes, positive change won't come unless parents demand the need to unplug.[32]

Extra challenges are present when parents work from home. As a mother and father asked me during a talk, "Since we both work from home, how can we keep our work-related computer use from affecting our daughter?" I suggest parents set aside a specific space exclusively for work, carve out time for family and honor it. If an emergency intervenes, make sure your kids know when you'll make it up.

Working with Spouses on the Issue of Technology

Children's technology use is much like other aspects of parenting in two-parent homes. Many spouses aren't fully in sync about all aspects of how their kids use technology, however differences can often be reconciled through discussion and compromise. Nonetheless, some parents report that they're on completely different pages over the issue of their children's technology use. For example, the mother of a 13-year-old boy told me, "I'm concerned about my son's gaming obsession, but my husband's a big gamer so he doesn't really believe it's an issue."

If a major gulf in parenting styles exists between you and your partner, it's essential to address it. If such differences aren't resolved, technology problems are likely to remain because children tend to side with the parent who permits greater access to entertainment technologies.

If you'd like your co-parent to be a better technology role model, the first step is to talk with him or her about your concerns. If you meet with resistance, ask your partner to do some research on the topic, or provide some reputable, easy-to-read information. Your child's pediatrician can play a supportive role because kids' doctors are increasingly aware of these issues. Not making any headway in coming to agreement? In that case, professional family counseling may help. This may sound dramatic, yet it beats the alternative of watching a child's life harmed by an unhealthy technology obsession.

Parents in two-caregiver homes also need to consider how their relationship as a couple influences their child's technology use. When there's frequent conflict between parents, kids will often retreat to their rooms and devices. So do everything you can to make your relationship with your partner loving and strong. Spend time together as a couple, not just parents. If that's not working, seek couples counseling. In my experience, parents who are struggling often wait far too long before entering counseling. Once they do, seemingly intractable problems often melt away.

PARENTING LIKE A TECH EXEC

There's no doubt that the type of parenting I'm suggesting to address your child's tech use deviates greatly from the way American kids are typically raised. You may therefore look at the evidence presented in this chapter and say, "Sure, it makes sense to provide kids strong guidance on the issue of technology, but I just don't know if I want my kid to be different than his (or her) peers."

I completely understand. I have at times worried about how the tech limits my wife and I provide our kids would affect their relationships with peers. However, helping my wife and me stay firm is our determination to provide our kids the parenting they need—even if it's not the typical way to go. Most of us remind our kids, "Don't follow the crowd," so we sometimes need to be able to take our own advice. I also can honestly say that the tech rules my wife and I provide our kids have had no discernible effect on their peer relationships, except possibly encouraging them to form friendships with kids who play with tech less and focus on school more.

Nonetheless, perhaps you're still on the fence about taking what amount to bold actions on this issue. I suggest a credible source of guidance is the parenting method employed by many tech industry leaders to raise their own children and teens. Earlier in the chapter, we saw that Bill and Melinda Gates provided their kids strong tech limits growing up. Also elucidating is the *New York Times'* article "Steve Jobs Was a Low-Tech Parent."[33] Writer Nick Bilton says that while on a phone call with Steve Jobs in 2010 he asked him if his kids were enjoying the recently-released first-generation iPad. "They haven't used it," Mr. Jobs replied, "We limit how much technology our kids use at home."

If the Jobs' household wasn't bathed in gadgets, how did the family spend time? Walter Isaacson, who wrote Mr. Jobs' biography and who spent a great deal of time in the Jobs' family home, observes, "Every evening Steve made it a point of having dinner at the big long table in their kitchen, discussing books and history and a variety of things…. No one ever pulled out an iPad or computer."[34]

If both the Jobs' and Gates' families set strict technology limits, what type of parenting is employed by other tech industry leaders? In Mr. Bilton's interviews with a number of technology chief executives and venture capitalists, he found this same parenting strategy quite common, noting many "strictly limit their children's screen time, often banning all gadgets on school nights, and allocating ascetic time limits on weekends." For example, Chris Anderson, the former editor of *Wired* and now the CEO of the drone maker 3D Robotics, described why he and his wife set strict technology limits, noting it's "because we have seen the dangers of technology firsthand. I've seen it in myself. I don't want to see that happen to my kids." Anderson's concerns for his kids include being subjected to bullying online and the potential for developing a technology addiction.

The types of screen limits Bilton found commonly used by tech industry leaders include:

- no gadget use on weekdays and limits from 30 minutes to two hours on weekends for phones and tablets
- computers only being used for homework on school nights
- and a rule he found universal among the tech parents he polled: "No screens in the bedroom."

Why is the parenting approach applied by many tech leaders markedly different from that typically provided US kids? As Bilton notes, "These tech CEO's seem to know something that the rest of us don't." I believe their insiders' knowledge inoculates them from being deceived by the many digital-age myths outlined in this book. These business leaders understand the distressing reality that American kids' screen time is typified by long hours absorbed with entertainment technologies that pose the risk of addiction and often impair family togetherness and academic success.

Parents will benefit from noticing the contradictory messages coming out of the tech industry. On one hand, industry marketing claims it's vital we load kids up with ever more devices, and that video games, social networks, and texting promote kids' happiness and success. On the other, tech industry leaders speak volumes through the strong steps they take to limit their own kids' use of devices. Which counsel will you choose when raising your kids?

PROMOTING CHILDREN'S DIGITAL LITERACY

To parent authoritatively, we must teach our kids digital literacy. *Digital literacy* is the ability to understand how technology affects our thoughts, behavior, and lives.

When digital literacy is discussed in the popular media, it often refers to the ability to analyze the media and technology that is already being consumed, e.g., helping teens appreciate whether the marketing they see is really in their best interests. While this is important, I suggest that we also turn our focus to teaching kids another, often overlooked, component of digital literacy: *the ability to recognize the tremendous opportunity costs of spending long hours with amusement-based technologies.*[35]

Helping Kids See What's in It for Them

We are much more likely to be successful in teaching our kids digital literacy skills *if we start the process early* in their lives and make sure our efforts to talk with them about technology are *combined with firm limits.* That's because older kids who have developed obsessive tech habits often have a strong sense of denial about negative effects that impedes their ability to objectively discuss the issue.

These parent-child conversations might begin when they ask you a question about their use of technology. For example, if you delay providing digital devices until later in toddlerhood—remember the AAP suggestion of no more than 2 hours of high-quality content a day after the age of 2—and begin to put firm limits on entertainment technologies when your children are very young, they will likely come to you, at a younger age than you may expect, to ask the reason for limits.

Four-year-olds will ask why your family doesn't watch as much TV as other families. Six-year-olds will ask why they don't have the same gaming devices as their peers. Preteens and teens may wonder why their friends are getting smartphones and they're not, and so on. It's important to help our kids understand the reasons for such choices in language appropriate to their age and developmental maturity.

A good way to begin teaching kids about digital literacy is to help them understand how seemingly minor decisions that they make as a child or teen—how much time they spend gaming, social network-ing, or watching TV—can profoundly affect their future. We need to help kids see that their desire to become a veterinarian, a teacher, or any number of long-term goals can be easily thwarted if they become caught up in the heavy tech habits snaring many of their peers.

Too often parents avoid these conversations, because they ex-pect that their kids are already aware of potential consequences. Or some parents assume that their kids consciously choose to game, so-cial network, or text rather than study. Yet children, and even older teens (see Chapter 9), don't have the judgment needed to make such choices. They need help from parents, teachers, and others invested in their future.

When you talk with your kids about technology, you may be sur-prised to find what your child or teen has already noticed. A 3rd-grade boy told me, "Oh, I know kids who are gamers. That's all they talk about and they don't seem to care very much about school." And 4th or 5th graders may be aware of how their peers' technology use distances them from families and friends. A 10-year-old boy told his mother why he didn't like visiting a peer's house, "He just sits in his room and plays on his iPod and doesn't want to do anything else."

By the time kids reach middle school, they may realize that some of their peers are suffering as the result of being entangled in cyber drama. And most high-school-age students are aware of highly capable peers who struggle with grades because they're buried in video games, social networks, and other entertainment technologies.

We don't have to be heavy-handed when we talk with our kids about these issues, e.g., telling them that video games or social networks are "ruining" their lives. Instead, we can gently remind them that activities like school, reading, and extracurricular involvements bring them pleasure. This helps kids develop their own insight about appropriate uses of technology.

How Does It Feel to Be Manipulated?

Questioning authority is developmentally normal for kids, especially as they enter and move through their teen years. Entertainment-based tech companies co-opt this instinct, convincing kids to reject the conformity of their families so they can (supposedly) find their own way using trendy technologies.

We should help our kids understand that while they may not want to follow our lead for the rest of their lives, being played or controlled by giant tech corporations is a bad alternative. Ask your kids about their aspirations, and then ask them what they think commercial technology companies want most from kids. Do tech companies care if children or teens don't reach their own goals? What strategies do those corporations use to encourage kids to use, or even overuse, their products? If you have teens, consider watching with them the powerful documentary *Consuming Kids: The Commercialization of*

Childhood.[36] The segments in which child marketers talk about manipulating and branding kids for profit may open kids' eyes to a side of industry they don't know exists.

Teens can also work together to limit their use of entertainment technologies. The *New York Times* article "To Deal With Obsession, Some Defriend Facebook"[37] describes teens who set up peer support groups that help them deactivate their social network accounts or limit their use to improve their chances of academic success. "We decided we spent way too much time obsessing over Facebook, and it would be better if we took a break from it," 17-year-old Halley from San Francisco, CA said. Fifteen-year-old Neeka, a high school sophomore from Ann Arbor, MI, got better grades after making a pact with her sister to limit her Facebook time.

Schools' Role in Teaching Digital Literacy

Because our children's immersion in entertainment technologies often hinders their academic performance, elementary and secondary schools have an important role to play in teaching kids digital literacy. One goal of this literacy should be to help kids learn to resist social pressure to indulge in entertainment technologies. Boys, especially, experience pressure from peers to engage in intensive online gaming communities. Girls, more than boys, are coerced by peers to be constantly available by social network and text. All kids experience social pressure to get smartphones that provide them increased access to academics-thwarting technologies.

Schools can ease this pressure through broad-based efforts to talk with students and their parents about the research that shows the more kids use video games, TV, or social networks, the less well they do academically. When schools remain silent about kids' tech use, students suffer. A study of 9- to-17-year-old students found that those who spent more time social networking had lower grades than kids who spent less time using the technology. In what should be an eye-opener for schools, these heavy social networking kids acted as frequent recruiters—getting large numbers of fellow students to visit their favorite sites.[38] Such recruiting can drag down the academic performance of the greater student body.

Schools should talk with their students about the risks of being a peer-follower on matters of technology. They should help kids and their parents understand that the tech-focused lifestyle normalized by our culture is a poor fit with the increasingly rigorous admission requirements of colleges. Schools can also outline what a successful student's after-school schedule typically looks like: focused study and sports, arts, or community activities rather than multitasking between fun-based technologies.

HELP KIDS LEARN TO NAVIGATE THE REAL WORLD

Technology use tends to be self-reinforcing: Kids who live in the virtual world can grow fearful of venturing into the real one. We therefore need to help children develop real-world communication skills and encourage and support their face-to-face interactions with adults and peers.

In the revised edition of *Odd Girl Out,* leadership authority Rachel Simmons explores the emotional costs of online relationships compared to real-world connections and shows that parents can help.[39] Online exchanges deny the experience of registering the tone of comments, so that we can't understand their true meaning. For example, kids could interpret the online comment, "Kim likes your new boyfriend," a number of ways, potentially leading to confusion, a cascade of drama, hurt feelings, and the unnecessary loss of friends. An effective way to provide guidance is by raising examples like this, asking your child if he or she has ever experienced the misunderstanding of an online remark, and talking about the advantages of real-world interactions.

Another benefit to getting kids involved in real-world activities is that it can improve the quality of their relationships. Many children and teenagers find it easier to ridicule one another online than in the real world, since they don't have to see someone's reaction if they say something mean. Remember from Chapter 1 that kids who spend greater amounts of time online are more likely to cyberbully or be cyberbullied than kids who spend less time online. I therefore suggest encouraging younger children to be involved in sports, drama, or other experiences where they interact with peers and adults in real time. Teens are also well served by volunteer or occupational experiences that demand offline interactions.

7

Nurture Young Children's Brain Development

An advertisement for a device using the latest technology promises parents that it will help kids become "more interested in school work" and get "better marks in school." This device is also intended to double as a babysitter, since the ad promises it's great for "keeping small fry out of mischief... and out of mother's hair."[1] These claims are actually from a 1950 advertisement promoting what was then the most modern in high-tech screen devices: a Motorola television set.

Unfortunately television, on the whole, has not educated children well. Research suggests kids ages 2½ and up benefit from limited exposure to educational programming like *Sesame Street* or *Blue's Clues*,[2] but American kids typically spend long hours watching entertainment TV that displaces reading and homework.[3] The result? TV generally detracts from academic success.[4]

To give due credit, the Motorola ad is right about the ability of television to occupy children without their caregivers' attention. In 2006, a study published in *Pediatrics* reported that the time kids (birth to 12) spent watching TV without parents "was strongly negatively related to time spent interacting with parents or siblings."[5] This is concerning because a strong connection to a parent or other caregiver underlies children's emotional health, academic success, and overall well-being. All things considered, television is a crummy babysitter.

REHASHING CLAIMS OF AN ELECTRONIC EDUCATING BABYSITTER

Marketing for the current generation of interactive technologies also promises parents an educating babysitter. An article in *Parenting* touts, "Want to enjoy eating out, even with your little one? Distract kids of every age with more iPhone, iPod Touch and iPad applications and game[s]." This article claims that various apps provide "brain food for kids," "a healthy way to strengthen those memory muscles," or "teach math skills."[6]

Also advocating for young kids' use of technology are those whose job it is to promote gadgets and software that ostensibly foster young children's learning. Not surprisingly, their focus often appears limited to *which* screen products kids should use rather than on the more important question of *whether* using these products is in kids' best interests.[7] This contrasts with *child development* experts who have children's overall well-being as their primary interest, and who aren't financially invested in kids' use of screens or technology. Unfortunately, in a culture consumed with technology, those with a vested interest in endorsing tech stuff may decide our kids' fate.

Recently, the National Association for the Education of Young Children (NAEYC), the nation's leading early childhood professional organization, which accredits childcare providers, decided to update its technology guidelines for kids from birth to eight. Sadly, the NAEYC heavily weighted the guidelines' authorship towards those who promote young kids' use of technology.[8] Not surprisingly, the resulting guidelines strongly endorse young kids' tech use without mentioning the associated risks. This support for young kids' tech time is now being communicated to parents via childcare providers who follow their accrediting organization's guidelines.

Parents also may have become aware of the NAEYC's guidelines through the popular press. In her *Huffington Post* article "Saying Yes to Digital Media in Preschool and Kindergarten," Lisa Guernsey, director of the New America Foundation's Early Education Initiative, ballyhoos the NAEYC's position statement and the importance of exposing young children to technology.[9] Like many others advocating for early tech exposure, Guernsey is financially tied to companies invested in bringing such products to young kids—something she neglects to mention in her article. The New America Foundation has the stated purpose of promoting screen media in early education settings, and its biggest funders (at $1 million or more in 2013) include The Bill & Melinda Gates Foundation as well as Google executive chairman Eric Schmidt and his wife Wendy.[10] Both Microsoft (Xbox) and Google (Google Play Games) sell video games for young kids.

Filling Early Childhood with Digital Media

Assurances that the latest tech gadgets can both occupy and teach young ones help parents feel good about handing these devices to their kids. A *New York Times* article noted that there were nearly three million downloads of Fisher-Price's Laugh & Learn tablet and smartphone apps for babies in 2011–2012 alone.[11]

The belief that very young kids benefit from digital devices also increases their use time. While we don't know what portion of screen time is spent watching traditional TV vs. using a tablet, iPod, or smartphone, 29% of babies under the age of one watch TV and video content for about 90 minutes a day, while on average 64% of kids watch a little more than 2 hours a day between their first and second birthday.[12] By the time they're about four years old, on average children view a little more than four hours of television and video content each weekday.[13] An increasing percentage of this screen time is on mobile platforms such as tablets and smartphones.

Let No Childhood Moment Go Unscreened

As so much of young kids' lives is now taken up by screens, corporations have to dig deeper to find non-screen moments of childhood ripe for new products. Fisher-Price's Newborn-to-Toddler Apptivity™ Seat for iPad® device has gained recent notoriety. It's an infant bouncy seat that places an iPad directly above the baby's face. The Campaign for a Commercial-Free Childhood (CCFC), which is leading a recall effort, notes that the device blocks the baby's view of the rest of the world and "encourages parents to leave infants all alone with an iPad."[14] Nevertheless, packaging for the seat advertises "Play & learning at baby's fingertips!"[15]

Another product of an increasingly screen-ubiquitous childhood is the iPotty, a toilet-training device with an iPad stand in front of the child. Its manufacturer, CTA, promotes the "removable touchscreen cover to guard against messy accidents and smudges."[16] In 2013, the iPotty received a Toady, CCFC's public choice award for the Worst Toy of the Year. Michelle, a mother from Greenville, SC, explained that she voted for the iPotty as worst toy because: "Toilet learning should be a time of positive interaction between child and caregiver. Also, children should be aware of the cues in their bodies as they learn. This toy takes this social/emotional focus out of the process and substitutes the hypnotism of a screen."[17]

THE EFFECTS OF WIRING UP THE YOUNG

While many promise the benefits of the latest digital devices for young kids, what does science say? Unfortunately, these technologies are so new that their long-term impact—which is how they must be gauged—has not been determined. As the Center on Media and Child Health at Boston Children's Hospital, Harvard Medical School notes: "Although there are many products that offer lapware and educational computer games for young children, there is very little research evidence to show that these products are beneficial for learning."[18]

This doesn't mean we don't have some important indicators, many of which are pointing to some disturbing effects of the move to immerse young kids in the digital sphere. In fact, despite a lot of hype, in many cases the effects of the newer screen technologies appear to be much like those of the old-fashioned TV.

Teaching Kids to be Alone with Screens

The revised NAEYC guidelines described previously suggest that digital technologies "have the potential to bring adults and children together for a shared experience, rather than keeping them apart."[19] However, this contrasts with how popular mobile devices are actually used by most kids and their parents. The Center on Media and Human Development at Northwestern University, looking at how children (ages 2 to 5) use technologies like the iPad or iPod touch, found that only about a quarter of parents use the device *with* their kids at least most of the time.[20]

There's also evidence that these and similar devices *teach* kids to be alone with technology. According to the Center, by the time kids are between 6 and 8 years old, only 11% of parents use these gadgets with their children at least most of the time.[21] As many of us have seen in restaurants and other settings, young kids' use of these devices encourages them to be alone—unnaturally alone—even in the presence of their family.

Why the Strength of Interactivity is a Weakness for Young Kids

Advocates such as those who crafted the NAEYC's position statement claim that *interactive* technologies (for example, a device that responds when a child swipes a touch screen) are better for young kids than *passive* media such as television. The position statement reads: "Noninteractive media can lead to passive viewing and overexposure to screen time for young children and are not substitutes for interactive and engaging uses of digital media...."[22]

It's a mistake to believe that a digital machine's ability to respond to a child's action—especially when we talk about younger kids—conveys an advantage. Instead, the truth is likely just the reverse. The profoundly absorbing nature of interactive digital devices can blunt a child's natural drive to seek interaction with parents and other caregivers.

ABC's *Nightline* staff visited the Barnard College Center for Toddler Development. They joined child experts behind a two-way mirror to watch 3- to 5-year-olds using an iPad. As the *ABC News* article describes the visit, "The center tested for 'distractibility' by having researchers call out the names of the children who were playing with iPads and noted how readily the children responded. Many of the kids were so zoned in on the apps they were playing with, they didn't respond to the researchers at all."[23] Video from the story shows the troubling, but familiar to many parents, sight of iPad-involved kids apparently oblivious to an adult repeatedly calling their name.[24]

When traditional toys such as blocks were substituted for the iPads, Barnard researchers found that the kids became more verbal, social, and creative. "You see how much their vocabulary has gone up and they are talking to each other," Tovah Klein, the director of the Center noted.[25]

It's perhaps most upsetting for the families I work with when young kids begin to show a preference for "interacting with" electronic gadgets over their parents. This isn't really surprising. Raising young kids is tough business. Moms and dads can't be entertaining around the clock, but a tablet, phone, or other interactive device can.

Wall Street Journal reporter and father Ben Worthen described what happened when he and his wife provided an iPad to their toddler. Initially, Ben and his wife were hopeful, as the device appeared to encourage their son's language development. Then they noticed that their son could go into a trance-like state with his iPad and wouldn't respond when they called his name. It became a nightly battle to get him to put it down. These concerns led Ben and his wife to stop giving the iPad to their son.[26]

The latest brain imaging studies reveal that young children's interactions with parents and other adult caregivers shape the architecture of the developing mind, building brain cell connections and brain volume. A *use it or lose it* principle exists. Brain cells and synapses (the connections between brain cells) that aren't stimulated during a child's early years are pruned away, and may never fully develop later. Because infants and toddlers need lots of loving exchanges with real-life caregivers, the American Academy of Pediatrics states: "Young children learn best from—and need—interaction with humans, not screens."[27] We should therefore be especially disquieted by efforts to introduce interactive technologies to the young; the devices' very "interactivity" may interfere with the human connections young kids must have for optimal brain and emotional development.

Should We Really Be Surprised? More Screens Means More Screen Time

Digital advocates, like those at NAEYC, suggest that the use of newer technologies in children's lives should be expanded, while TV exposure should be minimized.[28] Nonetheless, the sad reality is that our children now use digital phones and other portable devices to increase their already incredible overuse of television. The Kaiser Family Foundation notes, "It seems clear that one of the main roles 'new' communication technologies play is to bring more 'old' media content into young people's lives. Being able to access TV online and on mobile platforms [including iPods and smartphones] has led to a substantial increase in the amount of time young people spend watching, to a total of just about 4½ hours a day [4 hours, 29 minutes], nearly 40 minutes more than 5 years ago [3 hours, 51 minutes]."[29] Meet the new screens, same as the old screens.

In addition to watching a lot of TV on new devices, what are kids doing? In spite of lofty promises, we need to be honest with ourselves about what the popular new technologies are designed for and how they are typically used. Former Apple CEO Steve Jobs said his company's iPod touch was "the number one portable game player in the world" and boasted that it outsold Nintendo's and Sony's portable game players combined.[30]

Likewise, how are iPads and iPhones typically used? As *USA Today* noted in its article "Games dominate Apple's all-time apps list," 15 of the 25 most-ever-downloaded paid apps for Apple's iPad are games, including 5 of the top 6: *Angry Birds HD, Angry Birds Seasons HD, Fruit Ninja HD*, etc. Similarly, 21 of the top 25 most-ever-downloaded paid apps for Apple's iPhone are games, including the top 3: *Angry Birds, Fruit Ninja*, and *Doodle Jump*.[31]

Communication theorist Marshall McLuhan said years ago, "The medium is the message."[32] How messages are conveyed (e.g., via tablet computer or book) may be as important as the content. Tablets, smartphones, and iPods are synonymous with gaming and entertainment—especially for kids. When we provide kids one of these devices, it sends a powerful message about how they should spend their time. In contrast, when we provide children a book, we send the message that reading is important.

Gateway Games

The early learning benefits marketers and pundits promise from digital technologies convince many parents to buy their young children "educational" video games. Unfortunately, I believe this helps prime generations of children to spend long hours with entertainment-based video games. A Pew Research Center report confirms my concern, showing that by the time kids reach the ages of 12 to 17, entertainment-based titles dominate their video game time.[33]

What shifts children from "educational" to entertainment games? Video game developer Marc Prensky says that while preschoolers may tolerate "educational" games, these games "aren't fun" as kids get older and aren't something they will "do on their own."[34] In all likelihood, learning-based games don't provide the addictive-level stimulation of entertainment-based games. The result is that "educational" games played by young children appear to act as *gateway games,* conditioning their users to later indulge in entertainment games that displace reading and homework.

PARENTS NEED GOOD, HONEST INFORMATION

It's abundantly clear that parents making choices about how their children and teens use technology should have unbiased, science-based guidance. But that can be difficult to find because tech companies know parents are looking for direction and make efforts to provide their own profit-driven guidance (much as the tobacco industry once did), often disguised as objective information. It is this industry manipulation of information that helps construct and promote technology myths that hurt children.

Constructing a Technology Myth

Some years ago, when social networks were just coming on the scene, questions surfaced about how this technology would affect children. Social networks were becoming popular with kids of all ages, from preschoolers who used "kiddie" social networks to middle- and high-school-age kids who used the same social networks as adults. Parents, understandably, were curious about the effects of this new technology, including how it would affect kids' ability to learn. On the other hand, tech corporations—knowing that parents had questions about social networking—had a financial incentive to convince moms and dads that this technology was the next great thing.

One seemingly good resource for parents and teachers was *Creating & Connecting*, a report released in 2007, which studied kids' (ages 9–17) use of this technology. It was a pivotal moment for the emerging phenomenon of social networking, because parents, schools, and even the popular media needed leadership on the issue. The report claimed to offer "research and guidelines"[35] on social networks, and was released by the seemingly objective National School Boards Association (NSBA) whose stated goal is improving student achievement.[36]

Less publicized was that the funders of *Creating & Connecting* included powerful corporations with a financial incentive to get kids to use social networks: News Corporation (which purchased the social network Myspace in 2005[37]), Microsoft (which became part owner of Facebook in 2007[38]), and Verizon (a cell phone company that kids commonly use to access social networks).[39] It's not surprising that the report's guidelines put a positive spin on kids' use of social networks.

The *Creating & Connecting* report lavishes praise on heavy child users of social networks, suggesting that they exemplify "leadership among their peers" and "seem to have an extraordinary set of traditional and 21st century skills."[40] Buried in the flowery language is the acknowledgement that heavy users of social networks "are significantly more likely than other students to have lower grades."[41] That finding is consistent with research in Chapter 3 linking heavier use of social networks with lower academic performance. Nevertheless, *Creating & Connecting* ended up strongly advocating for increasing children's and teens' access to and use of social networks.

The *Creating & Connecting* report's flawed advice—which carries weight because of the NSBA's name—is an example of how tech corporations create digital-age technology myths. These myths in turn deceive parents, in this case about the relative importance of social networks vs. schooling in children's life success. Such misleading advice undermines parents' ability to raise healthy, successful kids. I have worked with countless families in which parents have been blindsided when they find that their children's overuse of social networks (or other entertainment technologies) have led to poor grades that reduce their kids' college admission prospects.

Moving forward, child-serving organizations should recognize the potential harm that can be done by partnering with consumer tech companies to create technology guidelines. It's no different than joining with the fast food industry to create nutritional advice. If you're a parent or teacher searching for objective information, I suggest you look carefully at who is providing the counsel.

Health-based Organizations

I'm most familiar with the following organizations committed to providing fact-based, impartial advice on media and technology matters:

- **American Academy of Pediatrics** (www.aap.org): provides research-based information for pediatricians and parents on technology issues, including the use of screens in childcare settings
- **Campaign for a Commercial-Free Childhood** (www.commercialfreechildhood.org): advocates for restricting corporate marketers' access to children, and develops research-driven recommendations on children's use of media and technology
- **Center on Media and Child Health** (www.cmch.tv): offers research-based resources for parents and teachers on issues of technology, including recommendations on the appropriate use of technology for kids of different ages

TECH RECOMMENDATIONS FOR YOUNG CHILDREN

The reality is that many heavily touted benefits of young kids' tech use—when studied more closely using objective research—appear to be based on wishful thinking. I therefore suggest following the 2013 American Academy of Pediatrics' recommendation that children from birth to two years not be exposed to any screen media, including TV, tablets, smartphone apps, and the new formats being developed continuously.[42] As children reach 2½ years or older, evidence suggests that some *educational* television programming can benefit them. I suggest limiting this to one hour or less a day for toddlers and preschoolers. I also believe parents best serve their children by *not* exposing them to interactive technologies long past the age of two, difficult as that may be. Chapter 10 will look at more factors to help you guide children's introduction to technology.

LIMITING YOUNG CHILDREN'S SCREEN EXPOSURE

Raising young children with limited screen access provides long-term benefits but short-term challenges. In this section, we look at action steps that will help you achieve this goal and surmount these challenges.

Encourage Time in Nature and Outdoor Play

In his book *Last Child in the Woods,* renowned author Richard Louv notes that our children are experiencing "Nature-Deficit Disorder," as they rarely get out to play. Instead, they stay inside staring at screens.[43] Hopefully, your neighborhood is safe and your older kids can play outside safely. Since younger kids often need supervision outdoors, getting them out of the house may demand that we take part.

Families I work with tell me that taking walks with their children in nature—seeing a deer run, or a swooping owl at dusk, or even watching birds in the park or at backyard feeders—have helped their kids develop interest in a life away from screens. If natural environments aren't readily available, a family walk through the city to take in the sights or a subway ride to the museum or zoo can provide a welcome departure from screen time.

Read to Young Kids

In 2014, the American Academy of Pediatrics (AAP) announced a new policy that during routine visits children's doctors should recommend that parents read to their children daily, beginning in infancy and lasting at least through the age of entering kindergarten.[44] This is because emerging research indicates that much of the most important brain development occurs in children's first years of life and that reading to young kids greatly enhances language development important for later school and life success. The AAP observes, "In contrast to often either passive or solitary electronic media exposure, parents reading with young children is a very personal and nurturing experience that promotes parent-child interaction, social-emotional development, and language and literacy skills during this critical period of early brain and child development."[45]

This recommendation is critical now because in a world caught up with all things technology, parents can perceive reading to kids as less important. "The reality of today's world is that we're competing with portable digital media," Alanna Levine, a pediatrician from Orangeburg, New York, said in a recent *New York Times'* article, "So you really want to arm parents with tools and rationale behind it about why it's important to stick to the basics of things like books."[46]

Research shows that while higher- *and* lower-income parents struggle to read to their young children daily, this is much more pronounced in disadvantaged families.[47] Because one of the barriers to reading to kids is investing in books, the AAP says that as part of its new policy it will provide books to disadvantaged children at health visits. It's vital that we provide all children a home environment supportive of their literacy skills, including limiting TV and video games known to decrease the time kids' spend reading (see Chapter 3 for supporting research).

Reading to my daughters, now ages 7 and 11, has been—and continues to be—one of the most enjoyable and rewarding experiences of my life. My wife and I continue to read to our kids—picking out "family books" such as the *Harry Potter* series or *Charlie and the Chocolate Factory. The Read-Aloud Handbook,* by educational consultant Jim Trelease, is a great guide to choosing engaging books to read to kids of various ages,[48] and so are librarians and bookstore staff. Most public libraries have free activities that support literacy development and/or parent-child reading experiences, from interesting guest readers to entertaining events that offer young kids and their parents a fun moment in the company of books.

Granted, I know it's challenging to find the time and energy to read to our kids. When my girls were infants and toddlers, I sometimes found myself chugging tea or coffee at 9 or 10 o'clock at night so I could read to them after a long day of work and child care. Still, I remember sometimes waking up in the comfy chair where I read to them with one of my girls staring up at me, because I'd fallen asleep before she did. I also remember family vacations in which one large suitcase was chiefly devoted to children's books (luckily, the books they read now take up less space). These experiences are much more taxing strategies than handing over a device. However, make no mistake, the research is showing more than ever that efforts to build our children's early literacy are worth it.

What To Do About "Mom (Dad), I'm bored!"

When our children come to us and say they "need" something to do, our first impulse may be to find something to occupy them, which all too often ends up being a screen. Be secure in the knowledge that a little boredom is good for kids. Downtime has a bad label in our current zeitgeist. It has us believing that kids must constantly be engaged, often with a device. But boredom is often the precursor to imagination, learning, and creative thought.

What should we do when our kids complain of boredom? First, we need to judge if our children really could find something to do, or if they're truly challenged, perhaps because they're so dependent on screens. For kids who could find something to do themselves, gentle encouragement and our ability to tolerate a few grumbles is often enough to foster their inner resourcefulness. If your kids really press you, consider the method used by my wife (who learned it from her mother): Explain to your kids that if they're really bored, you'd be happy to assign them a chore. This often leads kids to become surprisingly resourceful.

Due to their young age or because they've grown used to screen entertainment, some children truly struggle to occupy themselves. In such cases, we may need to foster this ability in our kids. To begin with, make sure your kids have access to alternatives to screens. Creativity-promoting props (see Chapter 2) help provide your child with raw materials that can turn boredom into something interesting or even magical. You also can sit down with your kids for a few minutes to brainstorm alternative activities.

Non-Screen Activities for Young Kids

I find that what parents do to raise young children with limited screen time is unique to each family and often reflects the special interests of parents. When our kids were young, my wife would engage them in make-believe or floor play. While I did this as well, I especially liked wandering out into the world, so I would bundle up our girls and hit the road in a jogging stroller, stopping to talk with neighbors or dogs, or to explore a fish pond. Our kids also listened to books and sing-alongs on tape. Arranging play dates or enrolling kids in community programs are also good ways to keep young kids engaged.

I'm not pretending that raising young kids with limited screen use is easy. Even with the help of extended family and childcare, caring for my kids during their earliest years was exhausting—far more challenging than I was prepared for. Yet it's worth remembering that since young brains are so malleable, these early experiences have a tremendous impact on developing the skills that will serve them a lifetime.

Going Screenless in Restaurants and Other Out-of-Home Settings

Caring for young kids in places like restaurants poses its own difficulties. A common modern solution is to offer children a smartphone or tablet computer whose magnetic appeal allows parents to enjoy a dinner or time to themselves. While this may seem like a good solution at the time, later you may find yourself looking at your screen-fixated preteens and teens and wondering where things went wrong.

What's an alternative? Bring along books, crayons, and paper. Engage with kids during dinner. Draw a picture together or take your kids for a walk around the restaurant to talk about things that you see. This is much more demanding, but it's actually an enjoyable and rewarding way to connect with kids. Moreover, such experiences are an essential part of helping children realize the joy of engaging with real people and the real world. In any restaurant or other setting there will be someone who likes kids, and who's willing to chat for a little while. If one person isn't, the next may be.

Understandably, parents need alone time and time together as a couple if there are two parents at home. If at all possible, invest in a regular babysitter or obtain childcare so you can get out of the house, enjoy a dinner, go to a movie, etc. Find a trusted neighbor or family member with whom to trade child-care. Recharging our batteries allows us to be more present when we're with our kids.

It Takes a Village

One of the saddest consequences of digital myths is the diminished appreciation for the importance of extended families in raising children. Parents can question the need to see grandma because they believe time with an iPad is just as good. Decisions to move far away from extended family are made with too little consideration of the consequences, as technology is believed to be a good childcare option.

Since the beginning of humankind, extended families have played an invaluable role in raising kids. Digital devices, in contrast, have no stake in a child's future. They can't compete with an invested grandparent's or other family member's loving presence. Do all you can to reach out to extended family. If you are a grandparent or other extended family member, realize how important you can be in a child's life.

Many parents don't have the luxury of having grandparents or other relatives who can regularly participate in childcare. They still need help. So consider enrolling your child in a quality preschool or daycare that strongly limits or doesn't incorporate screen time if you have the resources to do so. I also suggest accessing mature babysitters who can engage your kids without screens.

8

Keep Your Kids Close

One reason many parents allow kids to spend long hours socially networking, online gaming, or texting—even if at the expense of family—is the belief that it's developmentally appropriate for kids to *detach from their parents and shift alliances to peers* as they mature. Since today those peers are accessed online as much as or more than in real life, it should make sense to support kids' open access to phones, computers, and online video gaming where peers are found, right? But the belief that *detachment* from family is a normal part of growing up is another harmful myth.

KIDS NEED PARENTS MORE THAN THEY NEED PEERS

In contrast to the picture painted by popular culture, children's relationships with parents are more important to their health and welfare than their relationships with peers. While many parents may believe that this is only true for young children, it's also true for preteens and teens. A study in *The Journal of Youth and Adolescence* reports that while a strong relationship with both parents and peers enhances the emotional health of kids 12 to 19 years old, the connection to parents actually matters more. The researchers write, "The quality of attachment to parents was significantly more powerful than that to peers in predicting well-being."[1] The study's authors also found that adolescents who experienced high levels of stress were helped by their relationship with parents, while relationships with peers provided no such benefit.

Why is it better for kids to have their primary bonds with parents? The reason is clear: Parents have more mature brains and a larger store of life experiences than children's peers, which allows them to more skillfully guide kids through the challenges of growing up. In addition, parents invest in their children in a way that peers never can. Most of us would give our lives for our kids. In contrast, the strongest-appearing peer relationships can slowly fade, or even evaporate over the course of a few hours.

As developmental psychologist Gordon Neufeld and family physician Gabor Maté note in *Hold On to Your Kids*, a book that spotlighted the problem of today's more peer- than parent-oriented kids: "Absolutely missing in peer relationships are unconditional love and acceptance, the desire to nurture, the ability to extend oneself for the sake of the other, the willingness to sacrifice for the growth and development of the other."[2] All too often preteens or teens I work with go to bed believing they have a best friend, only to find out when they arrive at school that late-night online drama has destroyed this relationship forever. Not surprisingly, as these kids watch the peer contact they so deeply depend on suddenly collapse, they can fall into depression and even consider suicide.

Children should also form their primary alliances with parents because dominant peer bonds put kids at greater risk for delinquent behaviors and drug use.[3] That's because peer-oriented kids are apt to follow peers who make poor choices. As noted by Geoffrey Canada, founder of the Harlem Children's Zone, an advocacy organization for lower-income families in New York City: "It is so much more dangerous for boys today because there aren't any role models around for them. There's some 15-year-old telling a 12-year-old what it means to be a man, and these children are really growing up under so much stress."[4]

Parents I work with who have encouraged their kids' strong bonds with friends sometimes find themselves asking why their kids followed friends into using drugs or other kinds of trouble. In contrast, kids who have strong and primary attachments to parents resist peer pressure more readily and make better life choices.

For the unfortunate circumstances in which children don't have access to a healthy parent figure, see the subsequent section, "Foster Mentor Relationships," for helpful strategies.

Misjudging Why Kids Struggle

Although it's best that kids maintain their primary bonds with parents until they reach adulthood, the myth of detachment is strong in our culture and often leads parents to misattribute reasons for their children's suffering.

Thirteen-year-old Kayla's parents brought her to counseling because she was hurt by the constant teasing of her friends at school and online. She was harassed daily about her appearance—her weight, clothes, and a mole on her cheek—even though nothing about her looks was out of the ordinary.

Kayla's parents felt that she most needed skills that would allow her to stand up for herself. When I met with Kayla, it became clear that her primary problem wasn't the inability to defend herself, but that she was missing a close connection with her parents. Not feeling the love she needed from her mom and dad, Kayla felt compelled to seek constant attention from peers (including those with behavior problems), making her an easy target for them. Strengthening the bond with her parents helped Kayla, which in turn diminished her need to seek affirmation from all-too-often destructive peer contacts.

HOW TECHNOLOGY SPEEDS DETACHMENT

The shift from parent- to peer-orientation in America has been occurring for decades, influenced by factors such as the increasing hours parents spend working and the loss of extended family. However, new communication technologies have dramatically accelerated the premature detachment of kids from their parents' love and attention. As Emory University professor Mark Bauerlein notes in *The Dumbest Generation:* "Peer pressure long preceded the microchip, of course, but e-mail, cell phones, and the rest have cranked it up to critical levels, fostering an all-peers-all-the-time network."[5]

It's now common practice for kids to use their phones or computers to engage with peers while ignoring and even dismissing their parents. Occasions that have long been the domain of the family—including dinners and family gatherings—are now continually interrupted or don't happen at all because kids are texting or chatting with friends on social networks.

Nonetheless, the myth of detachment damps down parents' concerns about their children's and teens' technology dependence. "We're a typical family of today," Ron, the father of three, told me, "We see each other around the house but the kids are usually caught up with their phones." For such parents, there's often no recognition that "family time" for kids—on a trip to the city or even around the home—has less to do with family and more to do with social networking and texting with friends, as well as the peer drama these technologies foster.

Throwing Kids into the Arms of Peers

Caught up in the myth of detachment, today's parents may intentionally buy their children interactive gadgets or encourage kids to use them with the belief that connecting to peers is what their child needs most. Twelve-year-old Robert's parents knew their son was depressed, so when he told them how much it helped to talk with friends, they were inclined to let him spend long hours on his phone, even if it meant less time with the family.

Yet many peers Robert reached out to were depressed themselves—the boy's own sadness was his passport to connecting with them. "Life sucks!," he would send in a group text, and a bevy of online friends would reach out to soothe him. Over time, such experiences helped Robert feel that his online friends cared for him more and understood him better than his parents. However, these friendships were focused largely around emotional problems. This quashed Robert's desire to feel better, as he knew deep down that if he told his friends he was no longer depressed, he might lose this clan. The preteen's online community—filled with kids suffering from their own mental health problems—was also a toxic environment, fostering unhealthy coping mechanisms like superficial cutting and blaming parents for woes.

Contrary to our current ethic, middle-school-age-and-up kids such as Robert should not spend most of their lives electronically engaged with everyone and everything but family. Sure, kids need time to themselves and to be able to talk with friends. Nevertheless, they most need parents to be their rock, to provide unwavering support, a role their friends can't be depended upon to play.

Robert was helped when his parents realized that their ritual of watching shows downstairs for most of the evening left him feeling less wanted, and also encouraged him to seek out online contacts. Robert's parents began to ask their son if there was a show he wanted to watch with them. They also shut off the TV for much of the evening. At first, everything seemed strangely silent, but then signs of family emerged—talk of school, peers, and other conversations which had long been absent. Such experiences helped Robert feel heard and important, which in turn lifted his mood.

Technology's Impact on Sibling Relations

While a main focus of this book is technology's impact on children's relationships with parents, it's important to consider how the overuse of technology is denying kids another family connection: their siblings. Growing up with my brother, who is my best friend, was immensely helpful to me. We were allies who shared the same experiences—good and bad. Like other close siblings, we developed our own language and jokes that helped us feel a part of our family.

Research confirms the power of positive sibling relationships to boost children's self-esteem and contribute other important qualities.[6]

Increasingly, I see the profound draw of technology denying kids a relationship with a brother or sister. More often it's younger siblings who tell me that an older sibling is consistently unavailable to them—headphones on, gaming, or door shut, texting. Older siblings sometimes need space from younger siblings, yet the pull of today's technologies can totally shift the focus of older siblings away from their younger brothers and sisters.

Most poignant are families struggling through a divorce, the death of a relative, or some other tragedy. During such times, the support of a brother or sister who is going through the same ordeal can really help kids. I used to encourage those with siblings to seek comfort in them, but as technology has increased the emotional distance between siblings I work with, I've become wary of making this suggestion in order to avoid false expectations.

HELPING KIDS MAINTAIN THEIR CONNECTION WITH FAMILY

Because it's so vital that kids keep their primary attachment with parents, consider the following steps to build and sustain a close relationship with your child or teen.

Don't Misinterpret Pleas for Peer Connection

When I suggest to parents that they are more important to their kids than peers, parents sometimes remark, "Not for my child. Mine constantly demands to be in touch with friends." There's no doubt that today's kids—especially girls—demonstrate a hunger for tech-accessed peer connections. As leadership authority Rachel Simmons says in her revised edition of *Odd Girl Out*, "It is not uncommon for a girl to say, 'I don't exist if I'm not on Facebook.' Many girls sleep with their cell phones on their chests, waiting for them to vibrate with news in the night. They treat their cell phones like extensions of their bodies and are inconsolable if they lose access."[7]

Nonetheless, kids' cravings for peer, rather than parent, connection should not be viewed as an indication of the strength of peer relationships, but instead of their weakness. While kids generally won't admit it, in their heart-of-hearts they know that without constant attention to maintaining these connections, even their best friendships can cool surprisingly quickly. Their friends may wander off to greener pastures to find someone who is more popular or serves their interests better.

Kids don't show the same urgency to connect with their parents because they understand the relative permanence of these relationships, that mom and dad are much less likely to walk away than their friends. The knowledge of the relative importance of parent vs. peer relationships should encourage you to reach out to your child or teen, and to feel good about setting technology limits that help your kids to bond more closely with you than with peers.

Show Your Child the Advantages of Parent Attachment

How can we help our children and teens understand that their relationship with us serves them best over time? Show them through words and actions every day.

Sure we should encourage our kids to have friends—and close ones at that. However, starting from about the time your children enter elementary school, let them know, in an age-appropriate way, what makes your relationship with them special. Help them understand that you will always love them, even when you disagree. Emphasize that you will always have their back, you will always advocate for their best interests. You may not always make the right decisions, but you will be accountable for your mistakes.

I also believe we need to help our kids recognize that no matter what is promised them, such attributes cannot be expected of friends.

While this may sound insensitive, the myth of detachment and its un-realistic expectations of what childhood friends can provide sets too many kids up for heartache and despair as they confront the realities of childhood and adolescence.

Because kids have a "show me" mentality, we need to back up our words with actions. Even after a bad day at work, we need to spend quality time with our kids. We need to attend their practices and games, and offer our time ("Hey, what do you want to do on Sunday?") We need to consider parenting less as something that happens on twice-yearly vacations, and understand that it's about the everyday responsibilities of helping our kids through their lives. If we have to work late sometimes, our kids will forgive us. Yet if we tell our kids repeatedly that we don't have time to be with them, and they find us watching the game on TV or chatting with friends online, our kids will turn against us and align with peers.

Something else we can offer our kids that their friends can't is the ability to uphold our relationship through difficult and stressful peri-ods. Disputes among childhood friends often lead to disconnection, sometimes short-lived, sometimes permanent. In contrast, we need to show our kids that our relationship with them is far more durable, outlasting any argument.[8] This means that even when we can't stand our child's or teen's behavior, we must do our best not to do or say hurtful things that damage the relationship. The strategies psycholo-gist Michael J. Bradley offers in *Yes, Your Teen is Crazy!* are helpful in maintaining the loving relationship our older kids need with us, even through hard times.[9]

Foster Mentor Relationships

For years, authors have raised red flags about the loss of adult men-tors in children's lives. Rightfully so, as raising healthy children is best accomplished with a supporting cast. Since the beginning of time, we have depended on grandparents, aunts, uncles, friends, and mem-bers of communities to lend a helping hand and provide an extended family. Today, kids who have less access to mentors are more likely to seek peers to connect with via technology.

What our children find online are primarily *horizontal connections*, meaning that they connect with peers of a similar developmental level. However, our kids most need *vertical relationships*, or connections in which they can look to someone older, wiser, with a fully mature brain and substantial life experience. We need to do a better job of cultivating kids' relationships with relatives, teachers, coaches, church leaders, and other adult caregivers who will provide kids the guidance they need to grow into healthy adults. This is especially important in preteen and teen years, as kids' hormonal and brain changes increase the likelihood of at least some conflict with parents.

One of the most important steps we can take to encourage kids' vertical connections is to limit their use of screens. In her book *The Shelter of Each Other,* psychologist Mary Pipher says that too many kids are denied intergenerational connections because, as soon as extended family arrive at the home, they slide away or are sent away to engage with a screen. Nevertheless, as Pipher reminds us, "Children learn from grown-ups. They hear their stories, their jokes, their trials and tribulations. They learn the rich and idiosyncratic use of language that occurs in families. They hear the cautionary tales and moral fables. They learn the wrong and the right ways to do things."[10]

An example of mentoring available to kids from many walks of life is an activity our older daughter has become involved in called Girls on the Run.[11] Offered in 200 locations across the US and Canada, the program provides 3rd- to 8th-grade girls a chance to run with and be coached by primarily female adult mentors (only females can be head coaches; males can be assistant coaches). The focus is less on athletic performance than building self-esteem.

Making it all work are the dedicated coaches, who by their example show girls the ways of strength and compassion. These coaches recognize the potential that each girl has, and with a well-timed comment or a pat on the back help them make the most of their abilities. The value of programs such as Girls on the Run needs to be recognized and made available to all our nation's children—both boys and girls.

Our nation also faces the particular challenge of providing kids with positive adult male role models. My practice is a microcosm of our nation's struggle to raise children with two involved parents, especially fathers. Increasingly, American children are raised in single-parents homes, mostly by moms.[12] After parents separate, many fathers become largely absent in children's lives.[13] Too many kids are starving for adult male mentors.

The parents of 12-year-old Cassie and 8-year-old Kenny separated soon after Kenny was born. For a few years, the parents split custody, but then the kids' father remarried and his attention shifted to his new family. Kenny and Cassie could no longer depend on their father to show up for visits, and he called less and less. The loss of their father would have been more destructive if their maternal grandfather hadn't stepped in to fill the void. Realizing his grandkids' loss, he moved closer to the family so he could pick the kids up from school and spend time with them either doing homework or at the park. This connection helped the kids emotionally and academically. It also curbed the children's craving for peer companionship online.

Far too many kids aren't as fortunate as Cassie and Kenny, and we therefore need a renewed emphasis on addressing the problem of fathers who are less involved in kids' lives. Joe Kelly, author of *Dads and Daughters*, says that dads who live at least some of their lives away from their kids can continue to have a positive influence on their upbringing, e.g., by ensuring kids aren't put in the middle of possible parental conflict and by doing their best to stay a part of their kids' lives, in person, through phone calls, etc.[14] Two national organizations which help kids connect with mentors are Big Brothers Big Sisters (www.bbbs.org) and Mentor: National Mentoring Partnership (www.mentoring.org).

9

Give Sensation-Seeking Teens
the Help They Need

The *Huffington Post* article "What Really Happens On a Teen Girl's iPhone" describes the life of 14-year-old Casey from Millburn, New Jersey. The 8th-grader's phone is the center of her existence as she texts, games, and closely scrutinizes the number of followers or friends she has on various social networks—about 580 on Instagram and 1,110 on Facebook. She's preoccupied with the number of "likes" her Facebook profile picture receives compared with her peers. As she says, "If you don't get 100 'likes,' you make other people share it so you get 100…. Or else you just get upset. Everyone wants to get the most 'likes.' It's like a popularity contest."[1]

There are costs to Casey's phone obsession; author Bianca Bosker says that "[Casey's] phone, be it Facebook, Instagram or iMessage, is constantly pulling her away from her homework, or her sleep, or her conversations with her family." Casey says she wishes she could put her phone down. But she can't. "I'll wake up in the morning and go on Facebook just… because," she says. "It's not like I want to or I don't. I just go on it. I'm, like, forced to. I don't know why. I need to. Facebook takes up my whole life."[2]

Casey's tech-obsessed life is much like that of Sean, a high school senior whose habits are described in Matt Richtel's *New York Times* article "Growing Up Digital, Wired for Distraction."[3] Sean concedes that the long hours he spends video gaming (four hours each weekday and twice as much on weekends) are hurting his school grades and physical health. Sean wishes his parents would step in to limit his gaming so he could focus on his studies because he struggles to quit on his own.

PROMOTING THE MYTH OF THE TECH-SAVVY TEEN

The real-life stories of these teens contrast with the manufactured vision of the tech-savvy teen typically portrayed by the media and tech industry. In his pro-industry book *Grown Up Digital,* strategy consultant Don Tapscott says present-day kids "can work effectively with music playing and news coming in from Facebook. They can keep up their social networks while they concentrate on work; they seem to need this to feel comfortable. I think they've learned to live in a world where they're bombarded with information, so that they can block out the TV or other distractions while they focus on the task at hand."[4]

This image of teens growing up happily and successfully surrounded by electronic amusements is frequently promoted in popular culture, especially by those invested in teens' open access to their highly profitable technologies. Alison Hillhouse, an MTV marketing researcher, contends that today's teens are in command of their tech use because they've been raised with it. "They have grown up with social media their entire life," she says, "They are more in control of it." Parents apparently don't need to worry about setting rules for their teens' use of the Internet, as Hillhouse says of adolescents, "They set rules and regulations for themselves."[5]

American culture apparently accepts this tech-savvy claim, and many parents evidently believe that teens can manage their own tech use capably. In Chapter 6, we saw that parents set remarkably few tech rules for kids of all ages. Unfortunately, lack of supervision becomes increasingly common as children move through their teens. According to the Kaiser Family Foundation, only 38% of 8- to 10-year-olds report they have at least some media rules that are enforced most of the time. As kids transition into their teen years, rules become even more scarce. Only 29% of 11- to 14-year-olds report they have at least some media rules that are enforced most of the time compared to a paltry 16% of 15- to 18-year-olds.[6]

What's the result of allowing teens to navigate the technology environment for themselves? Kids like Casey and Sean say *themselves* that they can't control their use of technology. They are much like teens in my practice who tell me that they truly want to spend less time gaming, social networking, or texting, and want to spend more time with their families and studying. However, their tech use has become compulsive—they literally can't keep their hands off their phones. Since these admissions are made in the confidence of a therapeutic relationship, I can't relay this information to their parents.

I encourage kids to talk with parents about these problems but they won't because it would risk their parents' intervention. Such is the tremendously difficult spot our teens are in: knowing at one level they need help yet refusing to admit it to their parents. To do so would reveal their limitations—something teens, who tend to believe they're invincible, are reluctant to do. So teens try themselves to rein in their own tech habits, and for reasons we discuss in this chapter, are coming out on the losing end.

Some would argue that Casey and Sean represent teens at the extreme end of the tech use spectrum, but I think their habits under-represent or at least accurately reflect what's typical for today's teens. American adolescents ages 15–18 somehow manage to spend nearly 5½ hours using entertainment-based screens plus a little more than 2½ hours talking and texting on their phones every single day.[7] That's a remarkable amount of time playing with technology for kids who need to be focusing on their transition to adulthood and all that it demands.

There are also those who view adolescents' immersion in digital play spaces as normal and benign, claiming that this is simply how today's teens spend their time, just as kids of prior generations hung out at the soda fountain or listened to jukebox music. However, earlier generations of teens didn't spend this much time engaged in similar self-amusements, nor did these "retro" activities have the harmful effects that research finds for obsessive screen and phone use.

The bottom line: The belief that teens are tech savvy in that they grasp how time spent with gadgets affects their future and can control their tech usage is another myth promoted by a self-serving industry. It's illogical to suggest that just by virtue of growing up with entertainment technologies teens can better manage their use of them. That's like suggesting that teens who have been raised on fast food can better manage their diet. Still, perhaps the best evidence that this belief is a myth is revealed as we peer deep inside the teen mind.

THE TEEN MIND: HEAVY ON THE ACCELERATOR, LIGHT ON THE BRAKE

Using the latest brain imaging techniques, scientists have found that as kids enter adolescence, there's a dramatic remodeling of the dopaminergic system,[8] the brain areas responsible for reward. Chemical reward sensitivity peaks in adolescence, so that for teens, rewards feel *mega*-rewarding. Think back a few years, and you may remember yourself how listening to a certain song or some other experience during adolescence filled you with overwhelmingly positive emotions you just can't replicate as an adult. These reward-amplifying brain changes turn teens into *sensation-seeking machines*.

At the same time, teens' ability to contain impulsive behavior is compromised, as their prefrontal cortex (the brain's judgment center) is not fully developed. During adolescence, this center is busy making connections with and gradually gaining the ability to regulate the lower brain structures. It's these lower structures that generate highly emotional and impulsive responses. So even as teen brains are programmed for peak pleasure from (often impulsive) reward seeking, behavior control is still very much a "work in progress" that lags behind.

These two brain systems, one that seeks reward and the other that controls behavior, interact to produce characteristic teen behavior.

Laurence Steinberg, psychology professor at Temple University and author of *Age of Opportunity*,[9] describes it this way, "One way to think about it is a kind of competition or balance between two different brain systems: A system that impels us to seek out rewards and go for novelty and excitement, sensation seeking, and then a brain system that really puts the brakes on impulses."[10]

What's the effect of the adolescent brain changes that put our teens in thrill-seeking mode without a fully mature judgment center? They compromise impulse control, insight, and the ability to make good decisions. As Steinberg says, "It's like starting the engine before a good braking system is in place."[11] I was not immune as a teen: jumping off cliffs into waters of unknown depth, driving too fast, and a number of other imprudent or reckless behaviors that seemed like a perfectly good idea at the time.

How do these brain changes run their course, and when do teen decision-making skills become on par with those of adults? Evidence suggests that sensation-seeking is typically at its peak between the ages of 15 and 17, so it makes sense that experimentation with alcohol and marijuana typically peaks around the age of 17, as does the commission of crime and car accidents.[12] And the prefrontal cortex—which could moderate impulses—is one of the last brain areas to mature, with development continuing through adolescence into the mid-20s. The result is that as young people move beyond age 17 and head into their 20s, they generally are able to make better decisions and are less likely to jump into poor choices.

A BAD FIT: TEEN BRAINS AND THE TECH-SAVVY TEEN MYTH

With risk comes opportunity. Throughout human history, the remodeling of the teen brain into a thrill-seeking machine has served a purpose, encouraging teens to do the seemingly impossible: to move beyond the safe confines of family to seek out new habitats, food sources, and a mate.[13] In more recent times, these brain changes have emboldened teens to leave home to attend college or seek jobs.

Unfortunately, these teen brain changes evolved so young people could succeed in a world that looks less and less like the one we live in now. For most of human existence, the rewards teens sought required great effort and were associated with something productive, such as building a new shelter or learning skills that promoted survival in dangerous circumstances. Yet in the modern world, unproductive activities provide powerful rewards. Drugs and alcohol divert too many teens. And with the advent of the digital-age, the thrill-seeking teen brain can find gratification in dopamine-rich, but easily obtained, rewards of entertainment technologies rather than seeking out the challenging rewards found in school and other real-life experiences.

That's why our teens have always needed—and until fairly recently typically received—lots of support from those who love and care for them to help them make good life choices. Nonetheless, the tech-savvy teen myth has convinced this generation of parents that adolescents know what they're doing with the technologies that take up so much of their lives. The consequences are apparent in the tremendous overuse of entertainment technologies by the typical American teen. They are also evident in my practice.

I see many 17- and 18-year-old kids whose anxiety and depression have a similar genesis: Their prefrontal cortices have developed enough for them to recognize that their earlier years spent playing with e-gadgets hasn't helped them, and instead they should have been studying and preparing for their future. By this time, a lot of damage has been done not only to parent-child relationships from constant arguments over tech overuse but also to teens' chances for college admission, as they've accumulated poor grades and little constructive out-of-school experience.

THE EROSION OF ADOLESCENT ACCOUNTABILITY

Our ancestors lived under challenging circumstances. Food and other resources were hard to come by, and a family's survival sometimes hung in the balance. Most earlier generations needed adolescents—with their strong bodies and minds—to play an important role. Consider the tasks entrusted to teenagers in 19th-century American frontier families: tending animals and crops, chopping wood, cooking, and hunting from dawn until dusk. Teens who didn't fulfill their role put their families at risk for economic disaster and even death.

Prior cultures relied on their adolescents out of necessity. However, such reliance also gave teens purpose, indelibly connecting them to family and community, and helped them stay focused and lead productive, fulfilling lives. While earlier societies didn't have access to brain imaging studies, they understood this. They knew through experience that teens, with their sensation-seeking minds, are helped when they're held accountable to their families, communities, and to themselves.

One of the most tragic consequences of the tech-savvy teen myth is that it erodes the accountability that adolescents need. Present-day US culture normalizes teens donning headphones, shutting their bedroom doors, developing a tunnel focus on screens, and losing themselves to self-amusement. Even when tech playtime clearly supplants duties at home or a focus on schoolwork (the two main jobs of today's teens), this myth assumes the destructive imbalance is a normal part of growing up.

Teens' insistence that continuous access to screens is what makes them happy also contributes to parents' difficulty recognizing the problems associated with diminished adolescent accountability. As we saw in Chapter 1, though, the more time our kids spend with screens, the less happy and fulfilled they are. That's because allowing teens to spend so much time in wired-up self-pleasure sends a dangerous message: Even if kids play with e-gadgets for most of the day, their family will do just fine; if they don't put much effort into school, it doesn't really matter. According to *Family Matters,* by Brown University sociology professor Gregory Elliott, this lack of "mattering," especially to one's family, causes significant emotional and behavioral problems for today's adolescents.[14]

THE PERILS OF SELF-FOCUS

Tech-heavy lives not only diminish teens' accountability, but also foster their self-absorption. San Diego State psychology professor Jean Twenge, who together with W. Keith Campbell authored *The Narcissism Epidemic,*[15] says in a recent article that the younger generation, compared to those prior, is "more Generation Me than Generation We." She goes on to say the latest research "demonstrates a rise in self-focus among American young people, including narcissism, high expectations, self-esteem, thinking one is above average, and focusing on personal (vs. global) fears."[16]

What is causing this shift towards self-focus in the young? Signs suggest those who spend greater amounts of time social networking tend to be more narcissistic than those who spend less.[17] Similarly, those who are addicted to online gaming are more likely to have narcissistic traits than those who aren't addicted.[18]

Does immersion in digital entertainment actually lead teens to become more self-focused? I see that evidence in my work. Today's interactive technologies have a unique ability to demand attention, leaving teens with less capacity to attend to their families. Wired-up kids are less likely to notice that mom had a rough day at work and could use help with the chores, or that dad is worried about a sick relative.

Moreover, the way our kids spend their time online may also affect what, or who, they view as important. Today's preteens and teens can spend endless hours focused on self-display: fussing over social networking profiles, making videos of themselves, or creating a new gaming avatar. Such focus on self-promotion can encourage teens' self-absorption at the expense of empathy for the needs of their families and others.

A Fantasy Gap

There are other costs. This generation's increasing narcissistic focus may also lead them to feel more entitled—that they deserve things without working for them. A recent study by Professor Twenge and Tim Kasser, Professor of Psychology at Knox College, found a "fantasy gap," or a divergence between teens' desire for material goods and their willingness to work to obtain them. In 1976–1978, while 48% of recent high school graduates reported that it was important to have a lot of money, by 2005–2007 this had jumped to 62%. Yet our teens' willingness to work to obtain such a lifestyle is going in the opposite direction. Of high school graduates from 1976–1978, only 25% admitted they didn't want to work hard, but by 2005–2007 a full 39% admitted this was the case.[19]

The Frontier Exercise

While heavy tech use increases the self-absorption and decreases the work ethic of many teens I see in counseling, these kids often struggle to recognize this even when it's brought to their attention. To help increase teens' insight, I have found something I call the *frontier exercise* helpful. In the case of game-obsessed 15-year-old David, the exercise not only helped him and his family see how self-focused he had become, it also helped him see the need to change.

David was brought to counseling by his parents, Janet and Ben, because he had abandoned chores, studying, and just about everything else except gaming. In one of our first meetings, David's parents turned to their son to express their frustrations. David responded angrily, "They're my games, it's my life, and I can do what I want!" Janet and Ben then turned to me to ask what could help their son become more aware of the needs of his family.

I suggested that we do the frontier exercise. The first step was to ask David and his parents to imagine that they were a frontier family 150 years ago, doing their best to survive in an inhospitable landscape. I asked each family member to describe their role. Janet went first, saying that she likely would be working in the fields from sunrise until sunset and cooking for the family. Ben went next, and said he would be plowing or hunting for most of the day. Then we all turned to David and asked him to envision his role on the harsh frontier. "I don't know," he replied, "I'd probably be outside with friends doing stupid things to entertain ourselves."

Ben and Janet stared at David with their mouths open. After a few moments, they collected themselves and began to ask how their capable son could have come to believe this should be his role. It was such discussions that helped Janet and Ben realize how the endless hours their son spent gaming diminished his understanding of his responsibilities to his family and himself. The discussions also helped them become determined to make changes.

In the case of David's and many other families, parents assume that as kids reach their teen years, increasing age will automatically provide them the insight they need to grow up, to become more responsible to family and for their schoolwork. Yet these attributes don't magically materialize. They must be learned, not only from what parents say, but through kids' position within a family of hardworking adults. It's such experiences that help teens realize that, while their parents go to work, their main jobs are to put effort into school and help out around the house. There's no doubt that Janet and Ben worked hard for the money to support their son. However, David had been too busy gaming to notice. His primary interest in his parents' work was that it supported his ability to acquire the next gaming title.

In ensuing meetings with David's family, we talked about the skilled sons of the frontier, of how their determination helped families survive. The concept of a frontier family resonated with David. He began to realize that his life should be more than gaming, and he considered what role he should take in his modern family. He came to understand that while most of today's teen boys don't chop wood or hunt, he could try hard each day at school and put in a good effort on homework.

Janet and Ben also changed things up at home, and no longer allowed David to disappear for long hours gaming. The family resolved to do more together, from working in the garden to errands and playing. This brought David outside of himself and closer to his parents. It also helped him realize how much he was capable of and how he could contribute to his family. Perhaps most of all, these experiences helped David feel that he mattered, that his actions had a real impact on the world.

CREATING A TEEN CULTURE OF ACCOUNTABILITY

We need to help our teens become part of something bigger and more important than high scores and "like" counts. We can help them understand their accountability to their families and themselves, and that they're responsible for putting a strong effort into their schoolwork. We can do this by not underselling teens' potential, and instead creating a culture of accountability at home. The actions described in the rest of this chapter suggest how.

Take the Lead in Building Your Relationship

A culture of accountability starts at home with actions that we, as parents, take to build a strong relationship with our teens and model healthy technology use. In my meetings with families, parents and teens frequently play out the modern equivalent of a wild west standoff, as both sides complain about the others' overuse of technology:

"You were the one with 4,500 texts last month." "Well, you check your phone every five minutes!" The solution often comes down to who should act first to gain control of his or her technology. The answer is simple. We, the adults, need to act first *because* we're the adults.

Sometimes teens feel rejected by a tech-obsessed parent and turn to their gadgets out of loneliness. If you feel that your overuse of technology might have hurt your relationship with your child, I suggest you apologize to him or her. Teens have a strong sense of fairness, and parents expressing their regret—if deserved and genuine—is often necessary to help teens admit their own shortcomings and commit to change.

The Power of the In-Person Connection

Pundits sometimes suggest that social networks are a great way for parents to maintain their connection with teens in a hectic world. In truth, we need to emphasize real-world rather than cyberworld connections. Why? Because in-person connections build and cement relationships better than wired communications.[20] Much of what's conveyed between parent and teen is nonverbal—through facial expressions, eye contact, hugs, and tone of voice. The human mind is specially attuned to these unspoken cues. They trigger dopamine, oxytocin, and other "feel-good" brain chemicals that foster and maintain attachment, including the one between parents and teens.

While the word *attachment* is often associated with young children, it remains vital at all ages. For teens, a strong bond with parents supports emotional health and academic success. Attachment also may influence how productively teens use their time. A study published in the *Archives of Pediatrics & Adolescent Medicine* found that teens who were closer to their parents spent less time playing on the computer or watching TV, and more time reading and doing homework.[21]

Do all you can to engage with your teen in the real world. Go to lunch or dinner as a family; take a walk, a class, or participate in sports together. Let your teen decide where the family will go on a weekend trip, or go to an event your teen chooses. Work on home-work or a school project together. Remember that all of these activi-ties must be done without technology interruptions. Put your phone aside and if your teen has a phone, have him or her do the same.

Talking's Not Enough

Well-meaning parenting authorities sometimes recommend that protecting teens from problems related to technology can be accom-plished solely by talking with them about the risks of overuse. These authorities suggest that it's unrealistic for parents to limit teens' ac-cess to what have become ubiquitous and continually available tech-nologies. Yet I have worked with many, many families in which parents talk with their teens about such risks until they are blue in the face, to no avail.

The latest research on the adolescent brain tells us why talking with teens is no substitute for setting limits. Temple University psy-chology professor Laurence Steinberg observes that while teens are as capable as adults in naming the risks of an activity, they often don't use this information.[22] That's because their still-developing prefron-tal cortices don't provide the judgment and self-control necessary to stop them from taking risks they are well aware of. As a teen myself, on a given day I could rattle off many good reasons why I shouldn't jump off cliffs into what could be shallow water. Yet the next day I would happily yell "Geronimo!" as I launched myself off a precipice.

We need to provide our teens with the limits and guidance they need to be successful. Steinberg suggests, "Rather than attempting to change how adolescents view risky activities a more profitable strat-egy might focus on limiting opportunities for immature judgment to have harmful consequences."[23]

In determining how to protect teens from unhealthy technology use, we can learn from recent efforts to reduce teen driving risks. Mile for mile, 16- and 17-year-old drivers have crash rates that are almost nine times higher than the rates of middle-age drivers.[24] Traditional teen safe-driving programs have focused on educating teens about the dangers of irresponsible and reckless driving, but research shows that even if teens learn about such risks they often ignore them. The result is that unsafe teen driving practices don't change.[25] As a consequence, all 50 states now have shifted to graduated driver licensing.[26] These programs put actual restrictions on teen drivers, such as not allowing them to carry young passengers or to drive at night without an adult. These newer programs have reduced accidents and saved lives.[27]

Such research supports the recommendation that parents shift away from simply talking with teens about the risks of overusing technology. Our adolescents need real limits, starting with the approaches discussed in the next section.

Be Proactive, Not Reactive

I often hear, "I took away her (his) phone... again," in my practice, as parents give teens consequences for poor school performance. Without access to their phones, these teens' academic standing typically improves, upon which parents give back the phones, resulting in more overuse, more poor grades, and a continuing cycle of school focus inevitably followed by lack of focus and so on.

This is an example of *reactive parenting*. Parents react to a teen behavior—phone overuse leading to poor grades—that could have been prevented. *Proactive parenting* gives kids the structure they need on the front-end, not after problems have already occurred.

The difference between reactive and proactive parenting is evident in the case of Chloe's family. Fourteen-year-old Chloe wanted to be a veterinarian. She told her parents that she was determined to get the grades she needed to gain admission to a highly-selective college that would help propel her into the profession. But left alone in her room, Chloe got lost for hours jumping between the web and incessant texts. As a result, she didn't complete assignments or put minimal effort into them. Her grades suffered.

Seeing a report card, Chloe's parents would respond by taking away her gadgets, and her grades would improve. Chloe's mother and father would then give their daughter her tech privileges back, with her pledge that things would be better. They would be... for a time. Soon Chloe would fall back into her old pattern, and her school performance see-sawed from semester to semester.

Chloe's parents didn't realize that their daughter, like teens in general, simply couldn't limit her own phone and tech use. She needed her parents to be proactive by setting and enforcing phone rules that applied all the time, not just after a semester of poor grades. In our meetings, Chloe's mother and father resolved to think in the long term. They also realized that "talking the talk" with their daughter wasn't enough—instead that they needed to "walk the walk." They provided Chloe a prescribed study period each day, and during this time she had to put her phone away. Their approach helped Chloe move towards the academic goals she had set for herself.

Other proactive parenting strategies include keeping screen technologies out of kids' bedrooms and turning computers off unless needed for a particular assignment.

A Reality Check for Tech-Obsessed Teens

As we saw earlier in the chapter, the teen brain's hunger for rewards easily sidetracks it to dopamine-rich entertainment technologies. Helping teens gain insight about how gadgets can divert them from a productive, fulfilling life is sometimes remarkably difficult, in large part because of the denial that often accompanies obsessive tech use. Despite flagging grades, teens will insist that nothing is wrong and that they'll easily make it to a top college and enjoy a lucrative career. Most really believe it.

"My grades are great," 16-year-old Caden told me, "I only got two Cs last semester." I then asked the game-heavy, homework-light teen, "Have you checked the grades of admitted freshman at UCLA?"

(UCLA was the school Caden told me he planned to attend). "I'll be fine," he said, waving off my suggestion.

When teens strongly deny their problem technology use, seeking professional help from a counselor familiar with such issues may be necessary. (I describe how to select a counselor in Chapter 4.) Before taking this step, however, I suggest a *reality check exercise* with your teen—a process that's likely to involve a number of talks over the course of weeks or months. This should only be done with kids who are underperforming academically because of a tech obsession and lack of effort, not with kids who are trying hard in school.

A reality check involves helping teens answer three questions:

- What do you want to do after high school?
- Are you on the path to meet your goal?
- If you are not on the path to meet your goal, how can we fix this?

Question 1. What do you want to do after high school?

While many teenagers are unsure what they want to do after high school, this is even more challenging for teens immersed in the cocoon of digital entertainment. It's important to help them find a passion that will motivate them to work hard and that might be translated into a career some day. This is much easier if you have a close relationship with your teen, so make sure you're spending lots of positive time together. During such moments you can ask questions that encourage self-exploration, such as:

- "Who is someone in your own life that you really admire, and why?"
- "What is something you have done that makes you really proud?"
- "If you have friends looking to find their own interests, what advice would you give them?"

Question 2: Are you on the path to meet your goal?

As kids develop their goals, encourage them to decide if they are on the path to meet them. This can start with considering your teen's goal and knowing what's required to reach it. You could say to your teen, "Okay, so you have an idea about the career you want. Does that mean going to college or vocational school? If so, have you looked at the requirements for getting into college (or vocational school)?"

Encourage a teen who wants to go to college to find out the admission demands of colleges they are interested in and that are within your family budget. You (and your teen) can find the average high school GPA and other admission criteria for freshman at various colleges on the websites of the College Board (a non-profit organization at www.collegeboard.org) or the prospective colleges.

Heavy video gamers may tell their parents that they don't need college, and instead say they plan to parlay their gaming skills into a career. However, the great majority of these kids are not developing the high-level skills required to gain employment. Although the media give splashy coverage to exceedingly rare tech geniuses who make millions before high school graduation, we'll see in Chapter 10 that high-tech companies are most likely to hire people with college and advanced degrees. But heavy gaming during teenage years makes it harder to attain this level of education.

You can help your teen research the credentials that high-tech and other companies look for in hires. Often the "employment opportunities" tab for such corporations, or doing an Internet search using the company's name and "employment opportunities" as key words, gives specifications for open positions. The US Bureau of Labor Statistics *Occupational Outlook Handbook* (http://www.bls.gov/ooh/) is another great resource for this purpose, and provides a tool for helping your teen understand how to do online job research. It's a way you and your teen can spend time together focused on his or her interests and concerns, and a way to use your life experience to help interpret information. If you don't feel confident about your skills in this arena, many public librarians can help, as can guidance counselors.

For kids whose career goal doesn't demand a college education, there are still good reasons to work hard in high school. Because of our struggling economy, military recruiters may give preference to kids who performed well in high school, and a lot of teenagers who are sure they don't want to go to college change their minds after trying the job market.

In any case, help kids decide if their current high school efforts match the goals they have for themselves.

3. If you are not on the path to meet your goal, how can we fix this?

For tech-obsessed teens, there's often a considerable gap between their goals and efforts to reach these goals. This is not the time for "I told you so." It's vital to stay positive and offer to work with your teen to bring their goals and actions in sync. Sit down together to decide on concrete steps to improve study habits: starting homework right after school; studying without phone and computer; attending an after-school homework club; or studying routinely at the library after school or for a few hours on weekends.

Appealing to Outside Help

Sadly, in families with a teen who overuses technology, a great deal of animosity often has built up due to constant arguments over a lack of school effort. This can lead teens to be highly resistant to working with parents on a reality-check exercise. If this is the case for your family, you may benefit from the assistance of an impartial party. I find that tech-obsessed teens are often willing to listen to the warm yet eye-opening advice of high school or college admissions counselors. In such a meeting, counselors can outline exactly what it takes for kids to reach their own goals.

While it's typical for families to seek out college counseling when teens are in the last two years of high school, for tech-obsessed kids I suggest meeting much sooner, preferably prior to the start of their high school freshman year. While this may seem early, the alternative is that kids may perform so poorly during their first years of high school that they can't make up for it later.

HELPING TEENS CHANNEL THEIR AMBITIONS

There's no doubt that teens can do some imaginative and interesting things with today's technologies—make music, create artful webpages, tweak video games, etc. Some kids will be able to develop these skills into a career in music, graphic design, or video game development, but I find too many teens forgo school-based learning without evidence that their preferred activities will eventually provide productive employment. These kids often later find that they need a college education for what they want to do—something that may not happen because of the overuse of these same technologies.

Some pundits make the argument that kids should be allowed to pursue their tech interests—even at the expense of school—based on the fact that Bill Gates, Steve Jobs, and Mark Zuckerberg all dropped out of college to pursue their own goals. What's often left out is that all three men did well enough in high school to gain admittance to top-quality universities. Moreover, dropping out of college to pursue a career is one thing. Forgoing study in middle or high school is another.

The upshot is that we should do our best to help our teens channel their ambitions into pursuits that improve rather than hurt their chances of long-term happiness and success. The following additional steps can help make this a reality.

Encourage Kids Not to Quit Their Day Job (School)

"School is boring…. There's nothing for me there," adolescents may complain. Before we give in to the notion that our teen will never like school, it's vital to make sure that their immersion in a digital playground isn't the reason behind this feeling. It may be that the more subtle joys found in school simply can't stack up to the drug-like rewards from entertainment technologies.

To give teens an opportunity to appreciate the payoffs at school, it's vital that we limit their use of entertainment technologies and do all we can to support healthy school involvement, e.g., by setting up a structured learning environment at home. Parents I work with find such steps increase their kids' learning effort and school enjoyment, as it's hard to appreciate academic experiences when you constantly show up to class unprepared and are dinged for incomplete or missing homework.

We also need to show why school is worth it, helping answer the question "What's in it for me?" If college is one of your goals for your child, or one he or she has identified, I suggest that families visit colleges, not starting when kids are in their junior year of high school, but from the time kids are young. Rather than using the opportunity to make heavy-handed comments about the importance of education, visit local schools or stop by a university when on vacation to enjoy a nice walk around the campus or eat at a local café. Sometimes it's possible to eat in a school's dining venue.

College campuses tend to be beautiful settings with tree-lined paths and young adults spending positive time together. Such experiences can prompt kids of all ages to think, "Oh, I'd like to be here," which boosts their motivation for trying hard at school. Follow up with a little research on admission requirements and costs if your child has shown interest.

Finding Inspiration in the Real World

How teens spend their time outside of school powerfully affects their chances of life success. Specifically, teens involved in extracurricular activities tend to do better academically,[28] and they demonstrate to prospective colleges or employers that they have gained real-life experience. So parents can play a constructive role in encouraging kids to explore the world through involvement in sports, music programs, civic organizations, and vocational experiences.

"But I can't interest my child in anything other than video games (or social networks)," parents tell me. I know. If we allow teens open access to their devices, that's how they'll spend their lives, so carefully consider your priorities as a family and give teens the help they need to find satisfying alternatives to technology.

A number of tech-obsessed teens I work with have benefitted from volunteering in the community. Philanthropic experiences can help kids realize that many are less fortunate than them, and that there are more important things than playing with gadgets. Community experiences also show kids their actions can make a difference, even if it's a small one. So aid your teen in a search for such opportunities, perhaps by checking with parents in your area or encouraging your child to ask a school counselor or other trusted adult about available volunteer experiences. Teens also may benefit from your assistance in creating a resume or filling out a job/volunteer application.

10

Achieve the Elusive: Kids' Productive Use of Technology

O ur technology goals for children and teens seem misplaced. Over and over we hear about the need to teach kids *how to use technology*, yet a quick glance reveals that this goal has already, and easily, been accomplished. With no training at all, American kids deftly navigate computers and the Internet, and they know all the ins and outs of the latest e-gadgets.

Unfortunately, this knowledge generally has not served them well, as they overuse entertainment technologies at the expense of connections to family and success in school. Our goal should therefore shift to something that actually helps kids, but is undoubtedly more difficult to achieve: teaching them *how to use technology productively*. In this chapter, we look at how to make this a reality.

FOCUS ON BUILDING A HEALTHY BRAIN, NOT A LITTLE TECH EXPERT

Children find it remarkably difficult to use technology productively, as a million and one diversions are always, always, a tempting click away. Kids need *self-control skills* in order to stick with beneficial applications. How do we promote children's self-control? As we saw in Chapter 2,

these skills are built by limiting kids' exposure to video games and entertainment TV, and immersing them in slower-paced activities such as
dramatic play and reading. In other words, *we have to engage our kids in
real-world activities so they can build the brains they need to use technology productively.* This is particularly important for children from birth through
the end of elementary-school, when young brains are especially plastic.

Controlling access to digital devices means rejecting the advice
of industry-linked pundits who claim that setting limits will somehow cheat our children of the ability to use technology well. That's a
self-serving myth perpetuated by tech industry spokesmen with a financial interest in tethering your kids to the devices they sell. As noted by early-childhood experts Susan Linn, Joan Almon, and Diane
Levin in *Facing the Screen Dilemma: Young Children, Technology and Early
Education,* "There is *no* [emphasis mine] evidence that introducing
screen technologies in early childhood means children will be more
adept when they're older."[1]

Widely used technologies are purposefully designed to be acces-
sible and simple to understand—that's how companies profit from
them. "It's supereasy. It's like learning to use toothpaste," says Alan
Eagle, who works in executive communications at Google. "At Google
and all these places, we make technology as brain-dead easy to use
as possible. There's no reason why kids can't figure it out when they
get older."[2]

FIRST USES OF TECHNOLOGY SHOULD BE LEARNING-BASED

I believe we should reject the popular practice of having our children's first forays into technology center around entertainment, especially video gaming. The assumption is that digital amusements
will acclimate kids to technology so they can transition to using their
gadgets more constructively. The problem is that our nation's kids

aren't switching, but getting stuck on pleasure-based applications. Remember in Chapter 4 we saw that the earlier kids are introduced to video gaming the more likely they will game obsessively as they grow older.

I see it with the kids I counsel. Once they've grown used to the drug-like rewards they find in many digital self-amusements, they often have difficulty changing over to less stimulating learning activities. Our children and teens are being conditioned to view technology primarily as a toy, and to value immediate gratification over longer-term gains.

I believe kids' first uses of technology should have learning value backed up by objective research, e.g., a high school curriculum proven to effectively teach students programming skills. Allowing schools, whose job it is to teach children, to direct when and how kids begin to use technology may help achieve this goal. At home, consider this for your kids' first foray into technology: using the Internet to search about something they experienced during a family outing or in nature. And, as with early reading, make that exposure something you do together.

Some parents will argue that it's difficult to get young children to use technology productively, as young kids often struggle to do much beyond play games or watch videos when left alone with computers, tablets, and phones. I agree. Rather than take this as a sign we should leave young kids alone to play with gadgets, I think it proves the point that we introduce technology to children long before their developmental stage allows it to be helpful to them.

What's the right age for kids to begin using technology? Brain researcher Jane Healy, author of *Your Child's Growing Mind*, suggests that children be at least seven years old before they begin to use a computer.[3] In Silicon Valley, many high-tech executives enroll their kids in a Waldorf school whose philosophy is that children don't benefit from technology until middle school.[4] Instead, their curriculum emphasizes real-world experiences and interactions with teachers and students, on the principle that this best promotes children's creative thinking, problem solving, and other important skills.

So far, research has just not identified the best age for introducing kids to technology. Instead, the research clearly shows us good reasons to wait. I see no problem with postponing kids' introduction to computers until late-elementary or middle school. When parents I work with take this route, I see kids who love school and learning, are connected to their parents, are goal-oriented and have the self-control needed to stay focused when they use technology. As a result, they seem more often to view technology primarily as a tool to advance their success.

WHY WE SHOULD FOCUS ON THE HUMAN CONNECTION

What can help kids to use technology productively? Evidently, it's loving relationships with us. A study by Israeli technology researcher Gustavo Mesch found that teens who had a strong relationship with their parents were more likely than peers less close to their parents to use the Internet for learning purposes.[5]

In my practice, a close bond with family tends to be a common denominator for families in which kids put technology to good use. Twelve-year-old Noah was brought to counseling by his single father out of concern that his mother wasn't involved in Noah's life. Nonetheless, Noah was doing well in school and his tech use was productive for the most part, as the boy had an early interest in computer science. He was also avoiding the pitfalls of many of his game-obsessed 7th-grade peers. So I asked Noah how he was able to spend most of his computer time focused on learning.

Noah thought about it for a moment and responded, "I really don't know." Yet I was quite sure that the time Noah's father devoted to him was a factor. Each session, Noah spent much of our time together talking about how his father, in spite of being busy, did a lot for him and his younger brother—he took them camping and devoted his spare time to them, playing catch in the yard and helping them with their schoolwork. Such efforts seemed to encourage the boy's desire to stay on track with schoolwork and in using the computer.

ANOTHER REASON TO LIMIT KIDS' ENTERTAINMENT TECH USE

In Chapter 4, we saw how mind experts use behavioral manipulation tools in video game and social network development to pull users away from other interests and focus them on their digital products. I believe that the industry's increasing reliance on these techniques helps explain why, much to the chagrin of parents and teachers, our children use technology almost exclusively for entertainment.

Sucked in by the gravitational pull of virtual rewards designed for maximal stimulation, kids understandably struggle to gain the escape velocity needed to explore the less flashy universe of learning-based technology applications. This typically occurs without conscious awareness. Kids simply look up after spending most of the evening playing on their phone or computer and wonder where the time went.

Disengagement from entertainment technologies gives children the psychic space to explore themselves and develop their own goals. Away from an "always-on" existence, kids can daydream about what it would be like to become an architect or scientist. This space helps them find their own voice. In turn, their ambitions help propel kids to use technology to get to where they want to be.

When I asked 16-year-old Carlos what helped him to stay focused when using technology, he replied, "I can't become an engineer if I'm goofing around on my computer all day." So help kids find a sense of purpose by limiting their opportunity to get caught up in entertainment technologies. Follow the advice in this book and encourage your kids to consider technology primarily as a means to a productive end.

KIDS SHOULD LEARN FUNDAMENTALS FOR A HIGH-TECH CAREER

A number of parents I work with allow their children to immerse themselves in various devices at the expense of their focus on school, because "Technology is their future," as a father told me. However, even if we believe kids *are* using their devices productively, there are risks to becoming overly specialized from a young age. That's because it's always difficult to judge future employment trends. As Leonard Fuld notes in *Fortune*, "In the 1920s, pundits estimated that by 1940 the rapidly growing telephone network would require 42 million women—or every adult female in the country—to work as switchboard operators (women dominated this profession). This forecast never came to pass because switching systems became increasingly automated."[6]

In a few decades, how much computer programming will be automated, carried out by increasingly sophisticated machines that are capable of programming themselves with a few initial commands? Moreover, how much will the increasing trend of outsourcing high-tech jobs affect US kids' chances of joining the high-tech profession? The US Bureau of Labor Statistics recently described how the demand for American computer programmers is being dulled: "Computer programming can be done from anywhere in the world, so companies sometimes hire programmers in countries where wages are lower. This ongoing trend is projected to limit growth for computer programmers in the United States."[7]

A recent Economics Policy Institute report by researchers from Rutgers, Georgetown, and American Universities also showed that outsourcing is diminishing the demand for American-trained high-tech graduates. The researchers found that about a third of American computer science graduates took jobs outside of the Information Technology (IT) sector. The researchers discovered that about half of those working outside of IT found jobs where the pay or working conditions were better, while about a third left the field because they couldn't find jobs in IT. "The supply of graduates is substantially larger than the demand for them in industry,"[8] the researchers conclude—a cautionary note for those who recommend tech immersion for kids at the expense of learning in other areas.

What will the demand be for various high-tech jobs when our kids reach employment age? It's hard to say, which is true for most vocations. For this reason, schools and colleges have long looked to provide kids with a strong base in educational fundamentals such as math, reading, writing, and problem-solving. These skills are always in demand from employers. They give kids the brain power and flexibility they'll need to find jobs in a rapidly shifting economy.

As a society caught up in digital fever, too often we seem willing to allow children to downplay learning school-taught fundamentals in favor of letting them spend a majority of their time with gadgets. Ironically, there is evidence this will actually *reduce* their chances of success in the high-tech workforce. It's helpful to consider the educational requirements of working in the high-tech field. As described by the US Bureau of Labor Statistics, "Job prospects will be best for programmers who have a *bachelor's degree or higher* [emphasis mine] and knowledge of a variety of programming languages."[9]

Clearly, employers are looking to hire computer scientists with college or graduate degrees, but American kids' time-swallowing tech habits can prevent them from mastering the academic fundamentals needed for college admission. US children score far below their global peers in reading, math, and science, so we must refocus them on basic learning to increase their long-term success in high-tech and other fields.

GIVE KIDS THE STRUCTURE THEY NEED

How can we make sure our kids understand that technology is a tool and not a toy? We have to give them lots of help. Children are born into this world seeking guidance—that's how they learn the skills to survive. If we don't provide help when it comes to tech, our kids are lost, but only for a moment, because gaming, social networking, and communications industries will give them direction as to how they should spend their lives.

What kind of guidance can you provide your child or teen to encourage the constructive use of technology? First, think carefully about what devices you provide your children at what age, considering the realities of typical use. The more devices kids get, and the earlier the age they get them, the more difficulty you will have fostering appropriate use. Also, use the recommendations throughout this book to monitor kids' screen use, such as keeping computers in a common area, and having your kids study along with you as you do your own work.

Parents have never been able to raise healthy children alone, and this applies to helping kids use technology constructively. Schools can assist kids by offering classes that teach uses of technology like computer programming and web-based research. Considering US students' academic struggles, computer instruction should not be at the expense of reading, math, science, and other core subjects. Teens I work with benefit when schools sponsor science fairs or other projects that require kids to use technology for purposes other than entertainment. When schools offer such learning opportunities, the curriculum demands and guidance of instructors help teens avoid straying into time-wasting technologies.

Please don't underestimate the amount of structure kids need to ensure their work on computers remains productive. A teacher commenting in the *New York Times* described what happened in her efforts to expose kids to Scratch, an application that teaches kids rudimentary programming skills as they design video games: "Left on their own to learn at the Scratch website, my students almost all spent their time simply playing the games other people created."[10]

One extracurricular program that provides kids the framework they need is Odyssey of the Mind. It has kids work together to solve science-based goals, such as building a robotic vehicle, that may require the use of computers. The combination of the Odyssey goals and its coaches helps kids stay focused. To see if Odyssey is offered in your area, go to their website (www.odysseyofthemind.com) or do an Internet search using the key words: "Odyssey of the Mind" and your city and state or school.

Parents I work with have found other extracurricular or community activities that encourage their kids' constructive use of technology. These include science camps for preteens or programming classes for teenagers at a library or community college.

Conclusion

President John F. Kennedy said technology "has no conscience of its own. Whether it will become a force for good or ill depends on man."[1] Swayed by digital-age myths, we are providing our children with remarkably little guidance on their use of technology. Kids are not without direction, however, for our absence has allowed tech corporations to exert tremendous influence over their lives. The result is a wired-for-amusement young generation.

In her book *Alone Together*, psychologist Sherry Turkle is optimistic that the time is right for improving the lives of kids distanced from their families by distracting technologies. As she says, "I believe we have reached a point of inflection, where we can see the costs and start to take action."[2] I am also hopeful we can make better lives for our children. To achieve this requires that we see through a host of digital falsehoods.

Debunking technology myths is challenging because of popular culture's incessant positive spin on the wired life. Years ago, the media industry helped expose Big Tobacco myths such as claims that cigarettes weren't marketed to kids. Now many of the media/tech corporations that bring us our news have a financial stake in selling us on even more gadgets and more screen time. Wise parents will be wary of these sales pitches.

It should be clear from reading this book that an enormous trove of important, objective research on the risks of children overusing technology is being ignored by the news media in favor of headlines touting the latest gadgets. It's vital that those who bring parents their health information—teachers, journalists, authors, and health providers—look to this research rather than biased sources when providing technology advice for kids. I also suggest that when you—as a parent, teacher, or other caregiver responsible for raising children—look for guidance, that you rely on resources whose providers have the primary aim of child health, not selling more e-stuff.

While much is known about the effects of our children's use of technology, there is much more that needs to be learned. In the wake of mass shootings perpetrated by boys and young men steeped in violent video games, we need to look more closely at the risks posed by children's use of interactive violence. I did not focus on the effects of video game violence in this book because my emphasis is on technology myths. It's difficult to portray benign effects for gaming violence as a myth, since studies show that most parents, along with most pediatricians and psychologists, already agree that virtual violence is contributing to real-life violence in kids.[3]

America is in fact falling behind other countries in the study of children's use of technology. Some of the United States' biggest global competitors—China, South Korea, and Japan—justifiably view their children's use of entertainment technologies as matters of public health and economic interest. So they fund extensive research in this field, especially on issues of technology addiction. However, in the US, an increasingly powerful video game industry lobby, which spent $18 million in lobbying over the past four years, is thwarting efforts to fund studies on the effects of video gaming on children.[4] This must change, as we owe it to our children (and our country) to make sure our kids' future lives aren't stunted by the dominance of screens and phones in childhood.

I have made it clear that children's use of technology is not the problem—instead concern is rightly directed at our kids' profound *overuse of entertainment technologies* that displace their involvement with family and school. We do need to help our kids use technology as a tool, to use it productively. This will not be accomplished easily because selling kids fun-based technologies that provide drug-like stimulation and create their own demand is much easier and more profitable than getting our kids to use technology in ways that will improve their future. Addressing this issue will require investment in equipment and teaching resources.

I am hopeful this book accomplished its goal of helping you understand that you are not alone in your struggles with kids' technology. It's clear we have a serious problem on our hands, considering the many families I have worked with who inspired the research in this book, along with countless studies that show millions of children and teens are experiencing similar concerns about tech overuse. Looking forward, where can you turn for guidance in a fast-changing tech environment?

I believe that one of our best hopes rests with schools, which are in a unique position to educate students and their parents about how screen and phone technologies are affecting kids' academic success and emotional health. Schools and teachers now shoulder much of the responsibility for American children's struggles to compete academically with students from around the world. Wholly ignored is the mountain of digital entertainment kids indulge in at the expense of learning fundamentals. I suggest that schools bring parents and teachers together to discuss (and decide how to change) the appalling reality that our kids spend far more time in front of playtime screens than in school. Unless this shifts, I can't see US kids catching up to their global peers.

Community, religious, and other organizations that have as their mission raising healthy children and helping families also have a pivotal role to play because they offer forums for fair-minded conversation. When parents, teachers, and others who care for children come together, I suggest one of the first orders of discussion be challenging the digital native-digital immigrant belief that suggests parents have no business guiding their kids' use of screens and gadgets. We must be the strong and wise caregivers our kids need us to be if we are to lovingly reclaim their childhood in this digital age.

Acknowledgments

I am privileged to have worked with two extraordinary editors. Karen Motylewski's remarkable vision was vital to shaping the book's course. Marilyn Elias' gift for grasping the big picture, but never missing a detail, honed the book's message and voice. I am also grateful to editors of my earlier writing that became the foundation of this book, including Alison Blake, Beth Bruno, Joe Kelly, Lisa Ross, and Elizabeth Zack.

I am heartened by the generosity of colleagues who have offered their guidance and encouragement on this project. Susan Linn and Josh Golin have been particularly supportive of my efforts to understand the effects of media and technology on children. I am also appreciative of friends who offered their suggestions on the manuscript, including Eve Cervantes, Katy Doran, Judy Haus, and Kristin Powell.

I am thankful for the opportunity to have worked with many caring families in clinical practice, making it through sometimes rough times together. And the team of clinicians I work with every day has taught me a great deal about what's needed to meet the challenges of improving the lives of children and their families.

My parents, Marion Odell and Stephen Diaz, have done so much to make this endeavor successful, and I am obliged to family friends that provided support along the way, including Monica Lin, Maggie Mariscal, and Lise Wise. The creation of this book would not have been possible without my wife Rae. Her loving support and insight provided both the will and the way for this project to be realized. Our daughters, Madeline and Elena, helped inspire the book's contents, and the girls' quiet faith in me helped get me to the end.

Notes

INTRODUCTION

1   Apple. (2013). Apple iPhone Christmas commercial 2013. [video]. *YouTube.* Retrieved April 10, 2014, from https://www.youtube.com/watch?v=v76f6KPSJ2w

2   Diaz, A. (2014, July 10). See the 2014 Emmy nominees for Outstanding Television Commercial. *Advertising Age.* Retrieved August 2, 2014, from http://adage.com

3   McGonigal, J. (2011). *Reality is broken: Why games can make us better and how they can change the world.* New York: Penguin; Colbert, S. (Executive Producer). (2011, February 3). *The Colbert Report* [Television broadcast]. Retrieved February 11, 2014, from http://www.colbertnation.com/the-colbert-report-videos/373360/february-03-2011/jane-mcgonigal; Prensky, M. (2006). *"Don't bother me mom—I'm learning!": How computer and video games are preparing your kids for 21st century success—and how you can help!.* St. Paul, MN: Paragon House

4   *Note: Data from the Kaiser Family Foundation shows that children's entertainment-based screen time has swelled from about 5 hours in 1999 to more than 7 ½ hours each day multitasking between various screens in the latest count:* Rideout, V. J., Foehr, U. G., & Roberts, D. F. (2010). Generation M2: Media in the lives of 8- to 18-year-olds. *Kaiser Family Foundation.* Retrieved March 1, 2014, from http://kaiserfamilyfoundation.files.wordpress.com/2013/01/8010.pdf

5   *Note: Figures derived from:* Rideout, V. J., Foehr, U. G., & Roberts, D. F. (2010). Generation M2: Media in the lives of 8- to 18-year-olds. *Kaiser Family Foundation.* Retrieved March 1, 2014, from http://kaiserfamilyfoundation.files.wordpress.com/2013/01/8010.pdf

6   Rideout, V. J., Foehr, U. G., & Roberts, D. F. (2010). Generation M2: Media in the lives of 8- to 18-year-olds. *Kaiser Family Foundation.* Retrieved March 1, 2014, from http://kaiserfamily-foundation.files.wordpress.com/2013/01/8010.pdf

7   Prensky, M. (2001). Digital natives, digital immigrants. *On the Horizon, 9*(5), 1-6.

8   Prensky, M. (2006). *"Don't bother me mom—I'm learning!": How computer and video games are preparing your kids for 21st century success—and how you can help!.* St. Paul, MN: Paragon House.

9   Frail, T. A. (2010, August 1) What will America look like in 2050? *Smithsonian Magazine.* Retrieved February 3, 2014, from www.smithsonianmag.com

10   Collier, A. (2012, June 5). Facebook access for under-13 kids is good – if parents involved. *Christian Science Monitor.* Retrieved February 3, 2014, from www.csmonitor.com; Magid, L. (2012, June 4). Letting children under 13 on Facebook could make them safer. *Huffington Post.* Retrieved February 3, 2014, from www.huffingtonpost.com

11   ConnectSafely. (2014). *Supporters.* Retrieved April 10, 2014, from http://www.connectsafely.org/about-us/supporters/

12   Koepp, M. J., Gunn, R. N., Lawrence, A. D., Cunningham, V. J., Dagher, A., Jones, T., et al. (1998). Evidence for striatal dopamine release during a video game. *Nature, 393*(6682), 266-268; Weinstein, A. M. (2010). Computer and video game addiction-a comparison between game users and non-game users. *The American Journal of Drug and Alcohol Abuse, 36*(5), 268-276.

13   Microsoft Corporation. (2011, November 16). *Connecting with technology: Microsoft survey finds technology is bringing families together.* Retrieved September 24, 2013, from http://www.microsoft.com/en-us/news/press/2011/nov11/11-16holitechpr.aspx

CHAPTER 1

1   Kennedy, T. L. M., Smith, A., Wells, A. T., & Wellman, B. (2008). Networked families. *Pew Internet & American Life Project*. Retrieved June 20, 2011, from http://www.pewinternet.org/~/media//Files/Reports/2008/PIP_Networked_Family.pdf.pdf, p. iii.

2   Microsoft Corporation. (2011, November 16). *Connecting with technology: Microsoft survey finds technology is bringing families together*. Retrieved September 24, 2013, from http://www.microsoft.com/en-us/news/press/2011/nov11/11-16holitechpr.aspx

3   Mesch, G. S., & Talmud, I. (2010). *Wired Youth: The social world of adolescence in the information age*. London: Routledge, p. 31.

4   Richards, R., McGee, R., Williams, S. M., Welch, D., & Hancox, R. J. (2010). Adolescent screen time and attachment to parents and peers. *Archives of Pediatrics & Adolescent Medicine, 164*(3), 258-262.

5   Lee, S. J., & Chae, Y. G. (2007). Children's Internet use in a family context: Influence on family relationships and parental mediation. *Cyberpsychology & Behavior, 10*(5), 640-644, p. 643; Mesch, G. S. (2006). Family relations and the Internet: Exploring a family boundaries approach. *Journal of Family Communication, 6*(2), 119-138; Mesch, G. S. (2003). The family and the Internet: The Israeli case. *Social Science Quarterly, 84*(4), 1038-1050.

6   Rideout, V. J., Foehr, U. G., & Roberts, D. F. (2010). Generation M2: Media in the lives of 8- to 18-year-olds. *Kaiser Family Foundation*. Retrieved March 1, 2014, from http://kaiserfamilyfoundation.files.wordpress.com/2013/01/8010.pdf

7   Cavoukian, R. (2013). *Lightweb darkweb: Three reasons to reform social media be4 it re-forms us*. Canada: Homeland Press, p. 91.

8   Arnold, J. E., Graesch, A. P., Ragazzini, E., & Ochs, E. (2012). *Life at home in the twenty-first century: 32 families open their doors*. Los Angeles: UCLA CIOA Press.

9   Wallis, C. (2006, March 27). The multitasking generation. *Time*. Retrieved October 17, 2012, from www.time.com

10   Center for Media Design, Ball State University. (2009). *Video consumer mapping study: Key findings report.* Retrieved February 4, 2012, from http://www.researchexcellence.com/ VCMFINALREPORT_4_28_09.pdf

11   Nie, N. H., Stepanikova, I., Pals, H., Zheng, L., & & He, X. (2005). Ten years after the birth of the Internet: How do Americans use the Internet in their daily lives? *Stanford Institute for the Quantitative Study of Society,* Retrieved August 10, 2011, from the DocStoc database, p. 12.

12   Gardner, A. (2009, June 18). Surging Internet use cutting into family time. *US News.* Retrieved June 1, 2011, from *www.usnews. com*

13   Turkle, S. (2011). *Alone together: Why we expect more from technology and less from each other.* New York: Basic Books, p. 267.

14   Steiner-Adair, C., & Barker, T. H. (2013). *The big disconnect: Protecting childhood and family relationships in the digital age,* Kindle Edition. New York: Harper.

15   Ogilvy & Mather, & Communispace. (2011). *Tech Fast Forward: Plug in to see the brighter side of life.* Retrieved September 25, 2012, from http://assets.ogilvy.com/truffles_email/techfastforward/ TechFastForward_PlugIn_Single.pdf; Ogilvy & Mather. (2011, October 20). *Embracing technology may brighten mom's outlook.* Retrieved September 24, 2012, from http://www.bizjournals. com/chicago/prnewswire/press_releases/Illinois/2011/10/20/ NY90682

16   Ogilvy & Mather, & Communispace. (2011). *Tech Fast Forward: Plug in to see the brighter side of life.* Retrieved September 25, 2012, from http://assets.ogilvy.com/truffles_email/techfastforward/ TechFastForward_PlugIn_Single.pdf, p. 9.

17   Ogilvy & Mather, & Communispace. (2011). *Tech Fast Forward: Plug in to see the brighter side of life.* Retrieved September 25, 2012, from http://assets.ogilvy.com/truffles_email/techfastforward/ TechFastForward_PlugIn_Single.pdf, pp. 21, 39.

18 Ogilvy & Mather, & Communispace. (2011). *Tech Fast Forward: Plug in to see the brighter side of life.* Retrieved September 25, 2012, from http://assets.ogilvy.com/truffles_email/techfastforward/TechFastForward_PlugIn_Single.pdf, p. 57.

19 Silver, K. (2011). Best baby apps. *Parents.com.* Retrieved October 15, 2012, from www.parents.com

20 Andrade, M. (2012, March 29). Concerns grow over children using tablet computers. *AFP.* Retrieved October 5, 2012, from http://www.google.com/hostednews/afp/

21 Madkour, Rasha. (2011, October 26). Squirmy toddler? There's an app for that. *Yahoo! News.* Retrieved October 11, 2012, from http://news.yahoo.com/squirmy-toddler-theres-app-165339272.html

22 Yahoo!, & Starcom MediaVest. (2012). *Brave new moms: Navigating technology's impact on family time webinar.* Retrieved September 15, 2012, from http://advertising.yahoo.com/video/brave-moms-navigating-technologies-impact-160000901.html; Yahoo! and Starcom MediaVest. (2012). *Brave new moms: Navigating technology's impact on family time.* Retrieved October 2, 2013, from http://advertising.yahoo.com/article/brave-new-moms.html

23 Yahoo!, & Starcom MediaVest. (2012). *Brave new moms: Navigating technology's impact on family time webinar.* Retrieved September 15, 2012, from http://advertising.yahoo.com/video/brave-moms-navigating-technologies-impact-160000901.html

24 Yahoo! & Starcom MediaVest. (2012). *Brave new moms: Navigating technology's impact on family time.* Retrieved October 2, 2013, from http://advertising.yahoo.com/article/brave-new-moms.html, p. 18.

25 Yahoo!, & Starcom MediaVest. (2012). *Brave new moms: Navigating technology's impact on family time webinar.* Retrieved September 15, 2012, from http://advertising.yahoo.com/video/brave-moms-navigating-technologies-impact-160000901.html

26 Yahoo! & Starcom MediaVest. (2012). *Brave new moms: Navigating technology's impact on family time.* Retrieved October 2, 2013, from

http://advertising.yahoo.com/article/cpg-insights-194919651. html

27 Yahoo!, & Starcom MediaVest. (2012). Brave *new moms: Navigating technology's impact on family time.* Retrieved September 15, 2012, from http://1.yimg.com/dh/ap/ayc/pdf/brave_new_moms_snapshot.pdf

28 Yahoo!, & Starcom MediaVest. (2012). *Brave new moms: Navigating technology's impact on family time webinar.* Retrieved September 15, 2012, from http://advertising.yahoo.com/video/brave-moms-navigating-technologies-impact-160000901.html

29 Siegel, D., & Hartzell, M. (2004). *Parenting from the inside out: How a deeper self-understanding can help you raise children who thrive.* New York: Jeremy P. Tarcher, p. 34.

30 National Scientific Council on the Developing Child. (2012). *The science of neglect: The persistent absence of responsive care disrupts the developing brain: Working Paper 12.* Retrieved November 21, 2013, from http://www.developingchild.harvard.edu

31 Karen, R. (1998). *Becoming attached: First relationships and how they shape our capacity to love.* New York: Oxford University Press; Siegel, D. (1999). *The developing mind: How relationships and the brain interact to share who we are.* New York: Guilford; Shochet, I., Homel, R., Cockshaw, W., & Montgomery, D. (2008). How do school connectedness and attachment to parents interrelate in predicting adolescent depressive symptoms? *Journal of Clinical Child and Adolescent Psychology, 37*(3), 676-681; Duchesne, S., & Larose, S. (2007). Adolescent parental attachment and academic motivation and performance in early adolescence. *Journal of Applied Social Psychology, 37*(7), 1501-1521; Mikulincer, M., & Shaver, P. (2007). *Attachment in adulthood: Structure, dynamics, and change.* New York: Guilford; Ooi, Y., Ang, R., Fung, D. S., Wong, G., & Cai, Y. (2006). The impact of parent-child attachment on aggression, social stress and self-esteem. *School Psychology International, 27*(5), 552-566; Brook, J. S., Brook, D. W., & Pahl, K. (2006). The

developmental context for adolescent substance abuse prevention. In H. A. Liddle & C.L. Rowe (Eds.), *Adolescent substance abuse: Research and clinical advances* (pp. 25-51). West Nyack, NY: Cambridge University Press.

32 Rideout, V. J., Foehr, U. G., & Roberts, D. F. (2010). Generation M2: Media in the lives of 8- to 18-year-olds. *Kaiser Family Foundation*. Retrieved March 1, 2014, from http://kaiserfamilyfoundation.files.wordpress.com/2013/01/8010.pdf, p. 4.

33 Page, A. S., Cooper, A. R., Griew, P., & Jago, R. (2010). Children's screen viewing is related to psychological difficulties irrespective of physical activity. *Pediatrics, 126*, e1011-e1017.

34 Walgrave, M., & Heirman, W. (2011). Cyberbullying: Predicting victimization and perpetration. *Children & Society, 25*, 59-72, p. 62.

35 Walgrave, M., & Heirman, W. (2011). Cyberbullying: Predicting victimization and perpetration. *Children & Society, 25*, 59-72.

36 Ybarra, M. L., & Mitchell, K. J. (2004). Youth engaging in online harassment: Associations with caregiver-child relationships, Internet use, and personal characteristics. *Journal of Adolescence, 27*(3), 319-336.

37 Ybarra, M. L., Diener-West, M., & Leaf, P. J. (2007). Examining the overlap in Internet harassment and school bullying: Implications for school intervention. *Journal of Adolescent Health, 41*(6 Suppl 1), S42-S50; Hinduja, S., & Patchin, J.W. (2010). Bullying, cyberbullying, and suicide. *Archives of Suicide Research, 14*(3), 206-221.

38 Ybarra, M. L., & Mitchell, K. J. (2004). Youth engaging in online harassment: Associations with caregiver-child relationships, Internet use, and personal characteristics. *Journal of Adolescence, 27*(3), 319-336.

39 Lenhart, A. (2009). Teens and sexting. *Pew Internet & American Life Project*. Retrieved July 1, 2011, from http://www.pewinternet.org/~/media//Files/Reports/2009/PIP_Teens_and_Sexting.pdf, p. 6.

40 Kotkin, J. (2013, May 13). America's new oligarchs—Fwd.us and Silicon Valley's shady 1 percenters. *The Daily Beast.* Retrieved May 18, 2014, from www.thedailybeast.com

41 Yahoo! & Starcom MediaVest. (2012). *Brave new moms: Navigating technology's impact on family time.* Retrieved October 2, 2013, from http://advertising.yahoo.com/article/brave-new-moms.html

42 Royal Council of the Real Fairyland, LLC. *The Real Tooth Fairies®.* Retrieved April 27, 2014 from www.therealtoothfairies.com/registration?gclid=CLTC_pTf-b0CFWuhOgod8jwA0g

43 Bus, A. G., & van Ijzendoorn, M. H. (1995). Mothers reading to their 3-year-olds: The role of mother-child attachment security in becoming literate. *Reading Research Quarterly 30(4),* 998-1015.

44 Scelfo, J. (2010, June 9). The risks of parenting while plugged in. *New York Times.* Retrieved October 29, 2012, from www.nytimes.com

45 The National Center on Addiction and Substance Abuse at Columbia University. (2009). *The importance of family dinners V.* Retrieved January 7, 2012, from http://www.casacolumbia.org/articlefiles/380-Importance%20of%20Family%20Dinners%20V.pdf

46 Eisenberg, M. E., Olson, R. E., Neumark-Sztainer, D., Story, M., & Bearinger, L. H. (2004). Correlations between family meals and psychosocial well-being among adolescents. *Archives of Pediatrics & Adolescent Medicine, 158(8),* 792-796.

47 Payne, K. J., & Ross, L. M. (2009). *Simplicity parenting: Using the extraordinary power of less to raise calmer, happier, and more secure kids,* Kindle Edition. New York: Ballantine.

48 The National Center on Addiction and Substance Abuse at Columbia University. (2009). *The importance of family dinners V.* Retrieved January 7, 2012, from http://www.casacolumbia.org/articlefiles/380-Importance%20of%20Family%20Dinners%20V.pdf

49 Retrevo. (2010). *Mother's day special report: Parenting and social media.* Retrieved January 7, 2012, from http://www.retrevo.com/content/blog/2010/04/mothers-day-special-report-parenting-and-social-media

50 The National Center on Addiction and Substance Abuse at Columbia University. (2009). *The importance of family dinners V.* Retrieved January 7, 2012, from http://www.casacolumbia.org/articlefiles/380-Importance%20of%20Family%20Dinners%20V. pdf

51 Bost, K. K., Shin, N., McBride, B. A., Brown, G. L., Vaughn, B. E., Coppola, G., et al. (2006). Maternal secure base scripts, children's attachment security, and mother-child narrative styles. *Attachment & Human Development 8*(3), 241-260.

52 Bohanek, J. G., Fivush, R., Zaman, W., Lepore, C. E., Merchant, S., & Duke, M. P. 2009. Narrative interaction in family dinnertime conversations. *Merrill-Palmer Quarterly 55*(4), 488-515.

53 Steiner-Adair, C., & Barker, T. H. (2013). *The big disconnect: Protecting childhood and family relationships in the digital age,* Kindle Edition. New York: Harper.

CHAPTER 2

1 McFadden, M. (2011, April 20). High-action video games benefit brain. *WNDU.com.* Retrieved October 30, 2013, from www.wndu. com; Wawro, A. (2011, July 15). 7 games that expand your brain. *PCWorld.com.* Retrieved October 9, 2013, from www.pcworld.com

2 Olson, C. 8 reasons video games can improve your child. *Parents. com.* Retrieved October 9, 2013, from www.parents.com

3 Trudeau, M. (2010, December 10). Video games boost brain power, multitasking skills. *NPR.org.* Retrieved October 30, 2013, from www.npr.org

4 Sax, Leonard. 2007. *Boys adrift: The five factors driving the growing epidemic of unmotivated boys and underachieving young men.* New York: Basic Books.

5   Green, C. S., & Bavelier, D. (2007). Action-video-game experience alters the spatial resolution of vision. *Psychological Science,* *18*(1), 88-94; Green, C. S., & Bavelier, D. (2006). Effect of action video games on the spatial distribution of visuospatial attention. *Journal of Experimental Psychology: Human Perception and Performance, 32*(6), 1465-1478.

6   Roach, J. (2003, May 28). Video games boost visual skills, study finds. *National Geographic News.* Retrieved October 11, 2013, from http://news.nationalgeographic.com

7   Zamora, P. (2013, March 4). Virtual training puts the 'real' in realistic environment. *www.army.mil.* Retrieved October 30, 2013, from www.army.mil; Montalbano, E. (2011, June 10) Army's $57 million training system uses gaming tech. *Information Week.* Retrieved October 30, 2013, from www.informationweek.com; Beidel, E. (2011, December). Gaming technology puts soldiers' boots on ground. *National Defense.* Retrieved October 30, 2013, from www.nationaldefensemagazine.org

8   Carr, N. (2011). *The shallows: What the Internet is doing to our brains.* New York: Norton.

9   Bavelier, D., Green, C. S., Han, D. H., Renshaw, P. F., Merzenich, M. M., & Gentile, D. A. (2011). Brains on video games. *Nature Reviews Neuroscience, 12,* 763-768, p. 765.

10   Chan, P. A., & Rabinowitz, T. (2006). A cross-sectional analysis of video games and attention deficit hyperactivity disorder symptoms in adolescents. *Annals of General Psychiatry, 5*(1), 16; Lim, C. G., Swing, E. L., Khoo, A., & Gentile, D. A. (2012). Video game playing, attention problems, and impulsiveness: Evidence of bidirectional causality. *Psychology of Popular Media Culture, 1*(1), 62-70; Swing, E. L., Gentile, D. A., Anderson, C. A., & Walsh, D. A. (2010). Television and video game exposure and the development of attention problems. *Pediatrics, 126*(2), 214-221; Christakis, D. A., Zimmerman, F. J., DiGiuseppe, D. L., & McCarty, C. A. (2004). Early television exposure and subsequent attentional

problems in children. *Pediatrics, 113*(4), 708-713; Zimmerman, F. J., & Christakis, D. A. (2007). Associations between content types of early media exposure and subsequent attentional problems. *Pediatrics, 120*(5), 986-992.

11 Klass, P. (2011, May 9). Fixated by screens, but seemingly nothing else. *New York Times*. Retrieved October 15, 2013, from www.nytimes.com

12 Lehrer, J. (2009, May 18). Don't: The secret of self-control. *The New Yorker*. Retrieved January 9, 2012, from www.newyorker.com

13 Moffitt, T. E., Arseneault, L., Belsky, D., Dickson, N., Hancox, R. J., Harrington, H., et al. (2011). A gradient of childhood self-control predicts health, wealth, and public safety. *Proceedings of the National Academy of Sciences of the United States of America, 108*(7), 2693-2698.

14 Duckworth, A. L., & Seligman, M. E. P. (2005). Self-discipline outdoes IQ in predicting academic performance of adolescents. *Psychological Science, 16*(12), 939-944.

15 Lehrer, J. (2009, May 18). Don't: The secret of self-control. *The New Yorker*. Retrieved January 9, 2012, from www.newyorker.com

16 Richtel, M. (2012, November 1). Technology changing how students learn, teachers say. *New York Times*. Retrieved April 11, 2013, from www.nytimes.com

17 Schwarz, A., & Cohen, S. (2013, March 31). A.D.H.D. seen in 11% of U.S. children as diagnoses rise. *New York Times*. Retrieved October 30, 2013, from www.nytimes.com

18 American Academy of Pediatrics. (2011). Policy statement: Media use by children younger than 2 years. *Pediatrics, 128*(5), 1-6; American Academy of Pediatrics. (2013). Children, adolescents, and the media. *Pediatrics 132*(5), 958-961.

19 Zimmerman, F. J., & Christakis, D. A. (2007). Associations between content types of early media exposure and subsequent attentional problems. *Pediatrics, 120*(5), 986-992.

20 Zimmerman, F. J., Christakis, D. A., & Meltzoff, A. N. (2007). Associations between media viewing and language development in children under age 2 years. *The Journal of pediatrics, 151*(4), 364-368; Anderson, R. C., Wilson, P. T., & Fielding, L. G. (1988). Growth in reading and how children spend their time outside of school. *Reading Research Quarterly, 23*(3), 285-303; Rideout, V. J., Foehr, U. G., & Roberts, D. F. (2010). Generation M2: Media in the lives of 8- to 18-year-olds. *Kaiser Family Foundation.* Retrieved March 1, 2014, from http://kaiserfamilyfoundation.files.word-press.com/2013/01/8010.pdf

21 Bruni, F. (2014, May 12). Read, kids, read. *New York Times.* Retrieved May 13, 2014, from www.nytimes.com

22 Cummings, H. M., & Vandewater, E. A. (2007). Relation of adolescent video game play to time spent in other activities. *Archives of Pediatrics & Adolescent Medicine, 161*(7), 684-689.

23 Comstock, G., & Scharrer, E. (1999). *Television: What's on, who's watching, and what it means.* San Diego, CA: Academic Press.

24 Morrow, L. M. (1983). Home and school correlates of early interest in literature. *The Journal of Educational Research, 76*(4), 221-230.

25 Chiong, C., Ree, J., Takeuchi, L., & Erickson, I. (2012, Spring). Print books vs. E-books. *The Joan Ganz Cooney Center.* Retrieved October 30, 2013, from http://www.joanganzcooneycenter.org/wp-content/uploads/2012/07/jgcc_ebooks_quickreport.pdf

26 Chiong, C., Ree, J., Takeuchi, L., & Erickson, I. (2012, Spring). Print books vs. E-books. *The Joan Ganz Cooney Center.* Retrieved October 30, 2013, from http://www.joanganzcooneycenter.org/wp-content/uploads/2012/07/jgcc_ebooks_quickreport.pdf, pp. 1-2.

27 Parish-Morris, J, Mahajan, N., Hirsh-Pasek, K., Golinkoff, R. M., Collins, M. F. (2013). Once upon a time: Parent-child dialogue and storybook reading in the electronic era. *Mind, Brain, and Education, 7*(3), 200-211.

28 Vygotsky, L.S. 1978. *Mind in society: The development of higher psychological processes.* Cambridge, MA: Harvard University Press, p. 99.

29 Tough, P. (2009, September 25). Can the right kinds of play teach self-control? *New York Times.* Retrieved October 30, 2013, from www.nytimes.com

30 Diamond, A., Barnett, W. S., Thomas, J., & Munro, S. (2007). Preschool program improves cognitive control. *Science, 318*(5855), 1387-1388.

31 Vandewater, E. A., Bickham, D. S., & Lee, J. H. (2006). Time well spent? Relating television use to children's free-time activities. *Pediatrics, 117*(2), e181-e191.

32 Szabo, L. (2011, December 12). Smartest toys for kids can be the simplest. *USA Today.* Retrieved October 21, 2013, from www.usatoday.com

33 Lepper, M. R., Sethi, S., Dialdin, D., & Drake, M. (1997). Intrinsic and extrinsic motivation: A developmental perspective. In S. S. Luthar, J. A. Burack, D. Cicchetti, & J. R. Weisz (Eds.), *Developmental psychopathology: Perspectives on adjustment, risk, and disorder* (pp. 23–50). New York: Cambridge University Press.

34 Kohn, A. (1994, December). The risks of rewards. *ERIC.* Retrieved November 1, 2013, from http://www.alfiekohn.org/teaching/pdf/The%20Risks%20of%20Rewards.pdf

35 Lepper, M. R., Corpus, J. H., & Iyengar, S. S. (2005). Intrinsic and extrinsic motivational orientations in the classroom: Age differences and academic correlates. *Journal of Educational Psychology, 97*(2), 184-196.

36 Gottfried, A. E., & Gottfried, A. W. (2009). Development of gifted motivation: Longitudinal research and applications. In L. V. Shavinina (Ed.), *International handbook on giftedness, Part one* (pp. 617-631). Netherlands: Springer Science.

37 *Note: Helping kids see the relevance of what they are learning helps inspire intrinsic motivation:* Geiser, K., & O'Guinn, C. (2010). Youth in the middle: Envisioning and implementing a whole-school

youth development approach. *John W. Gardner Center for Youth and Their Communities at Stanford University.* Retrieved November 2, 2013, from http://gardnercenter.stanford.edu/docs/YIM_Toolkit_100429.pdf

38 Oliver, P. H., Gottfried, A. W., Marcoulides, G. A., & Gottfried, A. E. (2009). A latent curve model of parental motivational practices and developmental decline in math and science academic intrinsic motivation. *Journal of Educational Psychology, 101*(3), 729-739.

39 Henderlong, J., & Lepper, M. R. (2002). The effects of praise on children's intrinsic motivation: A review and synthesis. *Psychological Bulletin, 128*(5), 774-795.

40 Bronson, P., & Merryman, A. (2009). *Nurture shock: New thinking about children.* New York: Twelve.

41 Henderlong, J., & Lepper, M. R. (2002). The effects of praise on children's intrinsic motivation: A review and synthesis. *Psychological Bulletin, 128*(5), 774-795.

CHAPTER 3

1 Gee, J. P. (2003, May). High score education. *Wired.* Retrieved April 6, 2013, from www.wired.com

2 McGonigal, J. (2011). *Reality is broken: Why games can make us better and how they can change the world.* New York: Penguin; Colbert, S. (Executive Producer). (2011, February 3). *The Colbert Report* [Television broadcast]. Retrieved February 11, 2014, from http://www.colbertnation.com/the-colbert-report-videos/373360/february-03-2011/jane-mcgonigal

3 Lev-Ram, M. (2011, May 20). Zuckerberg: Kids under 13 should be allowed on Facebook. *CNN.* Retrieved April 10, 2013, from www.cnn.com

4 Taylor, P., Parker, K., Fry, R., Cohn, D., Wang, W., Velasco, G., et al. (2011). Is college worth it? College presidents, public assess value, quality and mission of higher education. *Pew Research Center.* Retrieved April 10, 2013, from http://www.pewsocialtrends.org/

files/2011/05/Is-College-Worth-It.pdf; Rampell, C. (2011, May 20). Once again: Is college worth it? *New York Times*. Retrieved August 12, 2011, from www.nytimes.com

5   Grusky, D. B., Red Bird, B., Rodriguez, N., & Wirner, C. (2013, January). How much protection does a college degree afford? The impact of the recession on recent college graduates. *Pew Charitable Trusts*. Retrieved April 10, 2013, from http://www. pewstates.org/uploadedFiles/PCS_Assets/2013/Pew_college_ grads_recession_report.pdf

6   ACT. (2008). *The forgotten middle: Ensuring that all students are on target for college and career readiness before high school*. Retrieved April 10, 2013, from http://www.act.org/research/policymakers/pdf/ ForgottenMiddle.pdf, p. 3.

7   Blum, R. (2005). School connectedness: Improving students' lives. *Johns Hopkins Bloomberg School of Public Health*. Retrieved April 11, 2013, from http://cecp.air.org/download/ MCMonographFINAL.pdf, p. 1.

8   Rideout, V. J., Foehr, U. G., & Roberts, D. F. (2010). Generation M2: Media in the lives of 8- to 18-year-olds. *Kaiser Family Foundation*. Retrieved March 1, 2014, from http://kaiserfamily-foundation.files.wordpress.com/2013/01/8010.pdf

9   *Examples of research on the connection between video games and lower academic performance:* Weis, R., & Cerankosky, B. C. (2010). Effects of video-game ownership on young boys' academic and behavioral functioning: A randomized, controlled study. *Psychological Science, 21*(4), 463-470; Sharif, I., & Sargent, J. D. (2006). Association between television, movie, and video game exposure and school performance. *Pediatrics, 118*(4), e1061-e1070; Gentile, D. A., Lynch, P. J., Linder, J. R., & Walsh, D. A. (2004). The effects of violent video game habits on adolescent hostility, aggressive behaviors, and school performance. *Journal of Adolescence, 27*, 5-22; Stinebrickner, T. R., & Stinebrickner, R. (2007, August). The causal effect of studying on academic performance. *National Bureau of Economic Research*. NBER Working

Paper No. 13341. Retrieved April 28, 2013, from http://www. nber.org/papers/w13341.pdf?new_window=1; *Examples of research on the connection between social networks and lower academic performance:* National School Boards Association. (2007). *Creating & connecting: Research and guidelines on online social—and educational—networking.* Retrieved September 24, 2013, from www.grunwald.com; Rosen, L. D., Carrier, M. L., & Cheever, N. A. (2013). Facebook and texting made me do it: Media-induced task-switching while studying. *Computers in Human Behavior, 29*(3), 948-958; Jacobsen, W. C., & Forste, R. (2011). The wired generation: academic and social outcomes of electronic media use among university students. *Cyberpsychology, Behavior and Social Networking, 14*(5), 275-280; Junco, R., & Cotten, S. R. (2012). No A 4 U: The relationship between multitasking and academic performance. *Computers & Education, 59,* 505-514; Kirschner, P. A., & Karpinski, A. C. (2010). Facebook® and academic performance. *Computers in Human Behavior, 26*(6), 1237-1245; Junco, R. (2012). Too much face and not enough books: The relationship between multiple indices of Facebook use and academic performance. *Computers in Human Behavior,* 28, 187-198.

10 Sax, L. (2007). *Boys adrift: The five factors driving the growing epidemic of unmotivated boys and underachieving young men.* New York: Basic, p. 63.

11 National School Boards Association. (2007). *Creating & connecting: Research and guidelines on online social—and educational—networking.* Retrieved September 24, 2013, from www.grunwald.com

12 *Note: Kids watch primarily entertainment programming:* Christakis, D. A., Garrison, M. M., Herrenkohl, T., Haggerty, K., Rivara, F. P., Zhou, C., et al. (2013). Modifying media content for preschool children: A randomized controlled trial. *Pediatrics, 131*(3), 431-438; *Examples of research on the connection between television and lower academic performance:* Christakis, D. A., Garrison, M. M., Herrenkohl, T., Haggerty, K., Rivara, F. P., Zhou, C., et al. (2013). Modifying media content for preschool children: A randomized

controlled trial. *Pediatrics, 131*(3), 431-438; Hancox, R. J., Milne, B. J., & Poulton, R. (2005). Association of television viewing during childhood with poor educational achievement. *Archives of pediatrics adolescent medicine, 159*(7), 614-618; Comstock, G., & Scharrer, E. (1999). *Television: What's on, who's watching, and what it means.* San Diego, CA: Academic Press.

13 Cummings, H. M., & Vandewater, E. A. (2007). Relation of adolescent video game play to time spent in other activities. *Archives of Pediatrics & Adolescent Medicine, 161*(7), 684-689.

14 National School Boards Association. (2007). *Creating & connecting: Research and guidelines on online social—and educational—networking.* Retrieved September 24, 2013, from www.grunwald.com

15 Weis, R., & Cerankosky, B. C. (2010). Effects of video-game ownership on young boys' academic and behavioral functioning: A randomized, controlled study. *Psychological Science,* 21(4), 463-470.

16 Sharif, I., & Sargent, J. D. (2006). Association between television, movie, and video game exposure and school performance. *Pediatrics, 118*(4), e1061-e1070.

17 Weis, R., & Cerankosky, B. C. (2010). Effects of video-game ownership on young boys' academic and behavioral functioning: A randomized, controlled study. *Psychological Science,* 21(4), 463-470.

18 Junco, R., & Cotten, S. R. (2012). No A 4 U: The relationship between multitasking and academic performance. *Computers & Education, 59,* 505-514; Jacobsen, W. C., & Forste, R. (2011). The wired generation: Academic and social outcomes of electronic media use among university students. *Cyberpsychology, Behavior and Social Networking, 14*(5), 275-280; Harmon, B. A., & Sato, T. (2011). Cell phone use and grade point average among undergraduate university students. *College Student Journal, 45*(3), 544-548; Junco, R. (2012). In-class multitasking and academic performance. *Computers in Human Behavior, 28*(6), 2236–2243; Lepp, A., Barkley, J. E., & Karpinski, A. C. (2014). The relationship

between cell phone use, academic performance, anxiety, and Satisfaction with Life in college students. *Computers in Human Behavior, 31*, 343-350.

19 Rosen, L. D., Carrier, M. L., & Cheever, N. A. (2013). Facebook and texting made me do it: Media-induced task-switching while studying. *Computers in Human Behavior, 29*(3), 948-958.

20 Chen, S., & Fu, Y. (2009). Internet use and academic achievement: Gender differences in early adolescence. *Adolescence, 44*(176), 797-812.

21 Rideout, V. J., Foehr, U. G., & Roberts, D. F. (2010). Generation M2: Media in the lives of 8- to 18-year-olds. *Kaiser Family Foundation*. Retrieved March 1, 2014, from http://kaiserfamily-foundation.files.wordpress.com/2013/01/8010.pdf

22 Vigdor, J. L., & Ladd, H. F. (2010, June). *Scaling the digital divide: Home computer technology and student achievement* (Calder Working Paper, No. 48). Retrieved April 10, 2013, from http://www.calder-rcenter.org/publications/upload/CALDERWorkingPaper_48.pdf

23 Richtel, M. (2010, November 21). Growing up digital, wired for distraction. *New York Times*. Retrieved February 11, 2014, from www.nytimes.com

24 Gee, J. P. (2007). *What video games have to teach us about learning and literacy*. New York: Palgrave Macmillan.

25 McGonigal, J. (2011). *Reality is broken: Why games can make us better and how they can change the world*. New York: Penguin, pp. 148, 277.

26 Saletan, W. (2011, February 11). The computer made me do it. *New York Times*. Retrieved April 22, 2013, from www.nytimes.com; Klavan, A. (2011, January 21). Upgrading the world. *The Wall Street Journal*. Retrieved April 22, 2013, from http://online.wsj.com

27 Kelly, D., Xie, H., Nord, C. W., Jenkins, F., Chan, J. Y., & Kastberg, D. (2013). Performance of US 15-year-old students in mathematics, science, and reading literacy in an international context: First

look at PISA 2012 (NCES 2014-024). US *Department of Education. Washington, DC: National Center for Education Statistics.* Retrieved December 3, 2013, from http://nces.ed.gov/pubsearch

28 Clayton, M. (2013, December 3, 203). PISA test shows 'stagnation.' Is US education reform failing? *Christian Science Monitor.* Retrieved December 5, 2013, from www.csmonitor.com

29 Bradsher, K. (2013, January 16). Next made-in-China boom: College graduates. *New York Times.* Retrieved December 18, 2013, from www.nytimes.com

30 Cooper, D., Hersh, A., & O'Leary, A. (2012, August). The Competition that really matters: Comparing U.S., Chinese, and Indian investments in the next-generation workforce. *Center for American Progress & The Center for the Next Generation.* Retrieved March 15, 2013, from http://www.americanprogress.org/wp-content/uploads/2012/08/USChinaIndiaEduCompetitiveness.pdf

31 Friedman, T. L., & Mandelbaum, M. (2011). *That used to be us: How America fell behind in the world it invented and how we can come back.* New York: Farrar, Straus, and Giroux.

32 Centers for Disease Control and Prevention. (2013, May 17). Mental health surveillance among children—United States, 2005-2011. *Morbidity and Mortality Weekly Report, 62*(Suppl. 2), 1-35; Barrocas, A. L., Hankin, B. L., Young, J. F. & Abela, J. R. Z. (2012). Rates of nonsuicidal self-injury in youth: Age, sex, and behavioral methods in a community sample. *Pediatrics, 130*(1), 39-45.

33 Eagan, K., Lozano, J. B., Hurtado, S., & Case, M. H. (2013). The American freshman: National norms fall 2013. *Higher Education Research Institute, UCLA.* Retrieved March 12, 2014, from http://www.heri.ucla.edu/monographs/TheAmericanFreshman2013.pdf; Pryor, J. H., Eagan, K., Palucki Blake, L., Hurtado, S., Berdan, J., & Case, M. H. (2012). The American freshman: National norms fall 2012. *Higher Education Research Institute, UCLA.*

Retrieved April 11, 2013, from http://www.heri.ucla.edu/mono-graphs/TheAmericanFreshman2012.pdf; Pryor, J. H., DeAngelo, L., Palucki Blake, L., Hurtado, S., & Tran, S. (2011). The American freshman: National norms fall 2011. *Higher Education Research Institute, UCLA.* Retrieved March 12, 2014, from http://www.heri.ucla.edu/PDFs/pubs/TFS/Norms/Monographs/TheAmericanFreshman2011.pdf

34 Cooper, H. (2010, December 10). Homework's diminishing returns. *New York Times.* Retrieved December 2, 2012, from www.nytimes.com

35 American Academy of Pediatrics. (2013). Children, adolescents, and the media. *Pediatrics 132*(5), 958-961.

36 Sharif, I., & Sargent, J. D. (2006). Association between television, movie, and video game exposure and school performance. *Pediatrics, 118*(4), e1061-e1070.

37 Google. (2013). Google Nexus 7 commercial. [video]. *YouTube.* Retrieved April 29, 2014, from https://www.youtube.com/watch?v=pN7dpnz8xg8

38 Frank N. Magid Associates/PlayFirst. (2013, July 9). *Tablets rule as preferred mobile gaming device: Tablet in-game virtual goods spending nearly 3x more than on smartphones.* Retrieved April 30, 2014, from http://www.prweb.com/releases/2013/7/prweb10908880.htm

39 Verizon. (2012). *Verizon foundation survey on middle school students' use of mobile technology.* Retrieved December 18, 2013, from www.thinkfinity.org/docs/DOC-10549

40 Verizon Foundation. (2012). *Kids finally have a case for why they are using mobile devices for homework.* Retrieved December 10, 2013, from http://www.howtolearn.com/2012/11/using-mobile-devices-for-homework/

41 Verizon Foundation. (2012). *Kids finally have a case for why they are using mobile devices for homework.* Retrieved December 10, 2013, from http://www.howtolearn.com/2012/11/using-mobile-devices-for-homework/

42 Rideout, V. J., Foehr, U. G., & Roberts, D. F. (2010). Generation M2: Media in the lives of 8- to 18-year-olds. *Kaiser Family Foundation*. Retrieved March 1, 2014, from http://kaiserfamily-foundation.files.wordpress.com/2013/01/8010.pdf, p. 3.

43 Lenhart, A., Ling, R., Campbell, S., & Purcell, K. (2010). Teens and mobile phones. *Pew Internet & American Life Project*. Retrieved December 18, 2013, from http://pewinternet.org/~/media//Files/Reports/2010/PIP-Teens-and-Mobile-2010-with-topline.pdf; Madden, M., Lenhart, A., Cortesi, S., & Gasser, U. (2013). Teens and mobile apps privacy. *Pew Research Center & The Berkman Center for Internet & Society at Harvard University*. Retrieved December 18, 2013, from http://pewinternet.org/~/media//Files/Reports/2013/PIP_Teens%20and%20Mobile%20Apps%20Privacy.pdf; Gould, J. (2013, December 9). Consumer insights: Nickelodeon's 'Story of Me'. *Nickelodeon*. Retrieved December 18, 2013, from http://blog.viacom.com/2013/12/con-sumer-insights-nickelodeons-story-of-me/; Rideout, V. J., Foehr, U. G., & Roberts, D. F. (2010). Generation M2: Media in the lives of 8- to 18-year-olds. *Kaiser Family Foundation*. Retrieved March 1, 2014, from http://kaiserfamilyfoundation.files.wordpress.com/2013/01/8010.pdf

44 Rideout, V. J., Foehr, U. G., & Roberts, D. F. (2010). Generation M2: Media in the lives of 8- to 18-year-olds. *Kaiser Family Foundation*. Retrieved March 1, 2014, from http://kaiserfamilyfoundation.files.wordpress.com/2013/01/8010.pdf, p. 2.

45 Vila, M. (2013, February 8). Keeping one step ahead of kids in a mobile world. *Mashable*. Retrieved December 9, 2013, from http://mashable.com

46 Silverstein, M. J., Fiske, N., & Butman, J. (2008). *Trading up: Why consumers want new luxury goods—and how companies create them*. New York: Portfolio.

47 Madden, M., Lenhart, A., Duggan, M., Cortesi, S., & Gasser, U. (2013). Teens and technology 2013. *Pew Research Center & The Berkman Center for Internet & Society at Harvard University.* Retrieved November 13, 2013, from http://www.pewinternet.org/~/media//Files/Reports/2013/PIP_TeensandTechnology2013.pdf, p. 7.

48 Meer, J. (2013, October 16). Distracted living. *Huffington Post.* Retrieved December 18, 2013, from www.huffingtonpost.com

49 Meer, J. (2013, October 16). Distracted living [Video]. *Huffington Post.* Retrieved December 18, 2013, from www.huffingtonpost.com

50 Wiseman, R. (2009). *Queen bees & wannabes: Helping your daughter survive cliques, gossip, boyfriends, and the new realities of girl world, Second Edition.* Three Rivers: New York, p. 34.

51 Rideout, V. J., Foehr, U. G., & Roberts, D. F. (2010). Generation M2: Media in the lives of 8- to 18-year-olds. *Kaiser Family Foundation.* Retrieved March 1, 2014, from http://kaiserfamilyfoundation.files.wordpress.com/2013/01/8010.pdf

52 Medina, J. (2008). *Brain rules: 12 principles for surviving and thriving at work, home, and school.* Seattle: Pear Press, p. 4.

53 Ophir, E., Nass, C., & Wagner, A. D. (2009). Cognitive control in media multitaskers. *Proceedings of the National Academy of Sciences* 106(37), 15583-15587.

54 Gorlick, A. (2009, August 24). Media multitaskers pay mental price, Stanford study shows. *Stanford Report,* Retrieved April 11, 2013, from http://news.stanford.edu/news

55 Rosen, L. D., Carrier, M. L., & Cheever, N. A. (2013). Facebook and texting made me do it: Media-induced task-switching while studying. *Computers in Human Behavior, 29*(3), 948-958.

56 Wein, H. (2010, February 12). Resting may boost memory. *NIH Research Matters.* Retrieved April 11, 2013, from www.nih.gov/researchmatters

57 Dworak, M., Schierl, T., Bruns, T., & Strüder, H. K. (2007). Impact of singular excessive computer game and television exposure on sleep patterns and memory performance of school-aged children. *Pediatrics, 120*(5), 978-985.

58 American Academy of Pediatrics. (2013). Children, adolescents, and the media. *Pediatrics 132*(5), 958-961.

59 Richtel, M. (2012, November 1). Technology changing how students learn, teachers say. *New York Times.* Retrieved April 11, 2013, from www.nytimes.com

60 Junco, R. (2012). In-class multitasking and academic performance. *Computers in Human Behavior, 28*(6), 2236–2243.

61 Sana, F., Weston, T., & Cepeda, N. J. (2012). Laptop multitasking hinders classroom learning for both users and nearby peers. *Computers & Education, 62,* 24-31.

CHAPTER 4

1 Couric, K. (2013, May 1). Are video games ruining your life? *Katie* [Television broadcast]. Retrieved August 5, 2013, from http://katiecouric.com/2013/05/01/daniel-petric-video-games/

2 Sangiacomo, M. (2008, December 15). Daniel Petric killed mother, shot father because they took Halo 3 video game, prosecutors say. *Cleveland.com.* Retrieved September 22, 2013, from www.cleveland.com; Harvey, M. (2009, January 13). Teenager Daniel Petric shot parents who took away Xbox. *TimesOnline.* Retrieved September 22, 2013, from www.thetimes.co.uk

3 The Plain Dealer. (2009, January 15). *Judge James Burge: Daniel Petric A.K.A. "Halo Killer"* [Video]. Retrieved September 22, 2013, from www.youtube.com

4 Elliot, L, Ream, G., McGinsky, E., & Dunlap, E. (2012). The contribution of game genre and other use patterns to problem video game play among adult video gamers. *International Journal of Mental Health and Addiction, 10*(6), 948-969; Ko, C. H., Yen,

J. Y., Chen, C. C., Chen, S. H., & Yen, C. F. (2005). Proposed diagnostic criteria of Internet addiction for adolescents. *The Journal of Nervous and Mental Disease, 193*(11), 728-733; Kuss, D. J., & Griffiths, M. D. (2011). Online social networking and addiction-A review of the psychological literature. *International Journal of Environmental Research and Public Health, 8*(9), 3528-3552.

5   Gentile, D. A., Choo, H., Liau, A., Sim, T., Li, D., Fung, D., et al. (2011). Pathological video game use among youths: A two-year longitudinal study. *Pediatrics, 127*(2), e319-e329.

6   Griffiths, M. D., Kuss, D. J., & King, D. L. (2012). Video game addiction: Past, present and future. *Current Psychiatry Reviews, 8*(4), 308-318; Weinstein, A., & Weizman, A. (2012). Emerging association between addictive gaming and Attention-Deficit/Hyperactivity Disorder. *Current Psychiatry Reports, 14*(5), 590-597; Mazurek, M. O., & Wenstrup, C. (2013). Television, video game and social media use among children with ASD and typically developing siblings. *Journal of Autism and Developmental Disorders, 43*, 1258-1271.

7   Yousafzai, S., Hussain, Z., & Griffiths, M. (2014). Social responsibility in online videogaming: What should the videogame industry do? *Addiction Research and Theory, 22*(3), 181-185; Gentile, D. A., Choo, H., Liau, A., Sim, T., Li, D., Fung, D., et al. (2011). Pathological video game use among youths: A two-year longitudinal study. *Pediatrics, 127*(2), e319-e329.

8   Koepp, M. J., Gunn, R. N., Lawrence, A. D., Cunningham, V. J., Dagher, A., Jones, T., et al. (1998). Evidence for striatal dopamine release during a video game. *Nature, 393*(6682), 266-268; Weinstein, A. M. (2010). Computer and video game addiction-a comparison between game users and non-game users. *The American Journal of Drug and Alcohol Abuse, 36*(5), 268-276.

9   Kuss, D. J., & Griffiths, M. D. (2012). Internet and gaming addiction: A systematic literature review of neuroimaging studies. *Brain Sciences, 2*(4), 347-374; Griffiths, M. D., Kuss, D. J., & King,

D. L. (2012). Video game addiction: Past, present and future. *Current Psychiatry Reviews, 8*(4), 308-318.

10 American Psychiatric Association. (2013). *Diagnostic and statistical manual of mental disorders* (5th ed.). Washington, DC: Author.

11 Young, K. S., & Abreu, C. N. (2011). Introduction. In K. S. Young & C. N. Abreu (Eds.), *Internet addiction: A handbook and guide to evaluation and treatment,* Kindle Edition. Hoboken, NJ: Wiley; Jiang, J. (2009, January 28). Inside China's fight against Internet addiction. *Time.* Retrieved September 23, 2013, from www.time.com; Sun, C. (2011, October 17). Online cravings. *The Daily Beast.* Retrieved September 23, 2013, from www.thedailybeast.com

12 Shlam, S., & Medalia, H. (Directors) (2014, January 19). China's web junkies. [Film documentary]. *New York Times.* Retrieved January 22, 2014, from www.nytimes.com

13 Xinhua (2009, March 20). *Anti-online game addiction system proves to be effective in China.* Retrieved September, 23, 2013, from http://news.xinhuanet.com; Tassi, P. (2012, January 9). South Korea's nightly gaming ban extends to Xbox live. *Forbes.com.* Retrieved September 23, 2013, from www.forbes.com

14 Hofilena, J. (2013, August 27). Japan to introduce camps for 'internet fasting' to help addicted kids. *Japan Daily Press.* Retrieved June 13, 2014, from japandailypress.com

15 Gartner. (2013, October 29). *Gartner says worldwide video game market to total $93 billion in 2013.* Retrieved June 14, 2014, from www.gartner.com

16 Keshet, S. (2011, January 13). Do video games cause mental health problems? *TG Daily.* Retrieved September 22, 2013, from www.tgdaily.com

17 American Psychiatric Association. (2013). *Diagnostic and statistical manual of mental disorders* (5th ed.). Washington, DC: Author, p. 585.

18 Davidow, B. (2012, July 18). Exploiting the neuroscience of Internet addiction. *The Atlantic.* Retrieved July 23, 2013, from www.theatlantic.com

19   Hon, A. (2010, August 16). One more turn. *Mssv.* Retrieved September 23, 2013, from http://mssv.net/2010/08/16/one-more-turn/

20   Bakan, J. (2011). *Childhood under siege. How big business targets children.* New York: Free Press, p. 29.

21   Hopson, J. (2001, April 27). Behavioral game design. *Gamasutra.* Retrieved August 6, 2013, from www.gamasutra.com

22   Poisso, L. (2010, July 27). 15 minutes of fame: Psychologist and games researcher John Hopson. *Joystiq.* Retrieved August 19, 2013, from www.joystiq.com

23   Microsoft/Channel9.*Playtestlabs: Getyourgamingvoiceheard.* [Video]. Retrieved September 23, 2013, from http://channel9.msdn.com/blogs/laurafoy/playtest-labs--get-your-gaming-voice-heard

24   Execution labs. (2012). *Bill Fulton.* Retrieved June 14, 2014, from http://executionlabs.com/en/mentors/bill-fulton

25   Edge. (2011, February 27). GDC preview: Mike Ambinder. *Edge.* Retrieved August 31, 2013, from www.edge-online.com

26   Morrison, A., & Gruman, G. (2012). Elements of effective game-based emotion design. *Technology Forecast/PricewaterhouseCoopers, Issue 3.* Retrieved August 28, 2013, from www.pwc.com

27   Turkle, S. (1995). *Life on the Screen: Identity in the age of the internet.* New York: Simon & Schuster; Turkle, S. (2005). *The second self: Computers and the human spirit*; Turkle, S. (2011). *Alone together: Why we expect more from technology and less from each other.* New York: Basic Books.

28   Hou, H, Jia, S., Hu, S., Fan, R., Sun, W., Sun, T., et al. (2012). Reduced striatal dopamine transporters in people with Internet Addiction Disorder. *Journal of Biomedicine and Biotechnology, 2012,* 1-5; Kim, S. H., Baik, S. H., Park, C. S., Kim, S. J., Choi, S. W., & Kim, S. E. (2011). Reduced striatal dopamine D2 receptors in people with Internet addiction. *NeuroReport, 22*(8), 407-411.

29   Hon, A. (2010, December 6). A new breed of computer games is creating compulsive behaviour. Someone is making a lot of

money out of this. *The Telegraph.* Retrieved August 19, 2013, from www.telegraph.co.uk

30 Sheffield, B. (2010, August 18). GDC Europe: To succeed in free-to-play, 'Exploit human weaknesses'. *Gamasutra.* Retrieved August 17, 2013, from www.gamasutra.com

31 Shokrizade, R. (2013, June 6). Monetizing children. *Gamasutra.* Retrieved September 2, 2013, from www.gamasutra.com

32 Block, J. J. (2008). Issues for DSM-5: Internet addiction. *The American Journal of Psychiatry, 165*(3), 306-307.

33 *Note: Parents frequently struggle to be satisfied with treatment outcomes for Internet addiction:* Eidenbenz, F. (2011). Systemic dynamics with adolescents addicted to the Internet. In K. S. Young & C. N. Abreu (Eds.), *Internet addiction: A handbook and guide to evaluation and treatment,* Kindle Edition, Hoboken, NJ: Wiley.

34 Kuss, D. J., van Rooij, A. J., Shorter, G. W., Griffiths, M. D., & van do Mheen, D. (2013). Internet addiction in adolescents: Prevalence and risk factors. *Computers in Human Behavior, 29,* 1987-1996, p. 1993.

35 Griffiths, M. D., & Hunt, N. (1998). Dependence on computer games by adolescents. *Psychological Reports, 82*(2), 475-480, p. 475.

36 Gentile, D. (2009). Pathological video-game use among youth ages 8 to 18. *Psychological Science, 20*(5), 594-602, p. 599.

37 Wagner, J. S. (2008, May 7). Addiction to video games a growing concern. *US News & World Report,* Retrieved September 23, 2013, from http://health.usnews.com

38 Grossman, D., & DeGaetano, G. (1999). *Stop teaching our kids to kill: A call to action against TV, movie, & video game violence.* New York: Crown, p. 99.

CHAPTER 5

1 Goldstein, D. (2012, June 7). How to fix the gender gap in technology. *Slate.* Retrieved April 9, 2013, from www.slate.com

2 Rideout, V. J., Foehr, U. G., & Roberts, D. F. (2010). Generation M2: Media in the lives of 8- to 18-year-olds. *Kaiser Family*

Foundation. Retrieved March 1, 2014, from http://kaiserfamily-foundation.files.wordpress.com/2013/01/8010.pdf; DePillis, L. (2013, March 28). How to close the tech industry's gender gap. *New Republic.* Retrieved July 17, 2013, from www.newrepublic.com

3   *Note: Statistics derived from the following study:* Rideout, V. J., Foehr, U. G., & Roberts, D. F. (2010). Generation M2: Media in the lives of 8- to 18-year-olds. *Kaiser Family Foundation.* Retrieved March 1, 2014, from http://kaiserfamilyfoundation.files.wordpress. com/2013/01/8010.pdf

4   Duckworth, A. L., & Seligman, M. E. P. (2006). Self-discipline gives girls the edge: Gender in self-discipline, grades, and achievement test scores. *Journal of Educational Psychology, 98*(1), 198-208.

5   Kristof, N. D. (2010, March 27). The boys have fallen behind. *New York Times.* Retrieved July 17, 2013, from www.nytimes.com

6   American Council on Education. (2010, Spring). *By the numbers: Gender gap in higher education holding steady.* Retrieved July 18, 2013, from www.acenet.edu

7   Goodwin, L. (2013, June 21). As court prepares affirmative-action decision, softer standards for men go unnoticed. *Yahoo! News.* Retrieved June 19, 2014, from http://news.yahoo.com

8   Ogletree, S. M., & Drake, R. (2007). College students' video game participation and perceptions: Gender differences and implications. *Sex Roles, 56*(7-8), 537-542.

9   Stinebrickner, T. R., & Stinebrickner, R. (2007, August). The causal effect of studying on academic performance. *National Bureau of Economic Research.* NBER Working Paper No. 13341. Retrieved April 28, 2013, from http://www.nber.org/papers/w13341.pdf?new_window=1

10   *Note: Women earn higher grades in and more likely to graduate from college:* Conger, D., & Long, M. C. (2010). Why are men falling behind? Gender gaps in college performance and persistence. *The ANNALS of the American Academy of Political and Social Science, 627*(1), 184-214: *Note: Women more likely to earn honors in college:*

Lewin, T. (2006, July 9). At colleges, women are leaving men in the dust. *New York Times*, Retrieved July 18, 2013, from www.nytimes.com

11 Autor, D., & Wasserman, M. (2013, March). Wayward Sons: The emerging gender gap in labor markets and education. *Third Way*. Retrieved July 3, 2013, from http://content.thirdway.org/publications/662/Third_Way_Report_-_NEXT_Wayward_Sons-The_ Emerging_Gender_Gap_in_Labor_Markets_and_Education. pdf

12 Sax, L. (2007). *Boys adrift: The five factors driving the growing epidemic of unmotivated boys and underachieving young men.* New York: Basic, p. 68.

13 Zimbardo, P., & Duncan, N. (2012). *The demise of guys: Why boys are struggling and what we can do about it,* Kindle Edition. Seattle: Amazon Digital Services.

14 Zimbardo, P., & Duncan, N. (2012). *The demise of guys: Why boys are struggling and what we can do about it,* Kindle Edition. Seattle: Amazon Digital Services.

15 Hoeft, F., Watson, C. L., Kesler, S. R., Bettinger, K. E., & Reiss, A. L. (2008). Gender differences in the mesocorticolimbic system during computer game-play. *Journal of Psychiatric Research, 42*(4), 253-258, p. 253.

16 Rideout, V. J., Foehr, U. G., & Roberts, D. F. (2010). Generation M2: Media in the lives of 8- to 18-year-olds. *Kaiser Family Foundation*. Retrieved March 1, 2014, from http://kaiserfamilyfoundation.files.wordpress.com/2013/01/8010.pdf

17 Duckworth, A. L., & Seligman, M. E. P. (2006). Self-discipline gives girls the edge: Gender in self-discipline, grades, and achievement test scores. *Journal of Educational Psychology, 98*(1), 198-208.

18 *Note: Figures derived from:* Rideout, V. J., Foehr, U. G., & Roberts, D. F. (2010). Generation M2: Media in the lives of 8- to 18-year-olds. *Kaiser Family Foundation*. Retrieved March 1, 2014, from http:// kaiserfamilyfoundation.files.wordpress.com/2013/01/8010.pdf

19 Rideout, V. J., Foehr, U. G., & Roberts, D. F. (2010). Generation M2: Media in the lives of 8- to 18-year-olds. *Kaiser Family Foundation*. Retrieved March 1, 2014, from http://kaiserfamilyfoundation.files.wordpress.com/2013/01/8010.pdf

20 Rideout, V. J., Foehr, U. G., & Roberts, D. F. (2010). Generation M2: Media in the lives of 8- to 18-year-olds. *Kaiser Family Foundation*. Retrieved March 1, 2014, from http://kaiserfamilyfoundation.files.wordpress.com/2013/01/8010.pdf

21 Lenhart, A. (2012, March 19). Teens, smartphones & texting. *Pew Internet & American Life Project*. Retrieved July 3, 2013, from http://pewinternet.org/~/media//Files/Reports/2012/PIP_Teens_Smartphones_and_Texting.pdf

22 Ma, C. Q., & Huebner, E. S. (2008). Attachment relationships and adolescents' life satisfaction: Some relationships matter more to girls than boys. *Psychology in the Schools, 45*(2), 177-190.

23 DePillis, L. (2013, March 28). How to close the tech industry's gender gap. *New Republic*. Retrieved July 17, 2013, from www.newrepublic.com

CHAPTER 6

1 Prensky, M. (2001). Digital natives, digital immigrants. *On the Horizon, 9*(5), 1-6. Retrieved June 12, 2014, from http://www.marcprensky.com/writing/Prensky%20-%20Digital%20Natives,%20Digital%20Immigrants%20-%20Part1.pdf

2 Prensky, M. (2001). Digital natives, digital immigrants. *On the Horizon, 9*(5), 1-6. Retrieved June 12, 2014, from http://www.marcprensky.com/writing/Prensky%20-%20Digital%20Natives,%20Digital%20Immigrants%20-%20Part1.pdf, p. 1.

3 Prensky, M. (2006). *"Don't bother me mom—I'm learning!": How computer and video games are preparing your kids for 21st century success—and how you can help!.* St. Paul, MN: Paragon House, p. xxiii.

4 Prensky, M. (2006). *"Don't bother me mom—I'm learning!": How computer and video games are preparing your kids for 21st century success—and how you can help!.* St. Paul, MN: Paragon House, p. xvi.

5   Prensky, M. (2006). *"Don't bother me mom—I'm learning!": How computer and video games are preparing your kids for 21st century success—and how you can help!*. St. Paul, MN: Paragon House, p. 4.

6   Prensky, M. (2006). *"Don't bother me mom—I'm learning!": How computer and video games are preparing your kids for 21st century success—and how you can help!*. St. Paul, MN: Paragon House.

7   Prensky, M. (2006). *"Don't bother me mom—I'm learning!": How computer and video games are preparing your kids for 21st century success—and how you can help!*. St. Paul, MN: Paragon House, p. 5.

8   Bennett, S. (2012). Digital natives. In Z. Yan (Ed.), *Encyclopedia of cyber behavior: Volume 1* (pp. 212-219). United States: IGI Global. Retrieved June 12, 2014, from http://ro.uow.edu.au/cgi/viewcontent.cgi?article=2364&context=edupapers, p. 3.

9   Selwyn, N. (2009). The digital native—myth and reality. *ASLIB Proceedings: New Information Perspectives, 61*(4), 364-379, p. 364.

10 Toddlers on Technology. *The book*. Retrieved June 2, 2014, from http://digitod.com/the-book/

11 Rosin, H. (2013, April). The touch-screen generation. *The Atlantic*. Retrieved June 12, 2014, from www.theatlantic.com

12 Rideout, V. J., Foehr, U. G., & Roberts, D. F. (2010). Generation M2: Media in the lives of 8- to 18-year-olds. *Kaiser Family Foundation*. Retrieved March 1, 2014, from http://kaiserfamilyfoundation.files.wordpress.com/2013/01/8010.pdf

13 Boyd, D. (2014). *It's complicated: The social lives of networked teens*, Kindle Edition. New Haven, CT: Yale University Press.

14 Boyd, D. (2014, March 24). Let kids run wild online. *Time, 183*(11), 40; *Note: Boyd makes similar comments about parenting in this article:* Simmons, R. (2014, February 24). danah boyd's exclusive q & a on her excellent new book on youth & social media. RachelSimmons.com. Retrieved March 17, 2014, from http://www.rachelsimmons.com/2014/02/danah-boyds-exclusive-q-a-on-her-excellent-new-book-on-youth-social-media/

15   Reuters. (2007, February 20). *Bill Gates keeps close eye on kids' computer time.* Retrieved December 5, 2012, from www.reuters.com

16   International Society for Technology in Education. (2014). *ISTE standards.* Retrieved October 3, 2014, from http://www.iste.org/standards

17   International Society for Technology in Education. (2012). *ISTE corporate membership.* Retrieved November 20, 2013, from https://www.iste.org/membership/join-renew/corporate-members

18   International Society for Technology in Education. *ISTE 2013.* Retrieved August 23, 2014, from https://www.isteconference.org/2013/about_us/past_conferences.php

19   Gray, P. (2012, March 9). The many benefits, for kids, of playing video games. *ISTE Connects Blog.* Retrieved January 6, 2014, from http://blog.iste.org/the-many-benefits-for-kids-of-playing-video-games/

20   Rideout, V. J., Foehr, U. G., & Roberts, D. F. (2010). Generation M2: Media in the lives of 8- to 18-year-olds. *Kaiser Family Foundation.* Retrieved March 1, 2014, from http://kaiserfamily-foundation.files.wordpress.com/2013/01/8010.pdf, p. 35.

21   Rideout, V. J., Foehr, U. G., & Roberts, D. F. (2010). Generation M2: Media in the lives of 8- to 18-year-olds. *Kaiser Family Foundation.* Retrieved March 1, 2014, from http://kaiserfamily-foundation.files.wordpress.com/2013/01/8010.pdf

22   Baumrind, D. (1996). The discipline controversy revisited. *Family Relations, 45*(4), 405-414; Maccoby, E. E., & Martin, J. A. (1983). Socialization in the context of the family: Parent-child interaction. In P. H. Mussen (Ed.), *Handbook of child psychology. Vol. 4: Socialization, personality, and social development* (pp. 1–101). New York: Wiley.

23   Milevsky, A., Schlechter, M., Netter, S., & Keehn, D. (2007). Maternal and paternal parenting styles in adolescents: Associations with self-esteem, depression and life-satisfaction. *Journal of Child and Family Studies, 16*(1), 39-47; Steinberg, L., Mounts, N. S., Lamborn, S. D., & Dornbusch, S. M. (1991).

Authoritative parenting and adolescent adjustment across varied ecological niches. *Journal of Research on Adolescence, 1*(1), 19-36.

24 Steinberg, L., Lamborn, S. D., Dornbusch, S. M., & Darling, N. (1992). Impact of parenting practices on adolescent achievement: Authoritative parenting, school involvement, and encouragement to succeed. *Child Development, 63*(5), 1266-1281; Steinberg, L., Mounts, N. S., Lamborn, S. D., & Dornbusch, S. M. (1991). Authoritative parenting and adolescent adjustment across varied ecological niches. *Journal of Research on Adolescence, 1*(1), 19-36; Turner, E. A., Chandler, M., & Heffer, R. W. (2009). The influence of parenting styles, achievement motivation, and self-efficacy on academic performance in college students. *Journal of College Student Development, 50*(3), 337-346.

25 Steinberg, L., Lamborn, S. D., Darling, N., Mounts, N. S., & Dornbusch, S. M. (1994). Over-time changes in adjustment and competence among adolescents from authoritative, authoritarian, indulgent, and neglectful families. *Child Development, 65*(3), 754-770; Aunola, K., Stattin, H., & Nurmi, J. E. (2000). Parenting styles and adolescents' achievement strategies. *Journal of Adolescence, 23*(2), 205-222; Cohen, D. A., & Rice, J. (1997). Parenting styles, adolescent substance use, and academic achievement. *Journal of Drug Education, 27*(2), 199-211.

26 Boyd, D. (2014, March 24). Let kids run wild online. *Time, 183*(11), 40.

27 Levine, M. (2012). *Teach your children well: Parenting for authentic success*, Kindle Edition. New York: Harper.

28 Levine, M. (2012, August 4). Raising successful children. *New York Times*. Retrieved January 7, 2014, from www.nytimes.com

29 Tanner, L. (2013, October 28). Docs to parents: Limit kids' texts, tweets, online. *The Washington Times*. Retrieved January 7, 2014, from www.washingtontimes.com

30 Scelfo, J. (2010, June 9). The risks of parenting while plugged in. *New York Times*. Retrieved October 29, 2012, from www.nytimes.com

31 Williams, J. C., & Boushey, H. (2010, January). The three faces of work-family conflict: The poor, the professionals, and the missing middle. *Center for American Progress, and the Center for Work Life Law, University of California, Hastings College of the Law.* Retrieved July 17, 2013, from http://www.americanprogress.org/wp-content/uploads/issues/2010/01/pdf/threefaces.pdf

32 Leibovich, L. (2013, September 4). 8 ways screens are ruining your family's life. *Huffington Post.* Retrieved June 12, 2014, from www.huffingtonpost.com

33 Bilton, N. (2014, September 10). Steve Jobs was a low-tech parent. *New York Times.* Retrieved October 2, 2014, from www.nytimes.com

34 Bilton, N. (2014, September 10). Steve Jobs was a low-tech parent. *New York Times.* Retrieved October 2, 2014, from www.nytimes.com

35 McCannon, B. *General tools of media analysis.* The New Mexico Media Literacy Project. Retrieved June 12, 2014, from http://www.medialiteracy.net/pdfs/general.pdf

36 Barbaro, A. (Director/Writer), & Earp, J. (Writer/Director). (2008). *Consuming kids: The commercialization of childhood* [Film documentary]. (Available from the Campaign for a Commercial-free Childhood at http://commercialfreechildhood.org/resource/consuming-kids)

37 Hafner, K. (2009, December 20). To deal with obsession, some defriend Facebook. *New York Times.* Retrieved January 7, 2014, from www.nytimes.com

38 National School Boards Association. (2007, July). *Creating & connecting: Research and guidelines on online social—and educational—networking.* Retrieved September 24, 2013, from www.grunwald.com

39 Simmons, R. (2011). *Odd girl out: The hidden culture of aggression in girls.* Boston: Mariner.

CHAPTER 7

1 Motorola. (1950, September 5). *How television benefits your children.* Retrieved March 3, 2013, from http://www.jumbojoke.com/tv_is_good_for_kids.html

2 Zimmerman, F. J., Christakis, D. A., Meltzoff, A. N. (2007). Associations between media viewing and language development in children under age 2 years. *The Journal of Pediatrics, 151*(4), 364-368.

3 Christakis, D. A., Garrison, M. M., Herrenkohl, T., Haggerty, K., Rivara, F. P., Zhou, C., et al. (2013). Modifying media content for pre-school children: A randomized controlled trial. *Pediatrics, 131*(3), 431-438; Comstock, G., & Scharrer, E. (1999). *Television: What's on, who's watching, and what it means.* San Diego, CA: Academic Press.

4 Comstock, G., & Scharrer, E. (1999). *Television: What's on, who's watching, and what it means.* San Diego, CA: Academic Press.

5 Vandewater, E. A., Bickham, D. S., & Lee, J. H. (2006). Time well spent? Relating television use to children's free-time activities. *Pediatrics, 117*(2), e181-e191, p. e181.

6 Rosario-Tapan, C., & Tahnk, J. L. 25 more iPhone, iPod Touch, and iPad Apps for kids. *Parenting.* Retrieved December 16, 2012, from www.parenting.com

7 Sigman, A. (2010, August). *The impact of screen media on children: A Eurovision for Parliament.* (Presentation given to the Quality of Childhood Group in the European Parliament). Retrieved July 14, 2013, from http://www.ecswe.org/downloads/publications/QOC-V3/Chapter-4.pdf

8 National Association for the Education of Young Children/Fred Rogers Center for Early Learning and Children's Media. (2012, January). *Technology and interactive media as tools in early childhood programs serving children from birth through age 8.* Retrieved July 14, 2013, from http://www.naeyc.org/files/naeyc/PS_technology_WEB.pdf

9 Guernsey, L. (2012, March 7). Saying yes to digital media in preschool and kindergarten. *Huffington Post.* Retrieved May 22, 2013, from www.huffingtonpost.com

10 Guernsey, L. (2010, August 2). Screens, kids and the NAEYC position statement. *New America Foundation.* Retrieved May 22, 2013, from http://earlyed.newamerica.net/blogposts/2010/screens_kids_and_the_naeyc_position_statement-35103; New America Foundation. *Our funding.* Retrieved July 2, 2014, from http://www.newamerica.org/about/funding

11 LaPorte, N. (2012, July 7). Where apps become child's play. *New York Times.* Retrieved July 2, 2014, from www.nytimes.com

12 Campaign for a Commercial-Free Childhood, Alliance for Childhood, & Teachers Resisting Unhealthy Children's Entertainment (2012, October). *Facing the Screen Dilemma: Young children, technology and early education.* Boston, MA: Campaign for a Commercial-Free Childhood; New York, NY: Alliance for Childhood.

13 Tandon, P., Zhou, C., Lozano, P., & Christakis, D. (2011). Preschoolers' total daily screen time at home and by type of child care. *The Journal of Pediatrics, 158*(2), 297-300.

14 Campaign for a Commercial-Free Childhood. *Tell Fisher-Price: No iPad bouncy seats for infants!* Retrieved July 2, 2014, from http://www.commercialfreechildhood.org/action/tell-fisher-price-no-ipad-bouncy-seats-infants

15 Fisher-Price. Packaging for Fisher-Price Newborn-to-Toddler Apptivity™ Seat for iPad® device. *ebay.com.* Retrieved July 2, 2014, from http://www.ebay.com/itm/NEW-FISHER-PRICE-NEWBORN-TO-TODDLER-APPTIVITY-SEAT-/231214295617

16 CTA. *Quality gaming and multimedia accessories.* Retrieved July 3, 2014, from http://www.ctadigital.com/item.asp?item=3016

17 Golin, J. (2013, December 9). And the TOADY goes to: The iPotty by CTA Digital. *Campaign for a Commercial-Free Childhood.* Retrieved July 3, 2014, from http://www.commercialfreechildhood.org/blog/toady-ipotty

18 Center on Media and Child Health. *Media and your child: Preschoolers: Ages 3-5.* Retrieved July 14, 2013, from http://www.cmch.tv/mentors_parents/preschool.asp; Center on Media and Child Health. *Media and your child: Infants and toddlers: Ages 0-2.* Retrieved July 14, 2013, from http://www.cmch.tv/mentors_parents/infants_toddlers.asp

19 National Association for the Education of Young Children/Fred Rogers Center for Early Learning and Children's Media. (2012, January). *Technology and interactive media as tools in early childhood programs serving children from birth through age 8.* Retrieved July 14, 2013, from http://www.naeyc.org/files/naeyc/PS_technology_WEB.pdf, p. 7.

20 Center on Media and Human Development at Northwestern University. (2013, June). *Parenting in the age of digital technology: A national survey.* Retrieved July 2, 2013, from http://web5.soc.northwestern.edu/cmhd/wp-content/uploads/2013/05/Parenting-Report_FINAL.pdf

21 Center on Media and Human Development at Northwestern University. (2013, June). *Parenting in the age of digital technology: A national survey.* Retrieved July 2, 2013, from http://web5.soc.northwestern.edu/cmhd/wp-content/uploads/2013/05/Parenting-Report_FINAL.pdf

22 National Association for the Education of Young Children/Fred Rogers Center for Early Learning and Children's Media. (2012, January). *Technology and interactive media as tools in early childhood programs serving children from birth through age 8.* Retrieved July 14, 2013, from http://www.naeyc.org/files/naeyc/PS_technology_WEB.pdf, p. 2.

23 Chang, J., Rakowsky, C., & Frost, M. (2013, April 1). Toddlers obsessed with iPads: Could it hurt their development? *ABC News.* Retrieved July 3, 2014, from abcnewsgo.com

24 Chang, J., Rakowsky, C., & Frost, M. (2013, April 1). Generation iPad: Could device hurt toddlers' development? [Video]. *ABC News.* Retrieved July 3, 2014, from abcnewsgo.com

25 Chang, J., Rakowsky, C., & Frost, M. (2013, April 1). Toddlers obsessed with iPads: Could it hurt their development? *ABC News.* Retrieved July 3, 2014, from abcnewsgo.com

26 Worthen, B. (2012, May 22). What happens when toddlers zone out with an iPad. *Wall Street Journal.* Retrieved July 1, 2013, from http://online.wsj.com

27 American Academy of Pediatrics. (2011, October 18). *Babies and toddlers should learn from play not screens.* Retrieved July 16, 2013, from http://www.aap.org/en-us/about-the-aap/aap-press-room/pages/Babies-and-Toddlers-Should-Learn-from-Play-Not-Screens.aspx

28 National Association for the Education of Young Children/Fred Rogers Center for Early Learning and Children's Media. (2012, January). *Technology and interactive media as tools in early childhood programs serving children from birth through age 8.* Retrieved July 14, 2013, from http://www.naeyc.org/files/naeyc/PS_technology_WEB.pdf

29 Rideout, V. J., Foehr, U. G., & Roberts, D. F. (2010). Generation M2: Media in the lives of 8- to 18-year-olds. *Kaiser Family Foundation.* Retrieved March 1, 2014, from http://kaiserfamilyfoundation.files.wordpress.com/2013/01/8010.pdf, p. 15.

30 Ong, J. (2010, September 13). Survey reveals over 40 million iOS gamers in the US. *Apple Insider.* Retrieved November 21, 2013, from http://appleinsider.com

31 Molina, B. (2013, May 4). Games dominate Apple's all-time apps list. *USA Today.* Retrieved November 22, 2013, from www.usatoday.com

32 McLuhan, M., & Fiore, Q. (1967). *The medium is the massage: An inventory of effects.* New York; Bantam.

33 Lenhart, A., Kahne, J., Middaugh, E., Macgill, A. R., Evans, C., & Vitak, J. (2008, September 16). Teens, video games, and civics. *Pew Internet & American Life Project.* Retrieved July 1, 2013, from http://www.pewinternet.org/~/media/Files/Reports/2008/PIP_Teens_Games_and_Civics_Report_FINAL.pdf.pdf

34 Prensky, M. (2006). *"Don't bother me mom—I'm learning!" How computer and video games are preparing your kids for 21st century success—and how you can help!*. St. Paul, MN: Paragon House, pp. 183-184.

35 National School Boards Association. (2007, July). *Creating & connecting: Research and guidelines on online social—and educational—networking.* Retrieved September 24, 2013, from www.grunwald. com, cover.

36 National School Boards Association. (2014). *Home page.* Retrieved June 30, 2014, from www.nsba.org

37 Chmielewski, D. C., & Guynn, J. (2011, June 30). News Corp. sells Myspace for $35 million. *Los Angeles Times.* Retrieved March 20, 2014, from www.latimes.com

38 Stone, B. (2007, October 25). Microsoft buys stake in Facebook. *New York Times.* Retrieved March 20, 2014, from www.nytimes. com

39 National School Boards Association. (2007, July). *Creating & connecting: Research and guidelines on online social—and educational—networking.* Retrieved September 24, 2013, from www.grunwald. com

40 National School Boards Association. (2007, July). *Creating & connecting: Research and guidelines on online social—and educational—networking.* Retrieved September 24, 2013, from www.grunwald. com, pp. 2, 4.

41 National School Boards Association. (2007, July). *Creating & connecting: Research and guidelines on online social—and educational—networking.* Retrieved September 24, 2013, from www.grunwald. com, p. 4.

42 American Academy of Pediatrics. (2013). Children, adolescents, and the media. *Pediatrics 132*(5), 958-961.

43 Louv, R. (2006). *Last child in the woods: Saving our children from nature-deficit disorder.* Chapel Hill, NC: Algonquin Books.

44 American Academy of Pediatrics. (2014). Literacy promotion: An essential component of primary care pediatric practice. *Pediatrics 134(2),* 1-6.

45 American Academy of Pediatrics. (2014). Literacy promotion: An essential component of primary care pediatric practice. *Pediatrics 134(2)*, 1-6, p. 2.

46 Rich, M. (2014, June 24). Pediatrics group to recommend reading aloud to children from birth. *New York Times*. Retrieved June 24, 2014, from www.nytimes.com

47 American Academy of Pediatrics. (2014). Literacy promotion: An essential component of primary care pediatric practice. *Pediatrics 134(2)*, 1-6.

48 Trelease, J. (2013). *The read-aloud handbook: Seventh edition*. New York: Penguin.

CHAPTER 8

1 Greenberg, M. T., Siegel, J. M., & Leitch, C. J. (1983). The nature and importance of attachment relationships to parents and peers during adolescence. *Journal of Youth and Adolescence, 12*(5), 373-386, p. 373.

2 Neufeld, G., & Maté, G. (2006). *Hold on to your kids: Why parents need to matter more than peers.* New York: Ballantine, p. 11.

3 Carter, M., McGee, R., Taylor, B., & Williams, S. (2007). Health outcomes in adolescence: Associations with family, friends and school engagement. *Journal of Adolescence, 30*(1), 51-62.

4 Del Rio, J. (2012, September 7). In the zone: Geoffrey Canada is changing the odds in Harlem. *Urban Faith*. Retrieved September 13, 2014, from www.urbanfaith.com

5 Bauerlein, M. (2009). *The Dumbest generation: How the digital age stupefies young Americans and jeopardizes our future.* New York: Tarcher/Penguin, p. x.

6 Yeh, H. C., & Lempers, J. D. (2004). Perceived sibling relationships and adolescent development. *Journal of Youth and Adolescence, 33*(2), 133-147.

7 Simmons, R. (2011). *Odd girl out: The hidden culture of aggression in girls.* Boston: Mariner, p. xvi.

8   *Note: Evidence that the parent-teen relationship is made stronger by staying related even during disagreements:* Allen, J. P., McElhaney, K. B., Land, D. J., Kuperminc, G. P., Moore, C. W., O'Beirne-Kelly, H., et al. (2003). A secure base in adolescence: markers of attachment security in the mother-adolescent relationship. *Child Development, 74*(1), 292-307.

9   Bradley, M. J. (2003). *Yes, your teen is crazy! Loving your kid without losing your mind.* Gig Harbor, WA: Harbor Press.

10 Pipher, M. (1996). *The shelter of each other: Rebuilding our families.* New York: Ballantine, p. 243.

11 Girls on the Run. (2013). *Grown up guide.* Retrieved September 22, 2013, from http://www.girlsontherun.org/What-We-Do/Parent-Resources

12 Rosiak, L. (2012, December 25). Fathers disappear from households across America. *Washington Times.* Retrieved July 7, 2014, from www.washingtontimes.com

13 Livingston, G., & Parker, K. (2011, June 15). A tale of two fathers. Pew Research Center. Retrieved July 7, 2014, from http://www.pewsocialtrends.org/2011/06/15/a-tale-of-two-fathers/

14 Kelly, J. (2002). *Dads and daughters. How to inspire, understand, and support your daughter when she's growing up so fast.* New York: Broadway Books.

CHAPTER 9

1   Bosker, B. (2013, May 23). What really happens on a teen girls iPhone. *Huffington Post.* Retrieved February 1, 2014, from www.huffingtonpost.com

2   Bosker, B. (2013, May 23). What really happens on a teen girls iPhone. *Huffington Post.* Retrieved February 1, 2014, from www.huffingtonpost.com

3   Richtel, M. (2010, November 21). Growing up digital, wired for distraction. *New York Times*. Retrieved February 2, 2014, from www.nytimes.com

4   Tapscott, D. (2009). *Grown up digital: How the net generation is changing your world*. New York: McGraw-Hill, p. 108.

5   Reaney, P. (2013, June 19). Teens more resilient, tech savvy than older millenials: Study. *Reuters*. Retrieved January 14, 2104, from www.reuters.com

6   Rideout, V. J., Foehr, U. G., & Roberts, D. F. (2010). Generation M2: Media in the lives of 8- to 18-year-olds. *Kaiser Family Foundation*. Retrieved March 1, 2014, from http://kaiserfamily-foundation.files.wordpress.com/2013/01/8010.pdf

7   *Note: Figures derived from:* Rideout, V. J., Foehr, U. G., & Roberts, D. F. (2010). Generation M2: Media in the lives of 8- to 18-year-olds. *Kaiser Family Foundation*. Retrieved March 1, 2014, from http://kaiserfamilyfoundation.files.wordpress.com/2013/01/8010.pdf

8   Steinberg, L. (2008). A social neuroscience perspective on adolescent risk-taking. *Developmental Review, 28*(1), 78-106.

9   Steinberg, L. (2014). *Age of Opportunity: Lessons from the New Science of Adolescence*, Kindle Edition. Boston: Eamon Dolan/Houghton Mifflin Harcourt.

10 Kaiser, E. (2013, May 15). 6 facts about crime and the adolescent brain. *MPR News*. Retrieved February 2, 2014, from www.mprnews.org

11 Jones, A. (2013, September 27). Laurence Steinberg on the legal and policy implications of teen brain development. *Duke Today*. Retrieved February 2, 2014, from http://today.duke.edu

12 Steinberg, L. (2012). Should the science of adolescent brain development inform public policy? *Issues in Science and Technology, 28*(3), 67-78.

13 Dahl, R. E. (2004). Adolescent brain development: A period of vulnerabilities and opportunities. Keynote address. *Annals of the New York Academy of Sciences, 1021*, 1-22.

14 Elliott, G.C. (2009). *Family matters: The Importance of mattering to family in adolescence.* Wiley-Blackwell, Oxford, UK.

15 Twenge, J.M., & Campbell, W.K. (2010). *The narcissism epidemic: Living in the age of entitlement.* New York: Free Press.

16 Twenge, J. M. (2013). The evidence for generation me and against generation we. *Emerging Adulthood, 1*(1), 11-16.

17 Buffardi, L. E., & Campbell, W. K. (2008). Narcissism and social networking web sites. *Personality and social psychology bulletin, 34*(10), 1303-1314; Panek, E. T., Nardis, Y., & Konrath, S. (2013). Mirror or megaphone?: How relationships between narcissism and social networking site use differ on Facebook and Twitter. *Computers in Human Behavior, 29*(5), 2004-2012; Mehdizadeh S (2010). Self-presentation 2.0: narcissism and self-esteem on Facebook. *Cyberpsychology, Behavior and Social Networking, 13*(4), 357-64.

18 Kim, E., Namkoong, K., Ku, T., & Kim, S. (2008). The relationship between online game addiction and aggression, self-control and narcissistic personality traits. *European Psychiatry, 23*(3), 212-218.

19 Twenge, J. M., & Kasser, T. (2013). Generational changes in materialism and work centrality, 1976-2007: Associations with temporal changes in societal insecurity and materialistic role modeling. *Personality & Social Psychology Bulletin, 39*(7), 883-97; Chee, B. (2013, May 1). Today's teens: More materialistic, less willing to work. *SDSU News Center.* Retrieved February 2, 2014, from http://newscenter.sdsu.edu

20 Goleman, D. (2007, February 20). Flame first, think later: New clues to e-mail misbehavior. *New York Times.* Retrieved August 13, 2014, from www.nytimes.com

21 Richards, R., McGee, R., Williams, S. M., Welch, D., & Hancox, R. J. (2010). Adolescent screen time and attachment to parents and peers. *Archives of Pediatrics & Adolescent Medicine, 164*(3), 258-262.

22 Steinberg, L. (2008). A social neuroscience perspective on adolescent risk-taking. *Developmental Review, 28*(1), 78-106.

23 Steinberg, L. (2008). A social neuroscience perspective on adolescent risk-taking. *Developmental Review, 28*(1), 78-106, p. 99.

24 Consumer Reports. (2014, June). *Risks of teen drivers*, 22-24.

25 Steinberg, L. (2008). A social neuroscience perspective on adolescent risk-taking. *Developmental Review, 28*(1), 78-106.

26 Zernike, K. (2012, August 13). Youth driving laws limit even the double date. *New York Times*. Retrieved February 2, 2014, from www.nytimes.com

27 Insurance Institute for Highway Safety. (2012, May 31). *States could sharply reduce teen crash deaths by strengthening graduated driver licensing laws.* Retrieved January 23, 2014, from http://www.iihs.org/iihs/news/desktopnews/states-could-sharply-reduce-teen-crash-deaths-by-strengthening-graduated-driver-licensing-laws

28 Eccles, J. S., Barber, B. L., Stone, M., & Hunt, J. (2003). Extracurricular activities and adolescent development. *Journal of Social Issues, 59*(4), 865-889.

CHAPTER 10

1 Campaign for a Commercial-Free Childhood, Alliance for Childhood, & Teachers Resisting Unhealthy Children's Entertainment (2012, October). *Facing the Screen Dilemma: Young children, technology and early education.* Boston, MA: Campaign for a Commercial-Free Childhood; New York, NY: Alliance for Childhood, p. 9.

2 Richtel, M. (2011, October 22). A Silicon Valley school that doesn't compute. *New York Times*. Retrieved July 2, 2013, from www.nytimes.com

3 Healy, J. (2004). *Your child's growing mind: Brain development and learning from birth to adolescence.* New York: Broadway Books; Your family. (2013, July). *Screen idol.* Retrieved April 22, 2013, from http://fitdv.com/new/articles/article.php?artid=811

4   Richtel, M. (2011, October 22). A Silicon Valley school that doesn't compute. *New York Times.* Retrieved July 2, 2013, from www.nytimes.com

5   Mesch, G. S. (2003). The family and the Internet: The Israeli case. *Social Science Quarterly, 84*(4), 1038-1050.

6   Fuld, L. (2014, May 13). America's tech talent shortage: Is it just myth? *Fortune.* Retrieved May 30, 2014, from http://tech.fortune.cnn.com

7   US Bureau of Labor Statistics. (2014). *Computer programmers.* Retrieved May 13, 2014, from http://www.bls.gov/ooh/compu-ter-and-information-technology/computer-programmers.htm#tab-6

8   Salzman, H., Kuehn, D., & Lowell, L. (2013, April 24). Guestworkers in the high-skill US labor market. *Economic Policy Institute, EPI Briefing Paper #359,* Retrieved May 30, 2014, from http://s3.epi.org/files/2013/bp359-guestworkers-high-skill-labor-market-analysis.pdf, p. 2.

9   US Bureau of Labor Statistics. (2014). *Computer programmers.* Retrieved May 13, 2014, from http://www.bls.gov/ooh/computer-and-information-technology/computer-programmers.htm#tab-6

10   Richtel, M. (2014, May 10). Reading, writing, arithmetic, and lately, coding. *New York Times.* Retrieved May 30, 2014, from www.nytimes.com

CONCLUSION

1   Kennedy, J. F. (1962, September 12). Address at Rice University on the nation's space effort. [video]. *Johnson Space Center/National Aeronautics and Space Administration.* Retrieved July 14, 2014, from http://er.jsc.nasa.gov/seh/ricetalk.htm

2   Turkle, S. (2011). *Alone together: Why we expect more from technology and less from each other.* New York: Basic Books, p. 296.

3   Strasburger, V. C., & Donnerstein, E. (2013). The new media of violent video games: Yet the same old media problems? *Clinical Pediatrics, XX*(X), 1-5.

4   Friedman, D. (2013, March 24). A proposal to study how violent video games may be affecting the minds of youngsters has stalled. *New York Daily News*. Retrieved March 27, 2014, from www.nydailynews.com; *Note: the Entertainment Software Association (ESA)—the video game industry's chief lobbying arm—spent more than $18 million on lobbying over the past four years:* Wilke, C., & Blumenthal, P. (2013, April 9). Game lobby steers gun violence debate away. *Huffington Post*. Retrieved March 27, 2014, from www.huffington-post.com

Index

CPSIA information can be obtained
at www.ICGtesting.com
Printed in the USA
LVHW090249120719
623858LV00005B/406/P